Doing Language Arts

IN

Morning Meeting

150 Quick Activities THAT Connect TO Your Curriculum

Jodie Luongo, Joan Riordan AND Kate Umstatter

ISBN: 978-1-892989-80-2
Library of Congress Control Number: 2014953016

Book design by Helen Merena
Illustrations for cover and introduction © Lynn Zimmerman,
Lucky Dog Design. All rights reserved.

Center for Responsive Schools, Inc.
85 Avenue A, P.O. Box 718
Turners Falls, MA 01376-0718

800-360-6332
www.responsiveclassroom.org

Printed on recycled paper

Contents

Language Arts Belongs in Morning Meeting

*"Language shapes the way we think,
and determines what we can think about."*

—BENJAMIN LEE WHORF, LINGUIST

Morning Meetings offer excellent opportunities to enhance children's language arts learning in pleasurable ways. Consider this kindergarten class:

> For the first week or so of school, students in Mr. Harrison's class begin their daily Morning Meeting with Hickety Pickety Bumble Bee, a chant that the whole class repeats until all students in the circle have had a chance to say their names. This simple greeting appeals to their sense of fun while helping them learn each other's names and practice speaking in the group. As the children repeat each classmate's name, they also clap the syllables. Later, when their teacher formally introduces syllabication during language arts time, they'll have prior knowledge to draw on. Right now, they're building skills informally and learning that language is intriguing and school is an enjoyable place to be.

Or this class of fifth graders:

> Divided into an "X" team and an "O" team, students in Ms. Denali's class are practicing their spelling words by playing a lively round of Human Tic Tac Toe for their Morning Meeting activity. As Ms. D calls out words, the teams take turns collaboratively figuring out the spelling. When they've got it, they send one player to stand somewhere on the human-size tic-tac-toe board taped to the meeting circle carpet. Just

as in paper-and-pencil tic tac toe, the object is to get three X's or O's in a row. Excitement mounts as both teams spell more words correctly and get more players on the board.

The teachers in both of these classes have found quick, easy, and fun ways to help children build their skill in using a powerful tool that is essential to their success in school and in life: language.

From their earliest days, children are surrounded by language. As infants, they learn to identify the adults who care for them in large part by their voices, and they respond to speech long before they can speak themselves or understand what language is. Then, as they grow, children use language as a tool to explore and explain their world. They experiment with words. They learn to speak and read, they inquire about words they don't know, they ask innumerable questions, and they listen to stories. As they grow older, many make up their own poems, plays, stories, and songs.

School adds rigor to that learning. As formal lessons in listening, speaking, reading, and writing begin, teachers strive to help students reach the highest levels of competence while keeping the fun in language exploration. The complexity of language lessons necessarily grows as students continue into the upper grades, but teachers remain mindful of the need to keep learning engaging by connecting it to students' lives and passions. And with the advent of guidelines like the Common Core State Standards, teachers are more aware than ever of the need to ensure that students have rich, daily opportunities to practice language arts.

The *Responsive Classroom®* practice of Morning Meeting gives teachers an excellent way to provide language arts learning in playful and engaging ways. Into each Morning Meeting component—greeting, sharing, group activity, and morning message—teachers can incorporate quick, lively ways for children to deepen their understanding of language arts skills introduced during formal lessons, all while having fun and building community.

And that's why we wrote this book. It gathers together many of our favorite ways of incorporating language arts into Morning Meeting. You'll find ideas for all four meeting components—ideas that get students greeting each other with expression, sharing opinions about books they're reading, wondering together about the meanings of new words, and acting out different points of view in a poem.

As classroom teachers ourselves, we took special care to make sure these activities are quick and easy to teach, fun to do, and connected to key Common Core standards. We hope these activities lead your students to connect to the joys of language and literature while helping them flourish in a world woven with words.

Morning Meetings and Language Arts

Responsive Classroom Morning Meeting offers teachers a structured, purposeful, and fun way to start each day on a positive note and build a strong sense of classroom community. Beginning in such a powerful way sets students up for success and enables them to approach learning with open minds and a willingness to take academic risks. Morning Meeting:

- Typically lasts 20 to 30 minutes, takes place in a circle, and follows a predictable structure, which students come to rely on.

- Gives teachers and students a chance to explore language arts and other academic topics and skills in playful and intriguing ways, while simultaneously building community and social skills.

Language Arts in Each Component of Morning Meeting

Each component of Morning Meeting—greeting, sharing, group activity, and morning message—has a specific purpose and offers different, but equally powerful, ways to explore language arts content.

GREETING

At the start of each Morning Meeting, students greet each other by name.

PURPOSES

- To provide a sense of recognition and belonging.

- To help children learn each other's names and foster friendships.

- To build friendly social skills.

EXAMPLES

- Students go around the circle and greet each other with a simple "Good morning,[classmate's name]."

- Students mix and mingle, greeting as many classmates as possible in a minute.

- For variety, students add a high five or shake pinky fingers instead of hands.

BRINGING LANGUAGE ARTS INTO GREETINGS

- Students greet classmates who have the same number of syllables in their first names.

- Students greet someone who has a sight word card that matches their own.

- The teacher chooses an adverb and students greet each other in the manner of that adverb (slowly, quickly, happily, etc.).

SHARING

During sharing, students present a brief bit of personal news or information.

PURPOSES

- To give students practice in speaking and listening.

- To develop children's vocabulary and language skills.

- To help children get to know classmates.

EXAMPLES

- **Around-the-circle sharing**—Each student briefly responds to the same prompt from the teacher, such as "What's one thing you like to do after school?"

- **Partner sharing**—Students talk about a specified topic with a partner.

- **Dialogue sharing**—A few children each day share in greater detail about an assigned or open topic.

BRINGING LANGUAGE ARTS INTO SHARING

- Students share about an important event in their lives, being sure to include the main point, supporting details, and a conclusion.

- Students share strategies for reading fluently.

- From a book they're reading, students choose a favorite character and explain what they admire about her or him.

GROUP ACTIVITY

Students play a game, sing a song, or do some other fun activity as a whole group.

PURPOSES

- To foster active, engaged participation.

- To develop a shared repertoire of activities, including energizers, chants, and songs.

EXAMPLES

- Play charades or other guessing games.

- Do cooperative beat-the-clock challenges.

- Sing or chant as a group or do simple dance steps together.

BRINGING LANGUAGE ARTS INTO GROUP ACTIVITIES

- Students count off into groups and take parts in a poem for two (or more) voices.

- Students act out the meanings of prepositions.

- Students act out a main event in a story.

MORNING MESSAGE

Before students arrive, the teacher writes a message to welcome them. Students read the message individually as they enter the classroom and again during Morning Meeting.

PURPOSES

- To reinforce reading and other academic skills.

- To engage children in exploring social and academic topics.

- To generate interest and excitement for the day's learning.

EXAMPLE

Dear Wordsmiths,

Spring is finally here. Yesterday I was able to go outside without a coat! Unfortunately, the forecast calls for snow on Wednesday, even though the weather is quite warm today.

How would you define "forecast"? Use context clues from the paragraph above, and be ready to share your idea during our Morning Meeting.

BRINGING LANGUAGE ARTS INTO MORNING MESSAGES

- Preview the day's upcoming language arts lesson.

- Review previously taught language arts content or skills.

- Post a language arts question for students to answer.

5

What's Special About the Activities in This Book?

All of the activities gathered here give students meaningful practice in key language arts skills while building community, nurturing students' confidence in themselves as learners, and fostering academic engagement. You'll find that these activities are:

Engaging ■ The activities in this book give students opportunities to get up and talk, reason, debate, sing, act, and create. This kind of active and interactive participation keeps students engaged and learning at their best.

Multilayered ■ Rather than focusing on just reading, writing, speaking, or listening, most activities incorporate several of these skills, which lets students practice them in an integrated way.

Flexible ■ These activities work well after Morning Meeting, too. Teachers can use them as energizers throughout the day or during end-of-the-day closing circles. Any activity could form the foundation for a formal lesson later in the day or week. And students can do some of them while waiting to enter the cafeteria or board the bus.

Adaptable ■ Teachers can easily make these activities simpler or more complex to fit students' needs and abilities or tweak them to respond to what's happening in students' lives. Variations included with most activities help with these adaptations and keep the activities fresh. And for each activity, extensions show how teachers might continue the learning begun at Morning Meeting during formal language arts instruction.

Thematic ■ We've included ten themed meetings in which all four meeting components focus on one language arts topic, such as comma use, for those times when children need extra practice. Teachers can also use these as templates for designing their own themed meetings.

Morning Meeting Language Arts vs. Formal Language Arts Lessons

As the activities collected in this book demonstrate, students can do important language arts learning during Morning Meeting as well as during language arts instruction. But the primary purpose of Morning Meeting is to build children's confidence and sense of community and to set a positive tone for the day's learning. During language arts instruction, we still want to build confidence and community, but our primary purpose is to develop students' understanding of language concepts, sharpen their language skills, and deepen their content knowledge.

Because of these differing purposes, the learning that happens during Morning Meeting compared to a language arts block needs to look different, too. Some things to keep in mind:

- Do your extended introduction, teaching, and review of concepts and skills only during the language arts instructional block. Preserve Morning Meeting as a time to offer quick, engaging practice while focusing on community- and confidence-building.

- During language arts block, you work with small groups and differentiate instruction according to children's needs. But for Morning Meeting, children gather and participate as a whole group. You'll want to make sure, therefore, that every child can participate in and enjoy any activity that you choose.

- For language arts lessons, students work with myriad supplies—notebooks, pencils, pens, laptops, tablets, perhaps markers or crayons. For a few of the activities in this book, students need to bring a book to Morning Meeting, or the teacher passes out clipboards or notecards for a task. But otherwise students go through Morning Meeting empty-handed so that they can concentrate on their classmates and move freely during activities.

- Language arts block is the time for formal assessment, coaching, and extended feedback. Morning Meeting works best when you limit yourself to observing children's understandings and misunderstandings and making mental notes for later follow-up. This lets children relax and give their full attention to enjoying Morning Meeting with you and their classmates.

Getting the Most Out of This Book

You can use this book in lots of different ways: Flip through the pages and look for activities that you think would appeal to your students, try a themed meeting if students need extra practice in a particular skill, or explore all the activities for one Morning Meeting component. Need an activity to help you address a certain language arts skill or standard? The "Activities Listed by Language Arts Content" chart on page nn and the "Activities Listed by Common Core State Standard" chart on page nn will help you zero in.

Whichever way you choose to use the book, here are a few strategies that will help you make the most of it.

Prepare for Morning Meeting ■ It's wise to prepare for Morning Meeting just as you would for any other part of the school day. Some important steps:

> ■ Create a supportive physical environment that includes a space large enough for a circle in which everyone can see and be seen.

> ■ Teach, model, and practice with students the behaviors that will help Morning Meetings run smoothly and feel safe for everyone. For example, students need to know how to move to and from the circle; move their bodies safely during the active parts of the meeting; use appropriate voice volume when speaking, chanting, and singing; wait their turns; show attention when someone else is speaking; and ask for clarification when they don't hear or understand what someone said.

> ■ Be vigilant in ensuring that students follow through with the behaviors you've taught. You'll be conveying that Morning Meeting is a very important time during which you'll hold everyone to the same high standards as during the rest of the day.

Think strategically ■ Look for activities that will enhance your already existing curriculum and lesson plans. You'll boost students' skills while also saving some of the time you usually spend designing practice activities.

Also note that sometimes a greeting and a sharing, or a sharing and group activity, combine easily into one activity. The variety is refreshing for students and may save you a few minutes on days when time is especially tight. You'll see several such combinations throughout the book.

Look above, below, and beyond ■ Many activities assigned to the grades above and below yours may work well for your class. And consider inventing your own variations—ones that express the personality of your class.

Reduce ■ Decide if you need to reduce the length or complexity of an activity to meet students' needs. As students' skills grow, they'll enjoy tackling the longer or more complicated version.

Reuse ■ Although it's important to offer plenty of variety to keep students interested and engaged, we encourage you to reuse some activities throughout the year. Repetition helps students become adept, and repeating favorites lends a sense of comforting familiarity to their Morning Meetings.

Recycle ■ You can recycle many of the activities by using them as energizers whenever students need a quick movement break.

Stick close or fly free ■ For most activities, we've provided teacher language that you can follow pretty much as is. This option might particularly appeal to you if you're new to Morning Meeting, but you can always come up with your own language to suit your students and your style. And you can try other changes to make each activity your own; for example, if an activity is based on a song but you'd rather not sing, teach the song as a chant instead.

Adapt, Invent, Have Fun!

No matter how you decide to use this book—whether to follow the activities as is, adjust them to fit your students' needs, or create new activities of your own—remember this single important word: fun. Real fun—that is, deep engagement and enjoyment versus superficial silliness—matters a great deal to learning. Children who are having fun are children who are motivated, focused, and engaged, and that is the state of mind in which they are most likely to absorb your teaching—during Morning Meeting or any other part of the day.

Everything's in Order

How to do it:

Language Arts Content

Alphabetical order

Common Core Standards

RF.K.1d Recognize upper- and lowercase letters

SL.K.6 Speak audibly

L.K.1a Print upper- and lowercase letters

Materials Needed

A set of lowercase letter cards, one for each letter of the alphabet

Vocabulary

Alphabetical order, lowercase

1 With students standing in a circle, introduce the greeting: "We know many lowercase letters. Today during our greeting, we are going to put them in alphabetical order. We are also going to give high fives."

2 Model how to give a safe and gentle high five.

3 Shuffle the cards and then give one to each student.

➤ If you have more letters than students, put the extras face up in the middle of the circle.

➤ If you have more students than letters, have the students share cards.

4 Call the letter "a" and have the class repeat it after you. The child with that card moves to stand at your left, holding the card waist high, facing out, so everyone can see it. Next call the letter "b," have the class repeat it, and invite that child to stand to the left of the child with the letter "a."

5 Continue calling letters until students are standing in the circle in alphabetical order.

➤ When you call out an extra letter, have the class repeat it in unison, and then move that card from the middle of the circle to its rightful spot in the circle.

➤ When you call out shared letters, both students move to the correct spot in the circle.

6 Now say the alphabet slowly. When you say a child's letter, she turns and gives a high five to the person to her left.

➤ When you name a skipped letter, students call out "Yay for [letter name]!"

➤ When you come to a shared letter, the two students turn and give each other a high five.

7 Say the alphabet together as a class.

VARIATIONS

■ Use uppercase letter cards.

■ After some practice, let students get into alphabetical order silently, without your calling the letters out.

EXTENSIONS FOR A LATER LANGUAGE ARTS LESSON

■ Students put the letter cards into alphabetical order, saying each letter as they do so.

■ Invite students to make their own letter cards.

Hey Readers

Language Arts Content

Reading behaviors

Common Core Standards

RF.K.1 Understand the organization and basic features of print

RF.K.1a Follow words from left to right

RF.K.2 Demonstrate understanding of spoken words, syllables, and sounds

SL.K.6 Speak audibly

Materials Needed

A chart with the following on three separate lines:

"Hey _____, good to see you. Who's the reader to the left of you?"

"_____ is to the left of me."

"Good morning, _____."

How to do it:

1 Introduce the greeting and the chart: "We've been doing lots of reading this year. Today, we are going to celebrate all our reading by greeting each other as readers. Let's look at our chart. It has the words we'll use as we greet." Reinforce the point that when reading, we start at the top and go from the left to the right.

2 Teach the class the following greeting words and pattern, modeling and then coaching as they practice.

Class: "Hey Tysheka, good to see you. Who's the reader to the left of you?"

Tysheka: "Danny is to the left of me."

Class: "Good morning, Danny."

Class: "Hey Danny, good to see you. Who's the reader to the left of you?"

Danny: "Hermella is to the left of me."

And so on around the circle.

3 Start the greeting with the class posing the question to the student on your left. Continue around the circle. The student on your right will be the last child to be greeted by the class, with "Good morning, _____."

EXTENSION FOR A LATER LANGUAGE ARTS LESSON

■ Keep a running list of the things readers do. For example, readers think about what they are reading, sound out words they don't know, and use pictures to help them understand the story.

Set Your Sights on a Word

How to do it:

1 Introduce the greeting: "This morning, we are going to greet each other and practice sight words at the same time."

2 As students stand in a circle, give each a sight word card. Remind students to hold the cards quietly and carefully.

3 Tell students to read their word to themselves. They can ask someone next to them for help if they need it.

4 Teach the greeting by going first.

➤ Take a step into the center of the circle and read your sight word card: "I have 'said.'" Turn your card so the class can see it.

➤ Students look at their cards. The student who has the same word takes a step into the circle and says, "I have 'said,' too."

➤ Meet the student in the center of the circle and say, "Good morning, Leland." The student replies, "Good morning, Mrs. H." Both of you put your cards down in the middle of the circle and step back to your places.

5 Ask the person to your right to read his word. Continue the greeting around the circle until all the words have been read and everyone has been greeted.

6 Reinforce students' recall of the sight words and self-control throughout the greeting: "You're helping classmates read their words." "You're all holding your cards gently and quietly."

VARIATION

■ Instead of doing the greeting in a circle, students mix and mingle to find the person who has the same word. Partners read their word and greet each other. Then students find someone who has a different word. They read their words and greet each other. Finally, students find someone they haven't greeted yet, read their words, and greet each other.

EXTENSION FOR A LATER LANGUAGE ARTS LESSON

■ Use the sight word cards to play matching games like Concentration or Go Fish.

Language Arts Content

Sight words

Common Core Standards

RF.K.1b Recognize that spoken words are represented in written language by specific sequences of letters

RF.K.3c Read high-frequency words by sight

SL.K.1a Follow agreed-upon rules for discussions

Materials Needed

Two cards of each sight word. Make enough so each student has a card.

That's the Point!

Language Arts Content

Punctuation

Common Core Standards

RF.K.4 Read emergent-reader texts with purpose and understanding

SL.K.1a Follow agreed-upon rules for discussions

L.K.1d Use question words (who, what, where, when, why, how)

L.K.2b Recognize and name end punctuation

Materials Needed

A chart with the following on two separate lines:

"It's so good to see you, _____!"

"It's so good to see you, too!"

Vocabulary

Punctuation, expression, exclamation point

How to do it:

1 With students standing in a circle, introduce the greeting: "We've been learning about punctuation. Today we're going to practice using an exclamation point and speaking with expression."

2 Show the chart and explain how students will be using the sentences on it to greet each other today. Call attention to the exclamation points in the sentences and remind students that those exclamation points signal they should speak with expression.

3 Model with two students you've prepared in advance.

➤ Turn to face your first student modeler and say with expression, "It's so good to see you, Jed!"

➤ Jed replies, "It's so good to see you, too!" Jed then turns to face the second student modeler and says, "It's so good to see you, Kass!" Kass replies, "It's so good to see you, too!" Kass then turns as if she's about to greet the next person in the circle.

➤ Ask students what they noticed about how you greeted each other. Prompt them to comment about your expressiveness if needed.

4 Now the class does the greeting the way it was modeled. The last student greeted says to the whole class, "It's so good to see all of you!" The class replies, "It's so good to see you, too!"

VARIATIONS

■ Use a question mark in the greeting. For example: "How are you today, _____?" The child being greeted responds, "I'm fine [or okay]. How are you?"

■ Write a period, question mark, or exclamation point on index cards and place them face down in the center of the circle. Each student chooses a card and greets someone in the manner of the punctuation mark.

■ Have students choose which punctuation mark to use, and state their choice before greeting someone.

EXTENSION FOR A LATER LANGUAGE ARTS LESSON

■ Refer back to the greeting during reading and writing to remind students of the use of end punctuation and how to use it to read with expression.

Author? Illustrator? You Decide

Language Arts Content

Role of authors and illustrators

Common Core Standards

RL.K.6 Define the role of the author and illustrator in telling a story

W.K.2 Use drawing, dictating, and writing to compose informative/explanatory texts

SL.K.1 Participate in collaborative conversations about kindergarten topics and texts

L.K.1d Use question words (who, what, where, when, why, how)

Materials Needed

None

Vocabulary

Author, illustrator

How to do it:

1 Introduce this around-the-circle sharing: "We've been working hard as authors and illustrators. Today, we will share which role we like best. For example, I like being an author best because I love to work with words and I like to organize things. You might like being an illustrator best because you like to use different art materials or because you like figuring out how to show what you see."

2 Give students a moment to think about their answers. They put a thumb up when they are ready to share.

3 Provide sentence frames for students to use: "I like being an author because _____" and "I like being an illustrator because _____."

4 Invite one student to begin. Continue sharing around the circle.

5 After everyone has had a turn, invite students to ask questions or make comments about what classmates shared. Provide examples: "Johan, do you like to illustrate with crayons or markers?" "Eliza, you wrote a funny poem at writing time."

VARIATION

■ Students share with a partner rather than around the circle, and partners offer each other questions and comments. After a few minutes, have three or four students share with the class what they talked about with their partners.

EXTENSION FOR A LATER LANGUAGE ARTS LESSON

■ Have students draw themselves as an author or illustrator and caption their drawing with the appropriately completed sentence frame. Display the work or put it together to make a class book.

Book Share

Language Arts Content

Stating opinions

Common Core Standards

RL.K.1 Ask and answer questions about key details in a text

RL.K.10 Engage in group reading activities with purpose and understanding

W.K.1 Compose opinion pieces and state an opinion or preference about the topic or book

SL.K.1 Participate in collaborative discussions about kindergarten topics and texts

L.K.1d Use question words (who, what, where, when, why, how)

Materials Needed

Sharers each need a book they have read

Vocabulary

Opinion

How to do it:

Choose three or four sharers for each day. Alert students ahead of time to be ready to bring a book they've read to Morning Meeting and share their opinion about whether or not they liked the book.

1 Introduce this dialogue sharing: "This week, everyone will have a chance to share and take questions and comments about a book they've read. A few of you will share each day. You will give us your opinion about whether or not you liked the book."

2 Model the sharing: Holding up your book, say, "My book is *Jillian Jiggs*. I liked this book. Does anyone have a connection?" Students who also like the book show a thumbs-up. Then say, "I'm ready for questions and comments."

3 Brainstorm questions and comments; possibilities are "Why do you like the book?" "Where did you get that book?" "What is one thing that happens in the book?" "That looks like a fun book." "I'm glad you enjoyed your book."

4 Remind students that they can also share a book they do not like. Brainstorm a few additional questions and comments, such as "Why did you choose to share this book?" "Why don't you like this book?" "I'm sorry you didn't enjoy it." "I hope you find a book you like soon."

5 Have the sharers share their books and take three or four questions and comments each.

6 Reinforce the participation and careful listening of the class. For example: "Many students had questions or comments for the sharers." "Students kept their eyes on the sharers."

VARIATION

■ Do this as an around-the-circle sharing, with each student bringing a book to the meeting circle. After everyone has shared, invite a few students to direct a question or comment to a classmate of their choice.

EXTENSION FOR A LATER LANGUAGE ARTS LESSON

■ Remind students about their book sharing and have them draw and write about the book they shared. Give them a sentence frame: "My book is _____. I liked/did not like it because _____."

Reading Inquiry

Language Arts Content

Interrogatives

Common Core Standards

W.K.8 Recall information from experiences or gather information from provided sources to answer a question

SL.K.3 Ask and answer questions to seek help, get information, or clarify something

L.K.1d Use question words (who, what, where, when, why, how)

L.K.1f Produce and expand complete sentences in shared language activities

Materials Needed

A chart with words and visuals to identify each word, such as a question mark for "what," a house or apartment building for "where," a clock for "when," and a stick figure for "who"

How to do it:

1 Introduce the sharing: "This week, we are going to share about our reading preferences. Usually during sharing, you share and then you answer questions from individual classmates. This sharing will be different because you will answer questions that all of your classmates will ask you at the same time. These are the questions the class will ask: 'What type of book do you like? Where do you like to read? When do you like to read? Who is someone you like to read with?' Take a moment to think about your answers to these questions."

2 Explain that answers will be complete sentences and ask for a volunteer to go first. The class chorally asks the sharer the first question, "What type of book do you like?" The sharer answers in a complete sentence, such as "I like to read books about dogs." The class chorally asks the next question: "Where do you like to read?" Continue having the class ask the questions and the sharer answer.

3 Invite two or three more children to share.

4 Reflect on the sharing, asking questions such as "What books did more than one sharer name?" and "What other things did the sharers have in common?"

5 Throughout the week, invite the rest of the class to share.

VARIATION

▪ Do this as a partner share: One partner asks the questions and one answers. Then reverse the roles.

EXTENSION FOR A LATER LANGUAGE ARTS LESSON

▪ Have students write a story, making sure to tell the "what," "where," "when," and "who" about the plot of the story. Prompt them to refer to the Morning Meeting chart with the question words and visuals as an aid.

Talking in Circles

How to do it:

1 Introduce the sharing: "Today, we are going to share about a kindergarten topic. The topic is: 'What do you like to do in kindergarten?'" Brainstorm some things students like to do in kindergarten.

2 As students stand, help them form an inner and an outer circle with each child facing a partner.

3 Explain that the person in the inner circle will go first. Then the person in the outer circle will ask a question or make a comment. Next the person in the inner circle will answer (if a question was asked), and finally both people will be silent.

4 Model this with a student: Put yourself in the inner circle and say to your partner, "I like to read books to the students in kindergarten." Your partner responds, "Why do you like reading books to the students?" and you answer, "I like sharing stories that I think students will enjoy."

5 After you and your partner stand silently for a moment, signal students to begin sharing with their partners.

6 When partners are finished, the outer circle takes one step to the right. This time, the outer circle shares and the inner circle asks a question or makes a comment.

7 Continue with new partners as time allows.

VARIATION

■ Do this as an around-the-circle sharing and have each person say one thing they like to do in kindergarten. After everyone has shared, ask questions such as "Who can remember who likes to do something outside?" and "Who can remember someone who likes to sing songs?"

EXTENSIONS FOR A LATER LANGUAGE ARTS LESSON

■ Read books that take place in kindergarten.

■ Write a class book, *Things We Like to Do in Kindergarten.*

Language Arts Content

Speaking about a topic

Common Core Standards

RF.K.4 Read emergent-reader texts with purpose and understanding

W.K.2 Compose informative/explanatory texts

SL.K.1 Participate in collaborative conversations about kindergarten topics and texts

SL.K.3 Ask and answer questions to seek help, get information, or clarify something

SL.K.6 Speak audibly and express thoughts, feelings, and ideas clearly

Materials Needed

None

Vocabulary

Topic

1, 2, 3, Rhyme With Me

Language Arts Content

Rhyming words

Common Core Standards

RF.K.2a Recognize and produce rhyming words

RF.K.2e Add or substitute individual sounds to make new words

RF.K.3d Distinguish between words by identifying letter sounds that differ

Materials Needed

Chart of rhyming words and pictures (optional)

Vocabulary

Rhyme

How to do it:

1 As students sit in a circle, introduce the group activity: "We are going to practice rhyming words. Remember rhyming words sound the same at the end; only the beginning sound is different. One beginning sound takes the place of another. For example, cat–bat and rake–lake." Brainstorm a few more rhyming words or review the chart of rhyming words and pictures.

2 Coach students through the first round of this chant:

First student in the circle:	One
Second student in the circle:	Two
Third student in the circle:	Three
Fourth student in the circle:	Rhyme with me
Teacher says a word to be rhymed:	Hen
Class responds with rhyming words:	Pen (or any word that rhymes with "hen")

3 When students run out of ideas, begin the chant again with a new word.

VARIATIONS

■ Let a student announce the word to be rhymed. (It's fine for students to use made-up words.)

■ Let a student write the rhyming words the class calls out on a chart. Model first by writing the first word called out. Then invite a student volunteer to write the rest of the words.

EXTENSION FOR A LATER LANGUAGE ARTS LESSON

■ Write and illustrate a rhyming word book.

If Your Letter's on the Card

How to do it:

1 As students stand in a circle, give each student an uppercase letter card. (If necessary, give some children two cards until all uppercase letters are handed out.)

2 Introduce the following song, sung to the tune of "If You're Happy and You Know It."

If your letter's on the floor, pick it up
If your letter's on the floor, pick it up
If your letter's on the floor, it won't be anymore
If your letter's on the floor, pick it up.

3 Put four or five lowercase letters on the floor inside the circle.

4 Explain the group activity: "We're going to look carefully at the lowercase letters on the floor. If you have the matching uppercase letter, you'll walk carefully to the lowercase letter, pick it up, and return to your spot." Model for students.

5 Continue explaining: "Then we'll go around the circle and each person who found a match will say the name of the letter and the sound it makes. For example, someone might say, 'I have b, /b/.'"

6 Sing the song with the class as they search for their matching card. When the first set of students who found matching cards return to their spots in the circle, they take turns saying their letter and the sound, and then put the cards down in front of them.

7 Reinforce students' careful and calm behavior. For example: "I notice children are walking carefully around the cards and the other students while looking for a match." "Students are holding their cards quietly and gently."

8 Put four or five more cards on the floor inside the circle and continue the activity until all the letters have been matched.

VARIATION

■ In the beginning of the year, have students say just the name of the matching lowercase letter and not the sound. Later in the year, have students say the name of the letter, the sound, and a word that begins with that letter.

EXTENSION FOR A LATER LANGUAGE ARTS LESSON

■ Have students choose a matching uppercase and lowercase letter, write both forms of the letter, and draw an object that begins with that letter.

Language Arts Content

Letters and sounds

Common Core Standards

RF.K.1d Recognize upper- and lowercase letters

RF.K.3a Demonstrate basic knowledge of one-to-one letter-sound correspondence

SL.K.6 Speak audibly

L.K.1a Print many upper- and lowercase letters

Materials Needed

A set of uppercase letter cards and a set of lowercase letter cards

Vocabulary

Uppercase letter, lowercase letter

Grade Level

K

Group Activity

I See

Language Arts Content

Identifying topics and events

Common Core Standards

W.K.3 Narrate a single event or several loosely linked events

SL.K.4 Describe familiar people, places, things, and events

L.K.1f Produce and expand complete sentences in shared language activities

L.K.5c Identify real-life connections between words and their use

Materials Needed

None

Vocabulary

Topic, event, pantomime

How to do it:

1 Before Morning Meeting, determine a topic that students will be writing about later in the day—for example, events that happen in spring, such as riding bikes, eating ice cream, flying a kite, planting a garden, playing tag, and blowing bubbles.

2 With students standing in a circle, introduce the activity: "Later today, our writing topic will be events that happen in spring. In this activity, we'll act out some of those events. Remember to be careful with your bodies as you pantomime the events."

3 Coach students through the following call and response:

Teacher: I see . . .

Students: What do you see?

Teacher: I see children learning to ride a bicycle. *(Children pantomime learning to ride a bicycle.)*

Teacher: That's what I see! *(Children stop the pantomime and return to their places in the circle.)*

4 Repeat the call and response with more events that fit your topic. As students become comfortable with the group activity, let volunteers say your part and name the event.

EXTENSION FOR A LATER LANGUAGE ARTS LESSON

- Refer back to the group activity at writing time to remind students of ideas for the writing topic.

Grade Level

K

Group Activity

Let's All Do the Opposite

How to do it:

Language Arts Content:

Opposites

Common Core Standards

RF.K.3c Read high-frequency words by sight

L.K.5b Relating verbs and adjectives to their opposites

L.K.6 Use words acquired through conversations, reading and being read to, and responding to texts

Materials Needed

A list of opposite words with pictures

Vocabulary

Opposites

1 Introduce the group activity: "Yesterday, we made a chart of opposites. Today, we are going to have a chance to practice them by singing a song. I will sing a word and act it out. You will tell me the opposite and act it out. For example, I might sing 'I'm cold' and rub my arms. You would then sing 'I'm hot' and fan your face. Let's read over the chart to refresh our memories about opposites."

2 After reading the chart with students, teach the following song and movements: Let's All Do the Opposite (sung to the tune of "Did You Ever See a Lassie?").

Teacher and students:	Let's all do the opposite, the opposite, the opposite. Let's all do the opposite, until I say stop.
Teacher:	I'm hot. *(Teacher pantomimes being hot.)*
Students:	I'm cold. *(Students pantomime being cold.)*
Teacher:	I'm happy. *(Teacher pantomimes being happy.)*
Students:	I'm sad. *(Students pantomime being sad.)*
Teacher and students:	Let's all do the opposite, until I say stop.

3 Continue singing the song and substituting in various words. To end the activity, say "Stop the opposites!" after students have responded with the last opposite.

SOME OPPOSITES TO TRY

- Adjectives: quiet–loud, high–low, clean–dirty, dry–wet, slow–fast, healthy–sick, empty–full, tall–short, mean–nice, straight–crooked

- Verbs: stopping–going, sleeping–waking, pushing–pulling, floating–sinking, throwing–catching, shouting–whispering, opening–closing

VARIATION

- Do a speed round in which you say a word and pantomime it and students quickly say and pantomime the opposite. Time the class to see how long it takes to do ten opposites. On another day, see if you can beat your time.

EXTENSION FOR A LATER LANGUAGE ARTS LESSON

- Take photographs of students doing opposite activities—for example, throwing and catching a ball—or have students draw pictures of themselves doing these activities. Display the pictures or use them for a matching game, in which you distribute the cards and students mix and mingle looking for the person with the card that's the opposite of theirs.

One Is Never Enough

Language Arts Content

Plural nouns

Common Core Standards

RF.K.2e Add or substitute individual sounds to make new words

W.K.2 Compose informative/explanatory texts and supply information about the topic

L.K.1b Use frequently occurring nouns

L.K.1c Form regular plural nouns orally by adding /s/ or /es/

Materials Needed

One die

Vocabulary

Plural

How to do it:

1 With students sitting in a circle, choose one volunteer to be the child and one volunteer to be the mom or dad. They come to the center of the circle.

2 The child decides what animal he wants and chooses one classmate to be that animal—for example, a kitten. This classmate joins the child and mom or dad in the middle of the circle and acts out being a kitten. The child then asks, "Mom, can I have one kitten?" Mom answers, "Of course."

3 The class says the refrain, "One is never enough!"

4 The child rolls the die to determine how many kittens he should ask for now. (If he rolls a one, he rolls again.) He then chooses classmates to be that number of kittens—three, for example. They join the child and the mom in the center of the circle and act out being kittens. Then the child asks, "Mom, can I have three kittens?" Mom replies dramatically, "Three kittens are too many!"

5 Point out to the class that the first child asked for one kitten and then he wanted three kittens, emphasizing the /s/ on the end of "kittens."

6 Have the child, the mom, and the kittens sit back down in the circle and then choose new volunteers. Continue as time allows.

VARIATION

■ When the child chooses the animal that he wants, write "1" and the animal name on a chart, for example, "1 horse." After the child rolls the die to determine how many animals he'll ask for the second time, write that number and the animal name on the chart, for example, "3 horse." Then ask a volunteer to come up to the chart and add the "s" to the end of "horse." (Offer help if the animal name is an irregular noun like "pony" or "mouse.")

EXTENSIONS FOR A LATER LANGUAGE ARTS LESSON

■ Make a class number book of animals mentioned during this activity.

■ Look at number books such as Eric Carle's *Rooster's Off to See the World* to find the "s" at the ends of the plural words.

The Bookey Pokey

Language Arts Content

Parts of a book (informational texts)

Common Core Standards

RI.K.5 Identify the front cover, back cover, and title page of a book

RF.K.1 Understand the organization and basic features of print

RF.K.4 Read emergent-reader texts with purpose and understanding

W.K.8 Recall information from experiences or gather information from provided sources to answer a question

Materials Needed

A book for each student

Vocabulary

Front cover, back cover, title page, spine

How to do it:

Have each child bring a book to Morning Meeting and set it aside until it's time for the group activity.

1 As students stand in the circle holding their books, introduce the group activity: "We are going to do the Hokey Pokey, but this time we will be showing the parts of a book when we do it. Our activity is called the Bookey Pokey. Remember we have to be safe when we move our bodies and be gentle with our books. Now I'll show you how the activity will go."

2 Model for students by singing the song and doing the motions yourself:

You put the cover in *(hold book, arms extended toward the center of the circle, with cover facing out)*

You put the cover out *(pull book back in toward your body)*

You put the cover in *(put book back into the circle)*

And you wiggle it about *(gently wiggle the book)*

You do the Bookey Pokey *(pull book back in toward your body)*

And you turn yourself around *(turn around while wiggling the book gently)*

That's what it's all about. *(hold the book in front of you)*

The Bookey Pokey!

4 Students repeat the first line with you and do the motions.

5 Continue singing and putting the other parts of the book into the circle: back cover, title page, spine.

EXTENSIONS FOR A LATER LANGUAGE ARTS LESSON

■ Quickly assess a student's knowledge of the parts of a book by chanting quietly to him: "Show me the front cover. Show me the back cover. Show me the title page. Now read a page to me."

■ Give students an outline drawing of a book and have them label the parts.

The Long and Short of It

Language Arts Content

Long and short vowel sounds

Common Core Standards

RF.K.2d Isolate and pronounce initial, medial vowel, and final sounds in words

RF.K.3b Associate the long and short sounds with the five major vowels

Materials Needed

A chart with the first stanza of "This Old Man" written on it.

Vocabulary

Short vowel, long vowel

How to do it:

1 Display the chart of "This Old Man."

This old man, he played one.
He played knick knack on my thumb.
With a knick knack paddy whack,
Give the dog a bone.
This old man came rolling home.

2 Introduce the group activity: "Yesterday, we sorted long and short vowel sounds. In our activity today, we are going to listen carefully to words. If the word has a long vowel sound, we are going to stretch a long way down and touch our toes. If the word has a short vowel sound, we are going to bend a short way and touch our knees."

3 Read through "This Old Man" once without any movements so that students become familiar with it.

4 Say a word from the song that has a short vowel sound and emphasize the vowel sound. For example, say "this" and have children touch their knees. Repeat with a word that has a long vowel sound (such as "old") and have students touch their toes.

5 Continue calling out words from the song and have students touch their knees or toes accordingly. Mix up the short and long vowel words.

VARIATIONS

- Invite a student volunteer to choose a word from the song or poem and say the word for the class, emphasizing the vowel sound just as you did.

- As a challenge and after practice, say the entire rhyme slowly and have students do the movements for each long and short vowel sound they hear.

EXTENSIONS FOR A LATER LANGUAGE ARTS LESSON

- During reading and writing, use the motions of reaching for your toes for a long vowel sound or touching your knees for a short vowel sound as a visual cue for students.

- Write the words from "This Old Man" on cards and have students sort them by long and short vowel sounds.

What's That Sound?

How to do it:

1 Introduce the group activity: "Today, we are going to listen carefully to sounds. You will close your eyes or cover them and try to identify the sound you hear. Remember, we are relying on our sense of hearing, so no peeking!"

2 Name the three noise makers and demonstrate the sounds they make.

3 When students have covered their eyes, make one of the sounds. Call on a volunteer to tell you which sound she heard.

4 Repeat a few times with the different sounds.

5 Introduce a challenge: "This time I am going to make things a little harder. I am going to do three sounds and you have to tell me which sound you heard at the end."

6 Make the three sounds and invite a volunteer to tell you which sound she heard at the end.

7 Repeat a few more times. Change the order of the sounds or ask children to identify the sound they heard at the beginning or in the middle.

VARIATIONS

- Have students listen only for the position of one sound. For example: "Listen for the bell and tell me if you hear it in the beginning, in the middle, or at the end."

- Substitute letter sounds for the noisemakers.

EXTENSION FOR A LATER LANGUAGE ARTS LESSON

- Have student volunteers use the noisemakers and call on classmates to identify the sound in each position.

Language Arts Content

Phonemic awareness, hearing beginning, middle, and ending sounds

Common Core Standards

RF.K.1b Recognize that spoken words are represented in written language by specific sequences of letters

RF.K.2d Isolate and pronounce initial, medial vowel, and final sounds in words

Materials Needed

Three noisemakers, such as a bell, a clapper, and a drum, or classroom objects that can serve as noisemakers, such as two blocks to hit together, a pencil to tap on a book, and an empty water bottle to crinkle

A Capital Idea

Language Arts Content

Capitalization, punctuation

Common Core Standards

RI.K.10 Actively engage in group reading activities with purpose and understanding

RF.K.1a Follow words from left to right and top to bottom

L.K.1a Print many uppercase letters

L.K.2a Capitalize the first word in a sentence

L.K.2b Recognize and name end punctuation

Materials Needed

None

Vocabulary

Capital letter, uppercase letter, punctuation, period, question mark, exclamation point

How to do it:

1 Display a version of the following message.

> Good Morning, Everyone!
>
> Today is _____.
>
> We will practice capitalizing the first letter of a sentence.
>
> Do you see more capital letters or more lowercase letters in this message?
>
> Write a capital letter below.
>
> J F Q

2 Students chorally read the message as you point to the words.

3 Review that every sentence begins with a capital letter and ends with punctuation such as a period, question mark, or exclamation point.

4 Invite student volunteers to circle capital letters in the message in green.

5 Choose other volunteers to circle punctuation at the end of the sentences in red.

6 As you reread the message, pointing to each word, students raise their hands in the air when they come to a capital letter. When they come to the punctuation at the end of each sentence, they say a word and make a corresponding motion for the punctuation as follows:

➤ Period—Hold one hand up at shoulder height, palms out and fingers splayed, and say, "Stop."

➤ Question mark—Hold hands out to the side with elbows bent and palms up, raise shoulders and say, "Huh?"

➤ Exclamation point—Hold hands up at shoulder height with palms out, wiggle hands back and forth and say, "Yay!"

EXTENSION FOR A LATER LANGUAGE ARTS LESSON

■ Give students a poem or a passage from a book. Have them circle the capital letters at the beginning of the sentences in green and the ending punctuation in red.

Give Me Space

Language Arts Content

Print concepts

Common Core Standards

RI.K.10 Actively engage in group reading activities with purpose and understanding

RF.K.1a Follow words from left to right and top to bottom

RF.K.1c Understand that words are separated by spaces in print

Materials Needed

Small stickers such as colored dots

How to do it:

1 Display a message like the following (be mindful of leaving obvious spaces between words):

Today   is   Wednesday.

_____   is   the   line   leader.

_____   is   the   caboose.

Yesterday,   we   learned   that   words   have   spaces   between   them.

Find   one   space   between   words.

---

2 Students chorally read the message as you point to the words.

3 Invite students to come up to the message and place a sticker in a space between words.

4 Reinforce students' effort and behavior: "Students are looking closely to find spaces between words." "Students are waiting patiently for their turns."

VARIATION

- Read through the message once. Then point to each word and space and have the children do a movement pattern to follow along. For example, each time you point to a word, students put their hands on their heads, and each time you point to a space, they put their hands in their laps.

EXTENSION FOR A LATER LANGUAGE ARTS LESSON

- On a simple piece of text such as a nursery rhyme, students put dots on the paper to mark the spaces between words. (Make sure that the spacing between the words is large enough.)

Phoneme Fun

Language Arts Content

Segmenting and blending sounds

Common Core Standards

RI.K.10 Actively engage in group reading activities with purpose and understanding

RF.K.1a Follow words from left to right and top to bottom

RF.K.2 Demonstrate understanding of spoken words, syllables, and sounds

RF.K.3 Apply grade-level phonics and word analysis skills

L.K.2d Spell simple words phonetically

Materials Needed

None

Vocabulary

Segment, blend

How to do it:

1 Display a version of the following message:

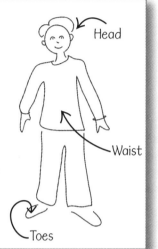

Good day, class.

Today is Wednesday, September 7, _____.

We have art.

We will segment words into sounds and blend them back together again.

Practice touching your head, waist, and toes.

Head

Waist

Toes

2 Invite a student to be the message pointer. Divide the class in half. One half reads the first sentence, the other half reads the next sentence. Continue alternating groups until you've read the entire message.

3 Have students stand and practice touching their head, then their waist, and finally their toes with two hands.

4 Say a word from the chart that only has three sounds—for example, "have"—and ask the class to repeat it.

5 Students slowly speak the word again and touch their head for the first sound, /h/, their waist for the second sound, /a/, and their toes for the last sound, /v/. They then stand up and blend the word back together again, "have."

6 Continue segmenting and blending other three-sound words from the chart.

VARIATIONS

■ For a two-sound word like "we," touch your head for the first sound, /w/, and your waist for the second sound, /e/.

■ For a word with a consonant blend at the beginning like "class," touch your head for the first sound, /c/, your shoulders for the next sound, /l/, your waist for the third sound, /a/, and your toes for the last sound, /s/.

EXTENSION FOR A LATER LANGUAGE ARTS LESSON

■ During writing, encourage students to touch their head, waist, and toes for each sound as they sound out words to write.

Typewriter

How to do it:

Before using a message like this, make sure students have some familiarity with a typewriter.

Language Arts Content

Print concepts

Common Core Standards

RI.K.10 Actively engage in group reading activities with purpose and understanding

RF.K.1a Follow words from left to right and top to bottom

Materials Needed

A visual of a typewriter from the Internet or a book such as *Click, Clack, Moo: Cows That Type*

1 Display a message like the following:

> Good morning, Kindergartners.
>
> Today is Monday.
>
> _____ is the line leader.
>
> _____ is the caboose.
>
> We will practice reading left to right and top to bottom.
>
> Can you believe we've been in school for a week already?

2 Tell students, "We've been talking about how readers read from top to bottom and left to right. Listen and watch as I read our message." Point to each word and emphasize the motion of your return sweep as you read the message.

3 Have the class choral read the message with you. Remind them about top to bottom, left to right. Point to each word and again emphasize the return sweep.

4 Explain the next step: "Now we will pretend to use typewriters as we reread the message. Put your hands out like this [hands extended with fingers ready to type]. As I read, move your fingers like you are typing and softly make a clickity noise." Model this for students. Then read the first sentence as the students "type" along with you.

5 Stop at the end of the first sentence and explain: "At the end of a line, when we go back to the left and down a row, this is what you have to do on a typewriter." (Move your right hand back to the left and down a row while making a *thwit* sound as if pushing the lever of a typewriter. Then bring that hand back into position to type again.) Have students practice.

6 Continue reading the message as students "type" along with you.

EXTENSION FOR A LATER LANGUAGE ARTS LESSON

■ Read a book that features a typewriter, such as *Click, Clack, Moo: Cows That Type*.

Are You Curious, George?

Language Arts Content

Characters

Common Core Standards

RL.1.3 Describe characters using key details

RL.1.7 Use illustrations and details in a story to describe its characters

W.1.1 Write opinion pieces; introduce topic, state an opinion, supply a reason, and provide closure

Materials Needed

A list of common book characters, such as Curious George, Froggy, Fly Guy, and The Very Hungry Caterpillar

Vocabulary

Character

How to do it:

1 Introduce the greeting: "Today we are going to greet each other like book characters. You will get to make noises and do motions so you will also have to show a lot of self-control."

2 Brainstorm some book characters and some sounds and motions to go with them. For example, for Curious George, students might say "ooo-aaaa" while scratching at their ribs.

3 Model the greeting:

➤ Walk over to a student you've prepared ahead of time and say, "Good morning, _____! Let's greet like Curious George."

➤ That student stands up, and both of you do the monkey sound and motion. Then you return to your spot in the circle and sit down.

➤ Ask the class what they noticed about the way you and the student greeted each other.

4 Begin the greeting. The student you greeted moves to stand in front of another student in the circle, greets that student, and names a character for the two of them to act out, the way you modeled it. Repeat until everyone has been greeted and only one person is standing.

5 The last student standing stays in her spot in the circle and says, "Good morning, everyone! Let's greet like [character name]." The entire class stands up, says the word or sound, and does the action for this last character.

EXTENSIONS FOR A LATER LANGUAGE ARTS LESSON

■ Have students draw a small picture of a favorite book character; then use the pictures to create a graph showing how many students chose each character.

■ Invite students to write a sentence or two about why they like a certain character or a connection they have to that character.

Final-E Decoded

Language Arts Content

Long and short vowel sounds, final -e

Common Core Standards

RF.1.2 Demonstrate understanding of spoken words, syllables, and sounds

RF.1.3b Decode regularly spelled one-syllable words

RF.1.3c Know final -e for representing long vowel sounds

SL.1.1a Follow agreed-upon rules for discussions

L.1.4 Determine or clarify the meaning of unknown and multiple-meaning words and phrases

Materials Needed

Cards with the letter "e" on them (enough for half the class) and cards with CVC words on them (enough for half the class). Some possible CVC words to use: can, hid, dim, cod, hop, cub, tub.

Vocabulary

Long vowel, short vowel

How to do it:

1 Help students form an inner and an outer circle with each child standing and facing a partner. Give students in the inner circle a letter "e" card and those in the outer circle a CVC word card. Remind students to hold their cards quietly and carefully.

2 Introduce the greeting: "Today in our greeting, we are going to practice changing words with a short vowel into words with a long vowel by adding a final 'e.'"

3 Model the greeting:

➤ Stand in the outer circle facing a student in the inner circle.

➤ Say, "Hello, Stan." Stan replies, "Hello, Mr. Smythe."

➤ Show your word to Stan (for example, "can") and read it aloud.

➤ Stan holds his letter "e" card next to your word and together you say, "We final-e decoded the word 'cane.'"

➤ Have each pair of students greet each other and read their final -e words.

4 The outer circle passes their word cards to the person on their left, the inner circle takes one step to their left, and students repeat the greeting. Continue for a few more rounds as time allows.

VARIATION

■ Do the greeting as a group activity. As in the greeting, have an outer circle with CVC words and an inner circle with letter "e" cards. Partners read the CVC word and the final -e word and quickly pass their cards to the person on their left. Partners stay together and continue decoding final -e words.

EXTENSION FOR A LATER LANGUAGE ARTS LESSON

■ Have students add to the CVC word cards and then sort the corresponding long vowel words into real words and nonsense words.

Me, Myself, and I

Language Arts Content

Pronouns

Common Core Standards

W.1.7 Participate in shared research and writing projects

L.1.1d Use personal, possessive, and indefinite pronouns

L.1.6 Use words and phrases acquired through conversations, reading and being read to, and responding to texts

Materials Needed

Cards with personal pronouns, one for each student—I, we, me, us, you, he, she, it, they, him, her, them, myself, himself, herself, themselves, itself. (Pronouns can be repeated.)

Vocabulary

Pronoun, singular, plural

How to do it:

1 Introduce the greeting: "This morning, we are going to greet each other using the pronouns we have been studying. Pronouns can be a bit tricky, so ask for help if you need it. We are also going to be giving pinky shakes. What are some things we have to remember so we can be kind and safe when we give a pinky shake?" Elicit answers such as "Give the pinky shake gently. Smile at the person we're giving a pinky shake to."

2 With students standing in a circle, give each a pronoun card.

3 Ask students to raise their card if their pronoun represents one person. Ask students to raise their card if their pronoun represents more than one person. Continue raising cards for other categories such as pronouns that represent a male, a female, an object, an animal, yourself, and someone or something else.

4 Name a category of pronouns, for example, singular pronouns or pronouns that have to do with one person or object. All the students who have a singular pronoun go to the middle of the circle. They take turns stating their pronoun, for example, "My pronoun is 'he.'" (If a student's pronoun does not fit the category, redirect her matter-of-factly. For example, "'We' represents more than one person. Return to your spot in the circle and listen for that category.")

5 Students in the middle of the circle pair up and give their partners a pinky shake. Reiterate the category: "All these pronouns are singular. They refer to one person or object." Students return to their spots in the circle.

6 Continue calling other categories of pronouns. Make sure everyone is greeted at least once.

VARIATION

▪ Use possessive pronouns (ours, mine, yours, its, theirs, his, hers) in addition to or in place of personal pronouns.

EXTENSION FOR A LATER LANGUAGE ARTS LESSON

▪ Invite students to make individual pronoun books. Each student can illustrate the pronoun in a way that will help him remember what the pronoun represents. For example, a page for "he" might show one child, while a page for "they" might show two children or two dogs.

That's Not Nellie's

Language Arts Content

Proper and possessive nouns

Common Core Standards

W.1.3 Write narratives; recount sequenced events, include details, use temporal words, provide sense of closure

SL.1.1 Participate in collaborative conversations about grade 1 topics and texts

L.1.1b Use proper and possessive nouns

L.1.1e Use verbs to convey a sense of past, present, and future

Materials Needed

A ball, bean bag, or other object to pass

Vocabulary

Proper noun, possessive noun

How to do it:

1 With students standing in a circle, introduce the greeting: "Today we are going to practice using the proper and possessive nouns that we have been studying. Pay careful attention to who has been greeted so you'll know who needs a turn."

2 Teach the greeting:

➤ Stand in front of a student ("Nellie" in this example). Give her the ball and say, "Good morning, Nellie." Nellie responds, "Good morning, Ms. Gennaro." Walk back to your spot in the circle and fold your arms to indicate you've been greeted.

➤ Have the class chant together, "That's not Nellie's. There's been a mistake."

➤ Now Nellie says, "I'll give it to Jimmy, for goodness' sake." As Nellie says this, she walks to stand in front of Jimmy. She hands him the ball and says, "Good morning, Jimmy." He responds, "Good morning, Nellie." Nellie walks back to her spot in the circle and folds her arms.

➤ The class chants, "That's not Jimmy's. There's been a mistake." And Jimmy replies, "I'll give it to Tess, for goodness' sake."

3 Continue until everyone has been greeted. The last person to have the ball says, "I'll put it away, for goodness' sake!" and does so.

4 Invite students to name proper and possessive nouns in the greeting.

VARIATION

▪ Ask a child, say Riley, to volunteer an object of hers to pass during the greeting. Riley should be the last person greeted. On her turn, the class says, "That is Riley's. There's been no mistake." And Riley replies, "I'll put it away, for goodness' sake."

EXTENSION FOR A LATER LANGUAGE ARTS LESSON

▪ Use "That's not Nellie's. There's been a mistake." as a sentence starter for a story.

Character Comparisons

Language Arts Content

Understanding character

Common Core Standards

RL.1.3 Describe characters, settings, and major events in a story, using key details

RL.1.9 Compare and contrast the adventures and experiences of characters in stories

W.1.1 Write opinion pieces; introduce topic, state an opinion, supply a reason, and provide closure

SL.1.2 Ask and answer questions about key details in a text read aloud or information presented orally

SL.1.3 Ask and answer questions about what a speaker says to gather additional information

Materials Needed

Each sharer needs a fiction book they are currently reading

Vocabulary

Character

How to do it:

Choose three or four sharers for each day. Have them bring a fiction book to Morning Meeting.

1 Introduce this dialogue sharing: "This week, everyone will have a chance to share about a character in a book you are reading. A few of you will share each day. You will share the name of the character and something that the character does."

2 Model the sharing: Hold up your book, for example, *Green Eggs and Ham*, and say, "A character in my book is Sam I Am. He tries to get another character to eat green eggs and ham. I'm ready for questions and comments."

3 Brainstorm questions and comments students might have, such as "What does Sam I Am do to get the other character to eat the green eggs and ham?" "Does he get the other character to eat the green eggs and ham?" "What's your favorite thing about the character Sam I Am?" "Sam I Am sounds like a funny character."

4 Have the day's sharers share about a character in their book and take three or four questions and comments each.

5 Reflect on the sharing, asking questions such as "How were some of the characters alike? How were they different?"

VARIATION

▪ Do this as a partner sharing. Each pair takes turns sharing their character, and offering questions and comments. Then invite a few partners to share about ways their characters are alike or different.

EXTENSION FOR A LATER LANGUAGE ARTS LESSON

▪ As a class or individually, make a Venn diagram to compare two of the characters discussed at Morning Meeting.

Fact Finding

How to do it:

1 Introduce the sharing: "We have been reading nonfiction books. Today you are going to share with a partner one fact you learned from your book. You can also share a text feature your book has. Remember to listen respectfully to your partner."

2 Model the sharing: Sit shoulder to shoulder with a student volunteer (whom you've prepared ahead of time). Show him your nonfiction book. Say, "I am reading a book about insects. I learned that a fly turns its food into liquid and then slurps it up with its tongue. I'm ready for questions and comments." Your student partner offers two or three questions and comments. Then he shares his nonfiction book and you offer him two or three questions and comments.

3 Brainstorm with the class questions and comments they could offer. For example: "What else did you learn from the book?" "Does your book have any nonfiction text features?" "Why did you choose to read this book?" "That's an interesting fact." "It might be fun to be a _____ [for example, an animal or a profession that the book is about]."

4 Students pair up. The partners take turns sharing their book and taking two or three questions and comments.

5 When the partners are finished sharing, ask a few students to share with the class facts they learned from their partners. Students can also share about nonfiction text features they saw in the books.

VARIATION

- Do this as a dialogue sharing. Ask three or four students a day to share their nonfiction books with the class. Continue throughout the week until everyone has had a chance to share.

EXTENSIONS FOR A LATER LANGUAGE ARTS LESSON

- At writing time, have students write a fact they learned at Morning Meeting. Gather the writings into a class book, *Facts Found at Morning Meeting*.

- At reading time, let Morning Meeting partners read together and continue to explore each other's nonfiction books.

Language Arts Content

Reading nonfiction (informational texts)

Common Core Standards

RI.1.1 Ask and answer questions about key details in a text

RI.1.2 Retell key details of a text

RI.1.5 Know and use text features to locate key facts or information in a text

W.1.7 Participate in shared research and writing projects

SL.1.1 Participate in collaborative conversations about grade 1 topics and texts

Materials Needed

Each student needs a nonfiction book they have read

Vocabulary

Nonfiction, text feature, fact

Proud Publishers

Language Arts Content

Stating opinions

Common Core Standards

W.1.1 Write opinion pieces; introduce topic, state an opinion, supply a reason, and provide closure

SL.1.1 Participate in collaborative conversations about grade 1 topics and texts

L.1.1j Produce complete simple and compound declarative, interrogative, imperative, and exclamatory sentences

L.1.6 Use words and phrases acquired through conversations, reading and being read to, and responding to texts, including frequently occurring conjunctions

Materials Needed

One published piece of writing by each student (a published piece is one that the student has edited and revised and considers finished)

Vocabulary

Opinion, edit, publish

How to do it:

1 Choose three or four sharers for each day. Have them bring a published piece of writing to Morning Meeting.

2 Introduce this dialogue sharing: "At writing, we have been working hard to edit and publish our writing. At sharing this week, we will share one thing about our work that makes us proud. We call this 'giving our opinion.'"

3 Model the sharing: Hold up a piece of your writing and share using the following sentence frame: "I wrote _____. I am proud of it because _____. I am ready for questions and comments." You might say, "I wrote a poem called 'Wild Wind.' I am proud of it because I used descriptive words like 'whoosh' and 'propel.' I am ready for questions and comments."

4 Brainstorm reasons students might be proud of their work. Some examples: "My illustrations have a lot of details." "I sounded out words on my own." "I took suggestions to improve my work."

5 Have the day's sharers share and take three or four questions and comments each. Reinforce sharing and listening efforts: "The sharers gave thoughtful reasons for being proud of their writing." "Everyone listened respectfully to the sharers and asked interesting questions."

6 Continue the sharing throughout the week until everyone has had a chance to share.

VARIATION

■ Do as a partner sharing and then have a few students share why their partners are proud of their work.

EXTENSIONS FOR A LATER LANGUAGE ARTS LESSON

■ Have students write about why they are proud of their work using the sentence frame "I wrote _____. I am proud of it because _____." Students can illustrate their writing. Display this writing with their published piece.

■ Invite students to read their published piece of writing to small groups or partners.

And, But, Because

How to do it:

Language Arts Content

Conjunctions

Common Core Standards

SL.1.1b Build on others' talk

L.1.1g Use frequently occurring conjunctions

L.1.1j Produce complete simple and compound declarative, interrogative, imperative, and exclamatory sentences

Materials Needed

A chart of the conjunctions "and," "but," and "because" (optional)

Vocabulary

Conjunction

1 Introduce the group activity: "This week, we have been learning about conjunctions. Today in our group activity, we will practice using the conjunctions 'and,' 'but,' and 'because' while making a group story. Each person will add a sentence on to the story."

2 Say a simple sentence, such as "We went to P.E. yesterday." Invite a volunteer to use "and," "but," or "because" to add on to the sentence. The volunteer might say something like "and we played soccer."

3 Choose a second volunteer to add another piece to the sentence with one of the conjunctions. The student might say "but we got muddy."

4 Repeat with a third volunteer, who might say "because it had been raining."

5 Now state another sentence starter, such as "We did a science experiment" or "We have a field trip tomorrow" and the next three students add to it.

6 Continue stating sentence starters until everyone in the circle has had a chance to participate.

7 As time allows, do more rounds with different conjunctions.

EXTENSIONS FOR A LATER LANGUAGE ARTS LESSON

- Look for conjunctions while reading and add them to a class list.

- Write and illustrate some of the sentences from Morning Meeting.

First, Next, Last

Language Arts Content:

Sequencing, temporal words

Common Core Standards:

W.1.3 Write narratives in which they use temporal words to signal event order

W.1.7 Participate in shared research and writing projects (for example, explore a number of "how-to" books on a given topic and use them to write a sequence of instructions)

L.1.1 Demonstrate command of standard English grammar and usage

Materials Needed:

None

Vocabulary:

Sequential order, sequencing, first, next, last

How to do it:

1 With the class standing in a circle, introduce the group activity: "Today, we are going to practice sequencing by using the words 'first,' 'next,' and 'last.' Three people will work together to act out making a peanut butter sandwich."

2 Have students whom you've prepped ahead of time model how to act out making a peanut butter sandwich:

➤ Point to one of the students and say "Peanut butter sandwich." The student holds one hand out, palm up, to be the bottom slice of bread, and says "First."

➤ The person to his left puts her hand on top of his hand to be the peanut butter, and says "Next."

➤ The third person puts his hand, palm down, on the second person's hand to be the top slice of bread, and says "Last."

3 The student who said "Last" now points to a classmate and says "Peanut butter sandwich" to start the activity around the circle. That classmate and the next two students in the circle form a trio to make a sandwich. The child who says "Last" in this trio points to the next student in the circle and says "Peanut butter sandwich," and so on until everyone has had a turn to be part of the sequence.

VARIATION

■ Introduce new action sequences, and invite the pointer to choose which will be acted out. For example, "Read a book": The first person holds her hands out with palms together, opens her palms as if opening a book, and says "First." The second person makes a motion as if turning the pages of a book and says "Next." The third person holds his hands out, palms together and facing up, closes them as if shutting the book, and says "Last."

EXTENSION FOR A LATER LANGUAGE ARTS LESSON

■ Have students write "how-to" books, using the group activity as an example of sequencing and temporal words. Support students in using standard English grammar and usage.

Have I Got a Preposition for You!

Language Arts Content

Prepositions

Common Core Standards

RF.1.4a Read grade-level text with purpose and understanding

W.1.6 Use a variety of digital tools to produce and publish writing

L.1.1i Use frequently occur-ring prepositions

L.1.6 Use words and phrases acquired through conver-sations, reading and being read to, and responding to texts

Materials Needed

A piece of yarn or rope about three feet long; a list of prepositions (optional)

Vocabulary

Preposition

How to do it:

1 Introduce the group activity: "Today, we are going to act out prepositions using this piece of yarn. Some prepositions are 'over,' 'in,' and 'across.' Prepositions connect other words together."

2 Model the group activity:

➤ "I can show the preposition 'on' this way. [Put the yarn on your head.] The yarn is on my head. Or I can show 'on' this way. [Stand on the yarn.] I am standing on the yarn."

➤ "Who can think of a way to show 'in' with the yarn?" Call on a few volunteers to show "in." A student might put the yarn in his pocket and say, "The yarn is in my pocket" or she might make a circle with the yarn, stand in it, and say, "I am standing in the yarn."

3 Continue naming prepositions and inviting students to act them out. Some prepositions to try: in, at, over, by, with, off, beyond, behind, above, across, under, against, along, by, around, beneath, between, beyond, through, near, underneath, upon, within, on.

VARIATIONS

■ Give each student a piece of yarn and have everyone act out the preposition at the same time.

■ Have students choose the prepositions to act out.

EXTENSIONS FOR A LATER LANGUAGE ARTS LESSON

■ Take digital photographs of the students demonstrating the prepositions and make them into a class book or webpage.

■ During reading time, have students notice the prepositions in the books they are reading.

If You're Jovial and You Know It

How to do it:

1 Introduce the group activity: "Yesterday we learned about adjectives. Today, we will practice using them in a song sung to a tune many of you may know, 'If You're Happy and You Know It.' Remember to be safe as we act out the motions of the song."

2 Sing and act out "If You're Jovial and You Know It."

If you're jovial and you know it, laugh out loud. *(Students laugh.)*
If you're jovial and you know it, laugh out loud. *(Students laugh.)*
If you're jovial and you know it, then your face will surely show it.
If you're jovial and you know it, laugh out loud. *(Students laugh.)*

3 Continue inserting different adjectives and motions for subsequent verses. Some adjectives and motions to try:

Drenched—Shake yourself off
Exhausted—Yawn loudly
Filthy—Scrub yourself
Successful—Take a bow
Thrilled—Jump for joy
Zany—Do several energetic motions at once, such as waving your arms around while turning your head from side to side and wiggling your hips

VARIATION

■ Pick a category and insert adjectives that belong in that category. For example, choose the category "sad" and insert adjectives such as glum, upset, blue, troubled, and grumpy. Talk about slight differences in the meanings of the adjectives and how that might impact the way you act out each one.

EXTENSIONS FOR A LATER LANGUAGE ARTS LESSON

■ Encourage students to use the adjectives practiced in the song in their writing.

■ Keep a running list of adjectives and decide on ways to categorize them. Have students add to the list from the books they're reading. Use the list to generate writing topics. For example, write about a time you were exhausted or about someone you know who is successful.

Language Arts Content

Adjectives

Common Core Standards

W.1.3 Write narratives; recount sequenced events, include details, use temporal words, provide sense of closure

L.1.1f Use frequently occurring adjectives

L.1.5c Identify real-life connections between words and their use

L.1.5d Distinguish shades of meaning among verbs and adjectives

Materials Needed

List of adjectives (optional)

Vocabulary

Adjective

I'm Thinking Of

Language Arts Content

Categories and attributes

Common Core Standards

SL.1.1a Follow agreed-upon rules for discussions

SL.1.4 Describe people, places, things, and events with relevant details

L.1.5b Define words by category and key attributes

L.1.6 Use words and phrases acquired through conversations, reading and being read to, and responding to texts

Materials Needed

None

Vocabulary

Category, attribute

How to do it:

1 Introduce the group activity: "In today's group activity, we will guess what a person is thinking of by using what we've been learning about categories and attributes. Our first category will be insects." (Choose a category familiar to your students.)

2 Brainstorm a list of insects.

3 Tell the class, "In this activity, a volunteer will choose an insect and list some of its attributes using the sentence frame 'I'm thinking of an insect that _____' and then call on classmates to guess the insect."

4 Model for students: "I'm thinking of an insect that is red and flies." Call on students to guess what insect you are thinking of (a ladybug). If students are unable to guess the insect after two tries, list another attribute. "I'm thinking of an insect that is red and flies and eats aphids."

5 Invite a student to go next and continue with new volunteers as time allows.

Other categories to try: sports, students in the class, art materials, colors, emotions, community

VARIATIONS

■ Invite students to choose the category for the group activity.

■ Let students think of words and determine the categories and attributes on their own. For example, one student might think of a cat and say, "I'm thinking of a pet that meows." Another student might think of a hammer and say, "I'm thinking of a tool that you hit nails with."

EXTENSION FOR A LATER LANGUAGE ARTS LESSON

■ Have students write and illustrate categories and attributes from the group activity. First they fold a piece of paper in half like a greeting card. On the outside they write, for example, "I'm thinking of a thing to play with that I take to the playground." On the inside, they might write "Frisbee" or "jump rope" and draw a picture of the object.

Just Say the Word

Language Arts Content

Sight words

Common Core Standards

RF.1.3 Know and apply phonics and word analysis skills in decoding words

RF.1.3g Recognize and read irregularly spelled words

L.1.2d Use conventional spelling

Materials Needed

Sight word cards, one for each person; chart with the following chant: "Just say the word and when you do, we will spell it back to you!"

How to do it:

1 Have students stand in a circle. Give each student a sight word card and introduce the group activity: "We are going to practice spelling sight words in a fun way. You will get to decide how we spell your word; for example, we might spell a word in a whisper voice or we might hop when we spell a word. Remember that we need to be safe during the activity, so we'll move our bodies carefully."

2 Brainstorm ways to spell the words, such as in a spooky voice, in a high voice, in a sing-song voice, or turn around as we spell, jog as we spell, slap our thighs as we spell.

3 Introduce the chant that you've written on the chart: "For each person's turn, we'll chant these words aloud together. Then the person will say their word in a special way and we'll all spell it together in the same way. Let's try it; I'll do the first word to show you how it will work."

➤ Class: "Just say the word and when you do, we will spell it back to you!"

➤ You (saying the word on your card in an excited voice while jumping gently up and down): "After."

➤ Class: Spells "a-f-t-e-r" in excited voices while jumping as you did.

➤ Class: Repeats the chant. The next student in the circle says the word on her card in her chosen manner and the class spells it in that manner.

4 Continue around the circle until everyone has had a turn.

VARIATIONS

■ Use word cards with a given spelling pattern such as silent -e words or consonant blend words.

■ Reverse the chant: "Just spell your word and when you do, we will say it back to you." Each child spells his word and the class states the word.

EXTENSION FOR A LATER LANGUAGE ARTS LESSON

■ Play "Just Say the Word" in pairs or small groups.

Lazy Mary

Language Arts Content

Understanding point of view

Common Core Standards

RL.1.4 Identify words and phrases that suggest feelings or appeal to the senses

RL.1.6 Identify who is telling the story at various points in a text

RL.1.9 Compare and contrast the adventures and experiences of characters in stories

RF.1.4 Read with sufficient accuracy and fluency to support comprehension

W.1.8 Recall information or gather information to answer a question

Materials Needed

A chart with the words to "Lazy Mary":

Lazy Mary, will you get up, will you, will you, will you get up?

Lazy Mary, will you get up, will you get up today?

No, Mother, I won't get up, I won't, I won't, I won't get up.

No, Mother, I won't get up, I won't get up today.

Vocabulary

Point of view

How to do it:

1 Introduce the group activity: "Today we are going to act out a poem that has different points of view: the mother's and Lazy Mary's."

2 Read the poem with the class. Ask, "How does the mother feel? How do you know that? How does Lazy Mary feel? How do you know that?"

3 Divide the class into Lazy Marys and Mothers, and reread the poem chorally: the mothers read their two lines, then the Lazy Marys read their two. Encourage students to read with expression.

4 Switch roles and act out the poem again.

VARIATION

■ Reread the poem, but this time have Lazy Mary answer, "Yes, Mother, I will get up." Ask the students how this will change the mother's tone and Lazy Mary's tone. Have them act this out.

EXTENSIONS FOR A LATER LANGUAGE ARTS LESSON

■ Brainstorm reasons the mother might give Lazy Mary to get out of bed. For example, "You have school today; your grandparents are visiting; you have to go to the dentist; it's your birthday; it's your turn to walk the dog." Students can sort the reasons into piles for reasons to get out of bed and reasons to stay in bed.

■ Have students write and illustrate a connection to Lazy Mary in response to questions like these: "When were you lazy? Think of a time when you didn't want to get out of bed. Have you ever tried to get someone else out of bed?"

My Son John

How to do it:

Language Arts Content

Understanding categories

Common Core Standards

RL.1.7 Use illustrations and details in a story to describe its characters, setting, or events

RL.1.10 Read prose and poetry of appropriate complexity

W.1.8 Recall information or gather information to answer a question

L.1.5a Sort words into categories

Materials Needed

A chart with the words to "My Son John":

Diddle, diddle, dumpling, my son John

Went to bed with his trousers on

One shoe off, one shoe on

Diddle, diddle, dumpling, my son John

Vocabulary

Categories

1 Introduce the group activity: "Today we are going to act out a poem. We will add motions to the poem, so make sure you have enough room to move carefully without knocking into anyone."

2 Display the chart of "My Son John." Read it with students and show them the following motions:

Diddle *(one hand on head)*, diddle *(other hand on head)*,

Dump . . . *(one hand on shoulder)* . . . ling *(other hand on shoulder)*

My *(one hand on hip)* son *(other hand on hip)* John *(clap hands together)*

Went to bed with his trousers on *(act out putting on a pair of pants)*

One shoe off *(point to right foot)*, one shoe on *(point to left foot)*

Diddle *(one hand on head)*, diddle *(other hand on head)*,

Dump . . . *(one hand on shoulder)* . . . ling *(other hand on shoulder)*

My *(one hand on hip)* son *(other hand on hip)* John *(clap hands together)*

3 Brainstorm other articles of clothing that John might wear to bed. Encourage students to think of clothing from different categories, such as outerwear (jacket or scarf), or sports clothing (baseball cap).

4 Act out the poem a few more times, inserting other types of clothing in the line, "Went to bed with his _____ on."

VARIATIONS

■ Change the setting of the poem and brainstorm with students different articles of clothing John might wear. For example, if John went to the beach, he might be wearing his bathing suit, and have one flipper off, one flipper on.

■ Change the character in the poem. For example, "Diddle, diddle, dumpling, my daughter Jane, went to bed with her _____ on, one _____ off, one _____ on, Diddle, diddle dumpling, my daughter Jane."

EXTENSION FOR A LATER LANGUAGE ARTS LESSON

■ Illustrate the poem. Allow students to choose which character (for example, John or Jane) and which of the brainstormed sets of clothing to use in their illustrations.

Shades of Meaning

Language Arts Content:

Vocabulary development

Common Core Standards:

RF.1.4c Use context to confirm or self-correct word recognition and understanding

SL.1.1 Participate in collaborative conversations about grade 1 topics and texts

L.1.5d Distinguish shades of meaning among verbs and adjectives

L.1.6 Use words and phrases acquired through conversations, reading and being read to, and responding to texts

Materials Needed:

None

Vocabulary:

Rank

How to do it:

1 Introduce the group activity: "Many words have similar meanings. For example, 'chilly' and 'freezing' both mean cold, but they represent different degrees of cold. Today we are going to use our bodies to rank some words with similar meanings."

2 Extend your hands out in front of you, horizontal to the ground, and explain, "This is the starting point for our ranking of words. For example, this is where we would put our hands to rank the word 'cold'—right in the middle. If the next word is colder than cold, we will move our hands down toward our feet. If the next word is warmer than cold, we will move our hands up."

3 Say "freezing" and move your hands down toward your feet. Say "chilly" and move your hands up. Explain that it's OK if people rank the words differently.

4 Begin stating words and having students rank them with their bodies. If students are confused about how to rank a word, stop to review the meaning of the word and the other words in its set and then rank the words together as a class.

5 Ask students to explain why they chose the rankings they did. For example: "Why did you rank 'noisy' between 'loud' and 'earsplitting'?"

Use sets of words that will give your students a "just-right" challenge. Some ideas:

- flow, gush, flood, trickle
- wave, flutter, flap, sway
- walk, march, stroll
- run, race, zoom, speed

- loud, earsplitting, noisy, booming
- large, enormous, gigantic, big
- small, itsy bitsy, teeny, tiny
- quiet, silent, noiseless, hushed

VARIATION

■ Divide the class into small groups. State the words and have each group rank the words. Then share and compare how each group ranked the words. Ask the groups to explain their thinking.

EXTENSION FOR A LATER LANGUAGE ARTS LESSON

■ Keep a running list of words with similar meanings. Encourage students to use the list when they read to ensure comprehension, and during writing time to find a just-right word or to replace a commonly used word with a more unique one.

What's Going On?

Language Arts Content

Verb tenses

Common Core Standards

SL.1.1a Follow agreed-upon rules for discussions

L.1.1e Use verbs to convey a sense of past, present, and future

L.1.4c Identify frequently occurring root words and their inflectional forms

Materials Needed

None

Vocabulary

Present, past, tense

How to do it:

Have the students stand in a circle.

1 Introduce the group activity: "We have been studying the present and past tenses of verbs. In this group activity, we will do movements and practice using different verb tenses. What are some safe movements that we can do in our places in the circle?" Brainstorm ideas such as jump, jog, twirl, clap, bow, stomp, and dance.

2 Do a simple movement, such as jumping up and down.

3 The class asks you, "Mrs. Jones, what's going on?"

4 Respond: "I am jumping."

5 The class asks the student to your left, "Jason, what's going on?"

6 Jason uses the past tense to state what you did, and he does that motion: "Mrs. Jones jumped" (Jason jumps). Then he uses the correct tense to name his own motion and does that motion: "And now I am running" (Jason runs in place).

7 Continue around the circle with the class asking each student, "What's going on?" Reinforce students' safe moving and use of the correct verb tenses. For example, "Students stayed in their own spots as they did the motions." "People remembered to use the past tense of verbs first." "Students had lots of ideas of actions to show their verbs."

VARIATION

■ Challenge students to remember the motions that all of the students before them did, for example, "Charlie hopped, Anna bowed, Kristen clapped, and now I am dancing."

EXTENSION FOR A LATER LANGUAGE ARTS LESSON

■ Use the verbs from the group activity and fill out a table like the following:

Root Word	Present	Past
jump	jumping	jumped
run	running	ran
bow	bowing	bowed

Greetings, Digraph Detectives

Language Arts Content

Consonant blends, digraphs

Common Core Standards

RI.1.5 Know and use various text features to locate key facts or information

RF.1.2b Produce single-syllable words by blending sounds, including consonant blends

RF.1.3a Know spelling-sound correspondences for common consonant digraphs

SL.1.1 Participate in collaborative conversations about grade 1 topics and texts

Materials Needed

None

Vocabulary

Consonant blend, digraph

How to do it:

1 Display a message like the following:

Greetings, Digraph Detectives,

Today is Thursday, April 23.

During Readers Workshop, we will review consonant blends and digraphs.

Think about how they are alike and different.

How many blends and digraphs can you find in this message? Write the number in the box.

		Blends	Digraphs
6 5 10 8			

2 Chorally read the message with the class.

3 Ask students to share their ideas about how digraphs and blends are alike and different.

4 Invite volunteers to come up to the chart and underline a digraph with a squiggle line and a consonant blend with a straight line.

5 Write each digraph or blend in the appropriate column of the t-chart on the morning message, and then count how many digraphs and blends are in the message.

VARIATION

■ Concentrate on finding only the consonant blends or only the digraphs.

EXTENSION FOR A LATER LANGUAGE ARTS LESSON

■ Write some digraphs and consonant blends on cards. Have students pick cards, say the letters and the sound they make, and sort the cards according to whether they are digraphs or consonant blends. To add a challenge, have students think of a word that contains that consonant blend or digraph.

Sentence Structure Models

How to do it:

1 Display a message that uses capital and lowercase letters, several of the punctuation marks students are learning, and at least one number:

Language Arts Content:

Capitalization, punctuation

Common Core Standards:

RF.1.1a Recognize the distinguishing features of a sentence

L.1.2a Capitalize dates and names of people

L.1.2b Use end punctuation

L.1.2c Use commas in dates and to separate single words in a series

Materials Needed:

None

Vocabulary:

Capitalize, comma, period, exclamation point, question mark

Dear Outdoor Adventurers,

Today is Wednesday, May 17. There are 14 days left in May.

We will take a nature walk with Ms. Elliot.

The weather is going to be warm, breezy, and bright!

What is one thing you might see, hear, or smell on the nature walk?

BIRDS   Flowers

GRASS

---

2 Divide the class into two groups and have the groups read the message, alternating sentences.

3 Call four volunteers to stand in a straight line near the message.

4 Explain how the class will interact with the message: "We are going to model the capital letters, punctuation marks, and numbers in our message. The salutation is 'Dear Outdoor Adventurers.' Maya represents 'Dear.' She is going to raise her hands up high to show the capital letter at the beginning of 'Dear' as she says that word. Juan and Danielle are 'Outdoor' and 'Adventurers.' They will raise their hands to show capital letters, too, as they each say their word. Michael represents the comma. He is going to bend at the waist to show it as he says 'comma.'"

5 Continue having groups of students model the remaining sentences in the message as time allows, assigning body positions for numbers and various punctuation marks. Periodically review why a capital letter or punctuation mark is being used: "Jillian is being a comma because when we write the date, we put a comma between the day of the week and the month."

EXTENSION FOR A LATER LANGUAGE ARTS LESSON

■ Give students a poem or a short passage from a story and have them each model the sentence structures as you read the poem or passage aloud.

What Do You Mean?

Language Arts Content

Using context clues

Common Core Standards

RI.1.4 Ask and answer
questions to determine
or clarify the meaning of
words and phrases

SL.1.1 Participate in collaborative conversations about
grade 1 topics and texts

L.1.4 Determine or clarify
the meaning of unknown
and multiple-meaning
words and phrases

L.1.4a Use sentence-level
context as a clue to the
meaning of a word or
phrase

Materials Needed

None

Vocabulary

Context, multiple meanings

How to do it:

1 Display a morning message like the following:

> Dear Star Students,
>
> Today is a fair day.
>
> In reading, we will check for clues to what words mean.
>
> Give a friendly wave to a classmate.

2 Explain the message: "All the underlined words in our message have multiple
meanings. We can use the words around each underlined word to figure out
what the underlined word means. As we learned this week, that's called
'using context clues.'"

3 State the first underlined word, "Star." Ask students what the word *star* can
mean. Elicit different meanings for the word, such as a bright light in the
night sky and someone who is very good at something.

4 Read the first sentence, "Dear Star Students," and ask students which of the
meanings of star fits in this context.

5 Continue discussing the multiple meanings of each underlined word and
then using context clues to determine which meaning fits.

VARIATION

■ Chorally read the message with the class. Invite students to partner up to
discuss the different meanings of one of the underlined words in the message.
Have partners share their thinking about the meaning and context clues for
each of the underlined words.

EXTENSION FOR A LATER LANGUAGE ARTS LESSON

■ Have partners work together to illustrate some words that have multiple
meanings. Display the work.

Emphatic Exclamations

Language Arts Content

Punctuation, inflection

Common Core Standards

RF.2.4b Read grade-level text orally with accuracy, appropriate rate, and expression

L.2.2 Demonstrate command of standard English capitalization, punctuation, and spelling when writing

L.2.3 Use knowledge of language and its conventions when writing, speaking, reading, or listening

Materials Needed

"Good morning!" posted on a chart

Vocabulary

Exclamation point, emphatic, salutation

How to do it:

As necessary, model for students how to move safely and carefully among their classmates.

1 Remind students that an exclamation point is used at the end of an emphatic salutation. Model the difference between saying "Good morning." and "Good morning!"

2 Tell students that they are going to act out the exclamation point after greeting a partner: "Today you'll be walking around inside the circle greeting classmates with an emphatic, 'Good morning!' and then moving your hands and bodies to create an exclamation point together. Let me show you what that will look like."

3 With a student volunteer you've practiced with beforehand, model acting out the exclamation point by high-fiving each other and then moving bodies and joined palms down toward the ground as you squat (or half-squat) down.

4 Students mix and mingle, greeting as many classmates as they can in one minute.

VARIATIONS

■ If your students do not yet have the self-control to do this greeting as a mix and mingle, do it as a greeting that travels around the circle.

■ As you act out the exclamation point, add a sound effect, such as "Zap!"

EXTENSIONS FOR A LATER LANGUAGE ARTS LESSON

■ Have students practice the appropriate inflections for periods and exclamation points when reading aloud.

■ Invite students to use exclamation points in their writing, but caution them to not overdo it.

Heading Hello

Language Arts Content

Using headings

Common Core Standards

RI.2.5 Know and use various text features to locate key facts or information

L.2.2e Consult reference materials as needed to check and correct spellings

Materials Needed

Heading cards (or slides on a projected screen) that represent the beginning letters of students' first names (for example, Ab–Da, De–Ji, Jo–Pe, and Pi–Zu); dictionary; chart with students' first names

Vocabulary

Heading, alphabetical

How to do it:

Before beginning, practice with a student volunteer who can model with you as you explain the greeting to the class.

1 Introduce the greeting: "We've been learning about dictionary headings. Today we're going to have headings of our own and greet each other as if we were inside a dictionary. I'm going to call out headings. When you hear the headings that your first name falls within, you'll come to the center of the circle and say 'Good morning' to everyone else who also came."

2 Call out "Ab through Da" and show that card or slide to the class.

3 All the students whose names fit within those headings (for example, Abeera, Barb, Carlos, and Dante) go to the center of the circle and say "Good morning" to one another before returning to their places in the circle.

4 Call out another heading. Repeat until all students have been greeted.

VARIATION

■ Use headings for last names or middle names.

EXTENSIONS FOR A LATER LANGUAGE ARTS LESSON

■ Students practice looking up a variety of vocabulary words using the headings in classroom dictionaries.

In the Manner of the Adverb

Language Arts Content

Adverbs

Common Core Standards

RF.2.4 Read with sufficient accuracy and fluency to support comprehension

L.2.1e Use adjectives and adverbs, depending on what is to be modified

L.2.5 Demonstrate under-standing of word relation-ships and nuances in word meanings

Materials Needed

Jar with adverb word cards (excitedly, sadly, happily, nervously, etc.)

Vocabulary

Adverb

How to do it:

1 Tell students that today they will be greeting each other in the manner of the adverb you draw from the jar.

2 Model the greeting:

➤ Draw an adverb from the jar (for example, "excitedly"). Show the word and say it aloud.

➤ Turn to the student next to you and say, "Good morning!" with wide-open eyes, a vigorous (but still gentle) handshake, and a bright voice.

3 Draw another card from the jar and say the adverb aloud. Students have one minute to greet as many classmates as they can in the manner of that adverb.

VARIATION

■ As students become more comfortable with this greeting, each can draw an adverb from the jar and then mix and mingle, greeting classmates in the manner of their own adverb.

EXTENSION FOR A LATER LANGUAGE ARTS LESSON

■ Have students practice their fluency by reading short passages in the manner of different adverbs you choose from the jar.

Irregular Plural Hello

Language Arts Content

Singular and plural nouns

Common Core Standards

RF.2.3 Apply grade-level phonics and word analysis skills in decoding words

L.2.1 Demonstrate command of standard English grammar and usage

L.2.1b Form and use frequently occurring irregular plural nouns

L.2.2d Generalize learned spelling patterns

Materials Needed

Pairs of cards, one with a singular noun and the other with its irregular plural (enough for each student to have one card)

Vocabulary

Noun, singular, plural, irregular

How to do it:

1 Introduce the greeting: "We've been learning about irregular plural nouns this week, and today you'll greet each other by matching singular and plural nouns. For example, 'mouse' is singular, so if I give you a card that says 'mouse,' you'll look for a person who has a card that says 'mice,' which is the plural of 'mouse.' Watch as Jared, Tina, Abby, and I show you how it's done."

2 Model the greeting with the three student volunteers (practice with them ahead of time):

➤ Choose two pairs of matching cards; give one card to each volunteer, and keep one yourself.

➤ Say, "Find your match!"

➤ You and the student volunteers mingle, looking for your match.

➤ When the pairs have found each other, they say "Good morning," "Hello," or "It's nice to see you today!" to each other and then return to their spots.

➤ Ask for questions; then say, "OK, let's all try it!"

3 Shuffle the cards and give each student one card.

4 When you say "Find your match!" students turn their card so others can see it and begin moving about the circle, looking for their match. When pairs find each other, they greet with a "Good morning" or any appropriate variation on that greeting.

VARIATION

■ After students become more comfortable with these pairs, mix in more challenging pairs (-is → -es pairs such as parenthesis → parentheses).

EXTENSION FOR A LATER LANGUAGE ARTS LESSON

■ During word study, have students classify the irregular plural nouns by spelling patterns, such as -ife → -ives (knife → knives, life → lives), -oo → -ee (foot → feet, tooth → teeth), no change (deer → deer, fish → fish), -ouse → -ice (mouse → mice, louse → lice).

What's in a Name?

Language Arts Content

Long and short vowel sounds

Common Core Standards

RF.2.3a Distinguish long and short vowels when reading regularly spelled one-syllable words

RF.2.3b Know spelling–sound correspondences for common vowel teams

Materials Needed

Chart with students' first names

Vocabulary

Short vowel sound, long vowel sound

How to do it:

1 With students standing in the meeting circle, explain the greeting: "Today we're going to greet each other in a few different categories. I am going to say a category, such as 'Anyone with a short *a* sound in their first name.' If this is true for you, you will come to the center of the circle. You'll greet all of the other students for whom this is also true with a 'Good morning.'" Model as needed.

2 Choose categories to ensure that most, if not all, students will have the opportunity to come to the middle of the circle. For example, names with a short or long vowel sound, names that include a long vowel sound that is spelled with a vowel digraph (ai, ee, oo, ea, etc.), or names with a consonant digraph (ch, ph, sh, etc.).

3 If any students have not been greeted after a few rounds, say, "Anyone who was not greeted, come to the center." Those students will greet each other or, if it is one person, the class will chorally say, "Good morning, _____" to that student.

VARIATIONS

■ Do the greeting with middle or last names.

■ Use different phonics rules after you introduce them in class; for example, names with "magic e" (Jake) or r-controlled vowels (Shirley).

EXTENSION FOR A LATER LANGUAGE ARTS LESSON

■ During word study, have students do a name sort by categorizing names into different columns—for example, names with the short "a" sound and names with only long vowel sounds.

It's All in the Details

Language Arts Content

Questioning

Common Core Standards

W.2.3 Write narratives in which they recount a well-elaborated event or sequence of events

W.2.8 Recall information from experiences or gather information to answer a question

SL.2.3 Ask and answer questions about what a speaker says

SL.2.4 Tell a story or recount an experience, speaking audibly in coherent sentences

SL.2.6 Produce complete sentences when appropriate to task and situation

Materials Needed

Chart with question words listed: who, what, when, where, why, how

Vocabulary

Question words

How to do it:

Choose three or four students to share each day. Practice beforehand with two student volunteers who can model with you.

1 Introduce the sharing: "Today you'll each have a chance to share some news. Then your classmates will use question words from this chart to learn more about your news. Kiefer, Gemma, and I will show you how it's done."

2 Model the sharing with the volunteers:

➤ You: "Last weekend I went to the movies."
Kiefer: "Who went with you?"
You: "I went with my husband."
Gemma: "What movie did you see?"
You: "We saw *Frozen*."

➤ When asking students what they noticed, if needed prompt them to name your use of complete sentences to tell your news and answer each question.

3 The first sharer of the day shares a simple piece of news and takes questions from three or four classmates, each time answering with a complete sentence the way you modeled. Encourage questioners to use different question words from the chart.

4 Repeat until all of the day's sharers have had a turn.

VARIATION

■ A student volunteer can keep track of which question words have already been used.

EXTENSION FOR A LATER LANGUAGE ARTS LESSON

■ As a writing exercise, students can write an elaborated version of their sharing, including the details they added in response to classmates' questions.

Readers Recommend

How to do it:

Language Arts Content

Stating and supporting an opinion

Common Core Standards

RL.2.1 Ask and answer questions to demonstrate understanding of key details

W.2.1 Write opinion pieces; state opinion, supply reasons, use linking words, provide concluding statement or section

W.2.5 Focus on a topic and strengthen writing by revising and editing

SL.2.1 Participate in collaborative conversations about grade 2 topics and texts

SL.2.3 Ask and answer questions about what a speaker says

Materials Needed

Each student who is sharing will bring one book

Vocabulary

Opinion, reason

1 Introduce this dialogue sharing: "This week, everyone will have the opportunity to practice giving an opinion and a reason for their opinion by recommending a book to the class." Model as needed, and consider setting up a schedule ahead of time to ensure students are prepared to speak.

2 Today's sharers bring their books to the meeting circle.

3 Have the first sharer begin. She might say, "I'd like to recommend *Miss Nelson Is Missing* because it's funny but also mysterious."

4 The sharer invites classmates to ask one question or make one comment (limit to three or four students). Classmates might offer, "What makes it so funny?" or "It sounds like you like books where there is a big problem to solve."

5 Reinforce students' clear sharing: "I heard sharers using specific reasons why they would recommend their books, just as we've been practicing."

VARIATION

■ Students give opinions about their school or home lives, and support their opinions with reasons. For example: "Lunch is the best time of the day because I get to talk with kids from other classes." "I think my big brother should be the one to give our dog a bath because I take her for a walk almost every day after school."

EXTENSION FOR A LATER LANGUAGE ARTS LESSON

■ During reading time, students can write, revise, and edit more fully developed reviews of their books. Display these reviews so that students are able to easily see the recommendations and use them to inform their own reading choices.

Syllable Sharing

Language Arts Content

Syllables

Common Core Standards

RF.2.3 Apply grade-level phonics and word analysis skills in decoding words

SL.2.1a Follow agreed-upon rules for discussions

Materials Needed

Chart with students' first names posted

Vocabulary

Syllable

How to do it:

1 Write this prompt on a chart or whiteboard: My first name is _____. My first name has _____ syllables. One special fact about me is _____.

2 Introduce the sharing: "For this morning's sharing, we'll tell about the syllables in our names and also share one special fact about ourselves. Watch as I show you how it's done."

3 Model the sharing:

➤ Say, "My first name is Gi-na," pronouncing your first name slowly and touching your hand to your chin for each syllable in your name.

➤ Then say, "My first name has two syllables. One special fact about me is that I know how to ride a unicycle—that's a bicycle with just one wheel."

4 Now invite a student volunteer to start the greeting: "My first name is Ed-win [student says name slowly, touching hand to chin for each syllable]. My first name has two syllables. One special fact about me is that I love learning magic tricks."

EXTENSION FOR A LATER LANGUAGE ARTS LESSON

■ To provide a visual representation of identifying syllables, list all students' names on a piece of paper and give a copy to each student. Have students scoop (that is, draw a semicircle) under each syllable of their classmates' names.

Alphabet Aerobics

How to do it:

1 Have students spread throughout the room so they'll have space to raise and lower their arms and bend over. If classroom space is limited, students can step apart just enough to draw an invisible arm's-length circle around themselves; this is the "safe zone" within which they'll make their movements.

2 Explain that students will take three different positions during this activity:

➤ Arms parallel and above head for letters with an ascender (b, d, f, h, k, l, t)

➤ Arms parallel and in front with knees bent for base letters (a, c, e, i, m, n, o, r, s, u, v, w, x, z)

➤ Arms parallel and down at sides with knees straight and head down for letters with a descender (g, j, p, q, y)

3 Begin saying and moving through the alphabet together; aim for a medium-fast pace, but adjust as needed to offer students the right amount of challenge.

VARIATION

■ Once students have mastered moving through the alphabet, challenge them to use their bodies to "spell" words, such as content vocabulary. For example, if you're studying the neighborhood, choose words such as "rural," "urban," and "suburban."

EXTENSION FOR A LATER LANGUAGE ARTS LESSON

■ When students are writing, remind them of what they learned about letter formation from this activity.

Language Arts Content

Letter formation, spelling

Common Core Standards

L.2.1 Demonstrate command of conventions of standard English grammar and usage

L.2.2 Demonstrate command of standard English capitalization, punctuation, and spelling when writing

Materials Needed

None

Vocabulary

Parallel, base letter, ascender, descender

Commonalities

How to do it:

1 With students standing in the meeting circle, introduce the activity: "For today's activity, you'll pretend that you're one of your favorite book characters. The character could be from one of our read-alouds, a library book, an independent reading book, or a book you have at home. Everyone take a moment to think of a favorite character."

2 Continue explaining: "I have a character in mind, too, and I'll go first to show you how this activity will work. I'm going to make a true statement about my character. If the statement is true for your character, you'll take a step toward the middle of our circle. If I say another statement that's also true of your character, you'll take another step forward. Let's try it."

> ➤ Teacher (from the middle of the circle): "I am Charlotte from *Charlotte's Web*. I am not human." Students who also chose non-human characters take a step forward.

> ➤ Teacher: "I am kind." Students whose characters are also kind take a step forward.

> ➤ Make one more statement, and then see which characters have the most in common with Charlotte. Everyone then returns to their place in the circle.

3 Take any questions and then invite a student volunteer to come to the center of the circle to begin the activity. She makes three statements about her character, each time inviting classmates whose characters share that trait to take a step forward.

4 Do several more rounds as time allows. Students may stay with their original character or they may change characters.

VARIATION

■ Have students substitute something they are studying in social studies (landmarks, states, countries, neighborhoods) for characters.

EXTENSION FOR A LATER LANGUAGE ARTS LESSON

■ During reading time, have pairs of students create Venn diagrams. They each write their character's name above a circle, discuss what their characters have (and don't have) in common, and note their conclusions in the diagram.

Language Arts Content

Understanding character

Common Core Standards

RL.2.3 Describe how characters respond to major events and challenges

RL.2.6 Acknowledge differences in the points of view of characters

RL.2.7 Use information from illustrations/words to demonstrate understanding of characters, setting, plot

SL.2.1 Participate in collaborative conversations about grade 2 topics and texts

SL.2.6 Produce complete sentences when appropriate to task and situation

Materials Needed

None

Vocabulary

Character, internal, external

Compound Charades

Language Arts Content

Compound words

Common Core Standards

RF.2.3 Apply grade-level phonics and word analysis skills in decoding words

L.2.4d Use knowledge of meaning of individual words to predict meaning of compound words

L.2.6 Use words and phrases, including using adjectives and adverbs to describe

Materials Needed

Cards with compound words, one card per group

Vocabulary

Compound word, individual word

How to do it:

1 Divide the class into groups of four or five students; designate spots in which each group can practice their charade privately and another spot where groups will take turns performing.

2 Review the guidelines: "Each group will receive a card with a compound word written on it. The group has to act out each individual word within the compound word. For example, if your group gets 'skateboard,' you would first act out 'skate,' followed by 'board.' Remember: no sounds, only actions."

3 Give each group a card and send them to their practice spots.

4 After a few minutes, students return to the meeting area. Ask for a volunteer group to go first.

5 As the group acts out the first individual word, the class calls out guesses. After the second individual word is guessed, the group pauses, the entire class calls out the compound word, and the group turns their card around for all to see.

If students try to guess the word without success after a minute or two, move things along: "This one's hard to guess! Group one, please show us your card now."

VARIATIONS

■ Students can work in pairs instead of groups. Each student gets a card and practices privately; the two students then try to guess each other's word.

■ After students have acted out the individual words, recycle the same cards, but now invite them to act out only the compound word, not the individual words.

EXTENSION FOR A LATER LANGUAGE ARTS LESSON

■ During word study, have groups illustrate the individual words as well as the compound word and write a sentence using them.

Describe It!

Language Arts Content

Describing

Common Core Standards

W.2.8 Recall information from experiences or gather information from sources to answer a question

SL.2.1a Follow agreed-upon rules for discussions

SL.2.1b Build on others' talk by linking comments to the remarks of others

SL.2.6 Produce complete sentences when appropriate to task and situation

Materials Needed

None

Vocabulary

Category

How to do it:

1 Have students count off by twos. Ones form an inner circle facing out; twos form an outer circle facing in, each opposite a one.

2 Introduce the activity: "Today I'm going to give you and the person facing you a task and a question to think and talk about. I'll give you ten seconds to think silently and then you and your partner will chat." Then say, "Think about some objects that are heavy. What are some of these objects? Describe what makes them heavy, using complete sentences."

3 Give ten seconds for silent thought. Then say, "Talk with your partner about some heavy objects and what makes them heavy. You'll have about a minute."

4 Partners chat. Signal students when it's time to stop, and use reinforcing language to point out comments that demonstrated understanding and helped move the conversations forward: "I heard some students listing a refrigerator and a car as heavy objects. Other students said that heavy objects are ones you can't lift very easily, or that small things are sometimes heavy and big things are sometimes light. A lot of thoughtful talk was happening, and that helped keep your conversations going."

5 Have the inner circle wave goodbye to their partners and move one space to their right.

6 Repeat using different categories, such as "Foods that are spicy" or "Activities that take a lot of energy." Students chat with a new partner each time.

VARIATION

■ Have students brainstorm different category ideas. Keep a jar handy to which they can add their suggestions.

EXTENSION FOR A LATER LANGUAGE ARTS LESSON

■ Have students elaborate in writing on ideas from this activity; they can also illustrate their ideas.

ReACT!

Language Arts Content

Understanding character

Common Core Standards

RL.2.1 Ask and answer questions to demonstrate understanding of key details

RL.2.3 Describe how characters respond to major events and challenges

RL.2.7 Use information from illustrations/words to demonstrate understanding of characters, setting, plot

W.2.8 Recall information from experiences or gather information from sources to answer a question

Materials Needed

Excerpts from a recent read-aloud marked with sticky notes

Vocabulary

React, neutral (and words describing various emotions and reactions)

How to do it:

Depending on your students' current skills, you might want to model this activity before beginning.

1 Students find a spot with space around them in the classroom.

2 Tell students that they will be "stepping into the shoes" of a character from a recent read-aloud. For example, if you've recently read *Brave Irene*, students will "become" Irene for the remainder of this activity.

3 Read a short section of the text. Ask, "How would Irene react?" Students may use facial expressions, physical movement, or sounds to show how they think Irene would react.

4 Signal students to return to a neutral body and face.

5 Repeat step 3 for two or three more sections of the book.

VARIATIONS

■ Choose a different character, perhaps a supporting one, from the same book.

■ Use this activity with a different picture book, or to reinforce how a character changes throughout a longer chapter book.

EXTENSION FOR A LATER LANGUAGE ARTS LESSON

■ During reading time, students use vocabulary for the feelings they demonstrated for the character. They can write sentences describing the character or respond to questions about the character, such as "What caused the character to feel _____?"

What a Character!

Language Arts Content

Understanding character

Common Core Standards

RL.2.3 Describe how characters in a story respond to major events and challenges

RL.2.6 Acknowledge differences in the points of view of characters

W.2.8 Recall information from experiences or gather information from sources to answer a question

Materials Needed

Chart with character traits and emotions (see step 1) and sentence starters (see step 4)

Vocabulary

Character, trait, emotion

How to do it:

1 On a chart or whiteboard, post different character traits (such as bold, mischievous, honest) and different emotions (such as afraid, joyful, jealous).

2 Invite a volunteer to the middle of the circle and tape to his back an index card with a character's name written on it (for example, a character from a recent read-aloud).

3 The volunteer turns slowly around so that everyone has a chance to see the card.

4 The volunteer calls on classmates to offer clues to help him guess the character. Clue givers use the following sentence frames, filling in the blanks with words listed on the chart.

You are _____ because _____.

When _____ helped you, you felt _____.

At the beginning of the story you were _____, but then you became _____.

Suppose the character is Patricia from *Thundercake* by Patricia Polacco. Students might use the following clues: "You are brave because you tried doing things even though you were scared. When your Babushka helped you, you felt confident."

5 After three clues, the student in the center tries to guess the character and book: "Am I _____ from _____?" If he guesses correctly, the activity is complete. If he guesses incorrectly, classmates continue giving clues. If after six or so clues the student still doesn't guess correctly, reveal the answer and end the activity so the guesser doesn't reach the point of being frustrated or embarrassed. For example, when you think it's time to stop, you might say, "That was a tough one! The answer is _____."

VARIATION

■ Move from main characters to supporting characters as children become more confident with this activity.

EXTENSION FOR A LATER LANGUAGE ARTS LESSON

■ Students can practice using trait and feeling vocabulary to describe characters, as well as evidence to support those ideas, when writing in their Readers' Notebooks. They can adapt the sentence frames from the activity.

Would You Rather?

Language Arts Content

Forming opinions

Common Core Standards

SL.2.1c Ask for clarification and further explanation about the topics under discussion

SL.2.3 Ask and answer questions

W.2.1 Write opinion pieces; state opinion, supply reasons, use linking words, provide concluding statement or section

Materials Needed

None

Vocabulary

Reason, opinion

How to do it:

Begin with students standing side by side in one line.

1 Ask a question that students can form an opinion about, such as "Do you think hamburgers or pizza make a better Saturday night dinner?"

2 Instruct students to take one step forward if they choose the first option (hamburgers) and one step backward if they choose the second option (pizza).

3 Invite a few volunteers to state the reasons for their opinions.

4 Have students return to their original positions.

5 Repeat steps 1–3 with a different opinion question, but on each of these subsequent rounds, invite a few students to ask classmates about the reasons for their opinions.

VARIATION

■ Link the opinions to different curricular topics. Sample questions: "Which do you think is more interesting to read, fiction or nonfiction? Why?" "What, in your opinion, is the most likely cause of global climate change? Why do you think so?" "Do you think it's healthier to live in the city, the country, or a suburb? What are your reasons for thinking so?"

EXTENSION FOR A LATER LANGUAGE ARTS LESSON

■ During writing time, have students write pieces in which they supply additional reasons that support their opinions. Help them to use linking words and phrases such as "one reason," "another reason," and "one example" to connect opinion and reasons.

Just Say Venn!

How to do it:

1 Display a message like the following:

Language Arts Content

Comparing and contrasting

Common Core Standards

RL2.2 Recount stories, including fables and folktales from diverse cultures, and determine their central message, lesson, or moral

RL2.9 Compare and contrast two or more versions of the same story by different authors or from different cultures

RF.2.4 Read with sufficient accuracy and fluency to support comprehension

SL.2.2 Recount or describe key ideas or details from a text read aloud or information presented orally or through other media

Materials Needed

None

Vocabulary

Compare, contrast, folktale

Dear _____ Listeners,

We've been listening to folktales from around the world. Sometimes we've read two versions of the same story. Today we'll compare and contrast two folktales we've recently read: *Stone Soup* and *Cactus Soup*. Help us get ready for our discussion by writing in the Venn diagram one thing both folktales have in common, or one thing that is different.

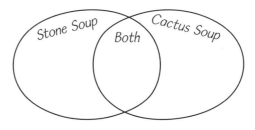

2 Ask students to brainstorm adjectives that could describe listeners, such as "attentive," "perceptive," and "conscientious." Use their words to fill in the blank preceding "Listeners" in the message.

3 Read through some responses students added to the Venn diagram. As a class, notice whether there were more similarities or differences.

VARIATION

■ Use the same Venn diagram activity to deepen your students' understanding of comparing and contrasting in other curricular areas. You might use characters from literature (Ramona vs. Pippi Longstocking), geography (mountains vs. deserts), or writing genres (narrative vs. poetry).

EXTENSION FOR A LATER LANGUAGE ARTS LESSON

■ During social studies or reading, have students do a partner chat to compare and contrast different versions of folktales they've read. Invite a few partners to share out.

Syllable Hunt

Language Arts Content

Decoding, syllables

Common Core Standards

RF.2.3 Apply grade-level phonics and word analysis skills in decoding words

RF.2.3c Decode regularly spelled two-syllable words with long vowels

L.2.2d Generalize learned spelling patterns

Materials Needed

None

Vocabulary

Syllable

How to do it:

Depending on students' skill levels, you might want to preview and circle the words with more than one syllable before doing step 3.

1 Display a message like the following:

_____ Decoders,

We have been practicing our word attack strategies as a class. You are becoming quite skilled when you decode two-syllable words with closed and/or "magic e" syllables.

Add a word to one of the categories below:

2-syllable word (Both syllables are closed)	2-syllable word (Both syllables are "magic e")	2-syllable word (One syllable is closed, one is a "magic e" syllable)

P.S.—Can you find any words in the message that fit into one of the categories?

---

2 Ask students to fill in the blank in the message by thinking of a salutation that could be used to greet the class, such as "Greetings," "Happy Tuesday," or "Bonjour."

3 Have students read through the message with one voice, placing a hand under their chins when they get to a word with more than one syllable.

4 Read through some of the words that were added to each category.

EXTENSIONS FOR A LATER LANGUAGE ARTS LESSON

■ During word study, have students scoop (that is, draw a semicircle) under each syllable in the words, and label and categorize the words.

■ Dictate and have students write two-syllable words.

Question Quest

How to do it:

1 Display a message like the following:

> Dear _____ Readers,
>
> We've been thinking deeply about the books we've read aloud as a class. Yesterday we finished reading *The Recess Queen*. Before we have our class book discussion, let's answer a few questions about the details of this thoughtful story:
>
> > Who are the characters?
> > Where does the story take place?
> > When does the main event happen?
> > What is the problem?
> > What is the solution?
>
> Be ready to share your ideas during our meeting.

2 Ask students to think of words that describe readers (for example, "thoughtful," "careful," "fluent"). Use their words to fill in the blank preceding "Readers" in the message.

3 Choose one of the fill-in words and invite the class to read the message in the manner of that word. (You may want to quickly brainstorm how this will look and sound.)

4 Invite three or four volunteers to share their thoughts about the questions asked in the message.

VARIATION

■ As students become more adept at answering explicit questions, ask inferential questions, such as "What made the character Mean Jean mean in the first place?"

EXTENSION FOR A LATER LANGUAGE ARTS LESSON

■ After a read-aloud, post a list of question words (who, what, when, where, why, how) and have students generate the questions.

Language Arts Content

Understanding story elements

Common Core Standards

RL.2.1 Ask/answer questions to demonstrate understanding of key details

RL.2.7 Use information from illustrations/words to demonstrate understanding of characters, setting, plot

RF.2.4c Use context to confirm or self-correct word recognition and understanding

SL.2.2 Recount or describe key ideas or details from a text read aloud or information presented orally or through other media

Materials Needed

None

What's It All About?

Language Arts Content

Identifying the main topic

Common Core Standards

RI.2.2 Identify the main topic of a text as well as the focus of specific paragraphs within the text

RI.2.8 Describe how reasons support specific points the author makes

W.2.8 Recall information from experiences or gather information from sources to answer a question

SL.2.2 Recount or describe key ideas or details from a text read aloud or information presented orally or through other media

Materials Needed

Paragraph of article (perhaps from *Time for Kids* or *National Geographic Kids*)

Vocabulary

Main topic, details

How to do it:

1 Display a message like the following:

Dear Focused Readers,

We've been reading a lot of interesting nonfiction articles lately. One challenge in nonfiction is to always keep in mind what the article is "mostly about"—the main topic. Read the paragraph of an article below. We'll dissect it during reading today.

> Light rays can go through some objects but not others. Some objects are transparent—most light goes through. Some objects are translucent—some light goes through. Some objects are opaque— no light goes through. We can use the words "transparent," "translucent," and "opaque" to describe all the objects we see around us.

What is this paragraph mostly about? Be ready to share your thoughts during Morning Meeting.

2 Choose a gesture for "main topic" and then invite the class to read the message chorally, making that gesture when they come upon the phrase "main topic."

3 Have another volunteer read the paragraph aloud.

4 Take a few ideas from students about the main topic of the paragraph.

5 Reinforce what good readers do: "I can see that you are attentive readers. Can you think of some other adjectives that describe the readers in our classroom?" Take a few ideas from students.

EXTENSION FOR A LATER LANGUAGE ARTS LESSON

■ Students can use a graphic organizer to help keep track of key details, reasons, and the main topic while examining the paragraph (and other paragraphs related to it).

Worth a Thousand Words

Language Arts Content

Analyzing illustrations

Common Core Standards

RL.2.7 Use information gained from illustrations to demonstrate understanding of characters, setting, plot

RI.2.7 Explain how specific images contribute to and clarify a text

SL.2.1 Participate in collaborative conversations about grade 2 topics and texts

SL.2.3 Ask and answer questions about what a speaker says

Materials Needed

One illustration from an upcoming read-aloud, posted or projected

Vocabulary

Character, plot, setting, observant

How to do it:

1 Display a message like the following and an illustration below it:

> Dear Observant Students,
>
> There is a saying that "a picture is worth a thousand words." We've spent a lot of time thinking about how illustrations help tell a story.
>
> Take a look at the illustration below. It is from a read-aloud you'll listen to later on today. Use your imagination to think about what is happening in the story.
>
> Who are the characters? Where is it taking place? What is happening?
>
> Be ready to share your ideas during our meeting.

2 Ask students to help define the adjective "observant." For example: "What in the message could help us figure out the meaning of this word? What root word do you see inside 'observant'?"

3 Read through the message in the manner of the word "observant." Perhaps students can pantomime looking through binoculars as they read carefully.

4 Elicit ideas about the illustration's characters, setting, and plot from student volunteers.

VARIATION

■ Post a photograph from a news magazine (*Time for Kids, National Geographic Kids*). Students can analyze the setting, subjects, and action of the photograph to get an idea of what news the photographer is trying to report.

EXTENSION FOR A LATER LANGUAGE ARTS LESSON

■ Studying illustrations and illustrators can keep even some of the most reluctant readers engaged. Create a Caldecott Medal Award Winners basket in your classroom library. Regularly pull out a book to study just how much illustrations help tell the story.

Comparatively Speaking

Language Arts Content

Degrees of comparison

Common Core Standards

RF.3.3 Know and apply grade-level phonics and word analysis skills in decoding words

L.3.1g Form and use comparative or superlative adjectives

Materials Needed

Cards with a sentence that is missing a comparative adjective; partner cards with a comparative adjective

Vocabulary

Comparative adjective

How to do it:

Before beginning, quickly review what comparative adjectives are.

1 Give each student a card on which you've written either a phrase with blanks where a comparative adjective would go, or a comparative adjective. For example, one student gets a card that says "A cheetah is _____ _____ a human"; another student gets a card that says "faster than."

2 Students mingle, looking for the classmate with the match for their card. When they find each other, they greet with a friendly "Good morning, _____!"

3 Students sit with their matching partner, their cards visible to the rest of the circle.

4 Going around the circle, partners hold up their cards and say their complete sentence, each saying the words on his or her own card.

VARIATION

■ Substitute superlatives for comparatives. For example, one card says "Mount McKinley is the _____ mountain in the United States" and the matching card says "tallest."

EXTENSION FOR A LATER LANGUAGE ARTS LESSON

■ Have students explore the different ways to build comparative adjectives, for example, tall → taller; pretty → prettier; beautiful → more beautiful. Students can begin to categorize these adjectives in terms of spelling patterns.

How Are You Feeling Today?

Language Arts Content

Using adjectives

Common Core Standards

RL.3.3 Describe characters in a story (e.g. their traits, motivations, or feelings)

SL.3.1c Ask questions to check understanding, stay on topic, and link comments

SL.3.3 Ask and answer questions about information from a speaker

L.3.1a Explain the function of nouns, pronouns, verbs, adjectives, and adverbs

Materials Needed

None

Vocabulary

Adjective

How to do it:

1 Students pair up to greet each other using the following format. (Model this first with a student partner you've prepped ahead of time.)

Student 1: "Hello, _____. How are you feeling today?"

Student 2: "I'm feeling tired."

Student 1 requests more information: "Why are you feeling that way?"

Student 2 responds by giving more information: "I'm feeling tired because I had to stay up to take care of my baby brother!"

2 Partners switch roles and repeat the greeting.

3 Encourage students to use a variety of adjectives; if needed, brainstorm a list with the class before starting the greeting.

VARIATION

■ Students move around, using this format to greet as many classmates as they can in a given amount of time.

EXTENSION FOR A LATER LANGUAGE ARTS LESSON

■ Collect the adjectives students used on a "Feelings Chart." Have students use these adjectives when describing how characters in their books feel. Challenge students to find evidence in the text that supports their choice of adjectives.

Interview and Introduce

Language Arts Content

Questioning

Common Core Standards

SL.3.1 Engage effectively in collaborative discussions on grade 3 topics and texts

SL.3.3 Ask and answer questions about information from a speaker

SL.3.6 Speak in complete sentences when appropriate to task and situation

Materials Needed

Chart with 2 or 3 interview questions, such as "What is your name?" "Where do you live?" "What is your favorite food?"

How to do it:

1 Students partner up with the person next to them. Get students ready to interview: "Today we're going to interview our partners and then introduce them to the class. What will we need to remember about speaking and listening for the interviews to work well?" Take student responses, emphasizing the importance of responding to questions in complete sentences.

2 In each pair, Partner A asks Partner B the interview questions from the chart, repeating back Partner B's answers to make sure she heard them correctly. Repeat, with A and B switching roles.

3 Partner A introduces Partner B to the class, saying something like "I would like to introduce Nate. He lives on 58th Street and his favorite food is grilled cheese."

4 The class responds, "Good morning, Nate!"

5 Partner B then introduces Partner A to the class.

6 Continue until all students have been introduced and greeted.

VARIATION

▪ Partners interview each other about any of the following: middle names, greatest fear, one wish, family members, or favorite subjects.

EXTENSION FOR A LATER LANGUAGE ARTS LESSON

▪ Students act as reporters, brainstorming initial and follow-up questions that would lead to deeper understanding of a classmate. For instance, the question "Where do you live?" might be followed by "Who lives in your home?" or "How many people live in your home?"

If I Were

How to do it:

1 Pose the following unfinished statement: "If I were a literary genre, I'd be _____."

2 Ask students to think about how they would finish that statement and to give a thumbs-up when they're ready. It might be helpful to post a list of literary genres (realistic fiction, historical fiction, poetry, mystery, biography, folktale, etc.).

3 When most students are ready, begin sharing around the circle.

VARIATIONS

■ Vary the content of the sharing. If you're studying Africa, the statement might be, "If I were an African animal, I'd be a _____."

■ Once students become comfortable with this sharing, have them elaborate by giving a reason for their choice. For example: "If I were an African animal, I'd be a cheetah, because I can run really fast."

EXTENSION FOR A LATER LANGUAGE ARTS LESSON

■ Continue elaborating on this idea during writing time. Have students write pieces that state their opinion and provide supporting reasons by using linking words and phrases (because, since, for example).

Language Arts Content

Elaboration

Common Core Standards

W.3.1 Write opinion pieces, supporting a point of view with reasons

W.3.1a Introduce topic or text, state an opinion, and create organizational structure that lists reasons

W.3.1b Provide reasons that support the opinion

W.3.1c Use linking words and phrases to connect opinion and reasons

SL.3.1d Explain their own ideas and understanding

Materials Needed

None

Vocabulary

Genre, elaborate

Special Interest Sharing

Language Arts Content

Staying on topic

Common Core Standards

W.3.2 Write informative/ explanatory texts and convey ideas and information clearly

SL.3.1 Engage effectively in collaborative discussions on grade 3 topics and texts

SL.3.1c Ask questions to check understanding, stay on topic, and link comments

SL.3.3 Ask and answer questions about information from a speaker

SL.3.4 Report on a topic or text with appropriate facts and relevant details, speaking clearly

Materials Needed

None

How to do it:

Invite two or three students to sign up for this sharing per day. If needed, post an anchor chart showing a sample sharing and one showing sample questions to ask a sharer.

1 Do a quick modeling to remind students how to do a brief, focused sharing by staying on topic and how to show respectful attention as an audience member.

2 The sharer states what her special interest is, what drew her to it, why she likes it, and when she does it. For example: "My special interest is singing. I became interested in singing because my mom sings a lot. I like singing because I get to be creative. I sing all the time: for example, at chorus and with my mom when we do dishes."

3 The sharer invites and answers a few questions from classmates.

4 Repeat steps 2 and 3 for the next sharer.

VARIATION

■ Have students bring in an object that represents something about their special interest. For example, a student with a special interest in singing might bring sheet music for a favorite song.

EXTENSION FOR A LATER LANGUAGE ARTS LESSON

■ Have students write expert books about their special interest to practice staying on topic. Encourage them to include appropriate facts and relevant details, such as how to do an activity associated with the interest, special gear or materials needed, etc.

State Your Opinion

Language Arts Content

Forming opinions

Common Core Standards

RI.3.2 Determine main idea; recount key details, explain how they support main idea

RI.3.6 Distinguish their own point of view from that of the author

SL.3.1 Engage effectively in collaborative discussions on grade 3 topics and texts

SL.3.2 Determine main ideas and supporting details of text read aloud

Materials Needed

None

Vocabulary

Point of view, agree, disagree

How to do it:

1 The sharer stands at the front of the room, facing a line of classmates who stand closer to the back of the room. To help students understand how the activity works, take your turn as sharer first.

2 The sharer states an opinion. For example: "I think leftover pizza makes a great breakfast." If students need the support, post sentence starters such as "My favorite . . ." and "I think . . ." or sentence frames such as "Doing _____ is more fun than doing _____."

3 Students who agree with the sharer's statement take one step toward the sharer; those who disagree stay where they are.

4 The sharer gives two to four more opinions. With each opinion, classmates either take one step forward or stay in the same spot.

5 When the sharer is finished, see who is closest and farthest from the sharer and briefly discuss some of the commonalities in the class: "We have lots of classmates who like pizza for breakfast! Lots of us think science is just as much fun as math."

6 Have the class return to the starting line and repeat the activity with a different sharer.

VARIATION

■ As students read different nonfiction texts, focus the sharing on opinions about a specific text.

EXTENSION FOR A LATER LANGUAGE ARTS LESSON

■ As a whole class, read aloud a published editorial and invite students to state whether they agree or disagree with the author's opinions. Next, ask students to explain why they agree or disagree, citing reasons and examples.

Weekend Focus

Language Arts Content

Constructing narratives

Common Core Standards

W.3.3 Write narratives using effective technique, descriptive details, and clear sequences

W.3.3c Use temporal words and phrases to signal event order

W.3.5 Develop and strengthen writing by planning, revising, and editing

SL.3.4 Report on a topic or text with appropriate facts and relevant details, speaking clearly

Materials Needed

Chart of temporal words, such as first, next, then, finally

Vocabulary

Sequence, temporal words

How to do it:

Let students know in the morning message that they'll be sharing something from their weekend.

1 Pair students up.

2 Introduce the sharing: "Today you'll have the opportunity to share about your weekend with your partner. You'll focus on one part of the weekend and recap the main points about that part in sequence. You can use our chart of temporal words to help you. You'll each have around thirty seconds to share."

3 Model by sharing something from your own weekend, highlighting the appropriate length, sequence, and use of temporal words and phrases. For example, "On Saturday morning, I had breakfast first. Then I went for a walk with my dog. Next I came home and washed the car. Finally, I collapsed on the couch to read my favorite magazine."

4 On your signal, partners choose who will share first and begin sharing.

VARIATION

■ Try this sharing after a vacation, such as winter or spring break.

EXTENSION FOR A LATER LANGUAGE ARTS LESSON

■ These weekend stories can become excellent foundations for narrative writing. As students plan, write, revise, and edit, they can elaborate more fully and add dialogue, specific actions, and internal thoughts.

Character Corners

Language Arts Content:

Understanding character

Common Core Standards:

RL.3.1 Ask and answer questions to demonstrate understanding of a text

RL.3.3 Describe characters in a story

SL.3.1a Come to discussions prepared; explicitly draw on that preparation to explore ideas

Materials Needed:

None

Vocabulary:

Character trait

How to do it:

1 With students gathered in the middle of the classroom, explain the logistics and main idea of the activity: "This morning you are going to choose one character to focus on. This character could be from our classroom read-aloud or an independent reading book. I'll make a statement about a character's traits or emotions along with four words that describe character traits."

2 Continue explaining: "As I say each of the four character traits, I'll point to a different corner of the room. You'll choose the trait that best describes your character and go to that corner of the room. For example, suppose you choose Harry Potter as your character. I read the statement, 'My character would best be described as . . . creative . . . generous . . . comical . . . serious' (point to the four corners of the room as you say this). You think 'creative' best describes Harry, so you go to the corner of the room by the fish tank."

3 Begin with your first statement; students move to the corner that best describes their character.

4 With others in their corner, students share the character they chose and their reasons for moving to this corner. For example, "I chose Harry Potter. I think he's creative because he comes up with solutions to problems that others haven't thought of."

5 Students move back to the middle of the classroom.

6 Repeat with students thinking of different characters and you naming different character traits for the corners of the room.

VARIATION

■ Once students have had the opportunity to think about their characters' traits, challenge them to think about those characters in certain imagined scenarios. Give them a sentence frame, such as "If my character could have one wish, I imagine it would be to . . ." Then offer them four options for completing the sentence, for example, "have lots of friends, win the lottery, be a famous athlete, be able to read people's minds."

EXTENSION FOR A LATER LANGUAGE ARTS LESSON

■ Have students use text evidence to support their ideas; for example, if a student chose "generous" to best describe their character, ask them to find evidence in the book that supports that choice.

Five-Minute Sleuths

Language Arts Content

Research, informational text

Common Core Standards

RI.3.5 Use text features and search tools to locate information efficiently

RI.3.7 Use information gained from illustrations/ words to demonstrate understanding

W.3.7 Conduct short research projects that build knowledge about a topic

W.3.8 Recall information from experiences/gather information from sources; take brief notes and sort evidence

SL.3.4 Report on a topic or text with appropriate facts and relevant details, speaking clearly

Materials Needed

Informational texts on a broad topic (for example, pandas or landforms); subtopic cards; pencil and paper (one per group)

Vocabulary

Text feature, subtopic

How to do it:

1 Divide the class into groups of five and introduce the activity: "Today each group is going to have five minutes to do some super-sleuthing about different subtopics related to pandas. Your job will be to use the text features of informational texts to help you track down new information."

2 Give each group a subtopic card (for example, what pandas eat, where pandas live, animal relatives of pandas) and a clipboard or notebook for taking notes.

3 Each group will have five minutes using the classroom library or computers to find as much information as they can find about their subtopic. One member of the group can be the scribe while the other four complete the research. Remind students to use text features such as table of contents, maps, headings and subheadings, and indexes to find information efficiently.

4 At the end of five minutes, ask each scribe to report some of the group's key findings.

EXTENSION FOR A LATER LANGUAGE ARTS LESSON

■ Using this activity as a launching pad, have students choose subtopics to research more fully. Students can record their new learning in various ways (for example, by creating tables or webs in research notebooks or online documents) and share their research with classmates.

Idiom-ania

Language Arts Content

Figurative language

Common Core Standards

RL.3.4 Determine the meaning of words and phrases as used in a text, distinguishing literal from nonliteral language

RF.3.4c Use context to confirm or self-correct word recognition and understanding, rereading as necessary

L.3.5a Distinguish literal from nonliteral meanings of words and phrases in context

Materials Needed

Cards with different idioms (for example, a dime a dozen, a drop in the bucket, a piece of cake, a picture is worth a thousand words)

Vocabulary

Figurative language, literal meaning, idiom, pantomime

How to do it:

1 Open with a brief review of what students have already learned about idioms and figurative vs. literal language.

2 Place idiom cards in the center of the circle. Have a student volunteer come to the center to choose a card.

3 The student pantomimes the literal meaning of the idiom printed on the card. For example, for "a drop in the bucket," the volunteer might pantomime putting a bucket on the floor and then dropping something into the bucket.

4 When the student has ended the pantomime, share the idiom's figurative meaning with the class: "'A drop in the bucket' is a colorful way of saying 'not enough to make any difference.' For example, a farmer might say, 'We got some sun this week, but it was only a drop in the bucket when you think about how much sun my crops really need.'"

5 Have students partner with a classmate and chat about the idiom. Offer a few prompting questions: "When might you use this idiom in a conversation with a friend or classmate? Where have you seen it in your reading? Who do you think might have invented the idiom?"

6 Repeat steps 2–5 with one or two more volunteers.

EXTENSION FOR A LATER LANGUAGE ARTS LESSON

■ Create a "Figurative Language" word wall. Have students illustrate idioms from their reading in both their literal and figurative meanings, encouraging them to reread as needed to confirm understanding.

Inquiring Minds

Language Arts Content

Listening, questioning

Common Core Standards

RI.3.1 Ask and answer questions to demonstrate understanding of a text

RI.3.7 Use information gained from illustrations/ words to demonstrate understanding

RF.3.4a Read grade-level text with purpose and understanding

SL.3.1c Ask questions to check understanding, stay on topic, and link comments

Materials Needed

Two different informational text paragraphs (from *Time for Kids*, *National Geographic Kids*, or other informational texts, including those with illustrations); question words posted (who, what, when, where, why, how)

Vocabulary

Inquire, informational text

How to do it:

1 Designate a specific place in the room for each question word.

2 With students gathered in the center of the meeting area, introduce the activity: "We've been learning a lot about how to work with informational texts. Listen carefully as I read aloud a paragraph from one of the texts we've been working on. Then you'll have a chance to ask questions, or inquire, about what you've heard."

3 Read the paragraph and give students a minute to think of one question about it. For example, after hearing a paragraph about elephants in danger, a student might wonder, "Why is ivory so valuable?" or "How do elephants use their tusks?"

4 Students move to the area in the room that corresponds to their question word.

5 Choose a few volunteers to share their questions and discuss possible answers.

VARIATION

■ Invite volunteers to read excerpts from their own informational writing.

EXTENSION FOR A LATER LANGUAGE ARTS LESSON

■ As students read informational texts, they write their questions in a reading notebook.

It's *How* You Do It

Language Arts Content

Understanding adverbs

Common Core Standards

RL.3.3 Describe characters in a story

SL.3.1 Engage effectively in collaborative discussions on grade 3 topics and texts

L.3.1a Explain the function of nouns, pronouns, verbs, adjectives, and adverbs

Materials Needed

None

Vocabulary

Adverb

How to do it:

1 Name a task (for example, washing the dishes) and ask students for specific actions performed when doing that task (for example, turning on the water, wetting the sponge, getting soap on the sponge, picking up a dirty dish, washing the dish with the sponge, etc.).

2 Pantomime those actions with a neutral body and facial expression and ask students what they noticed.

3 Students do the same actions with neutral body and facial expression.

4 Students brainstorm adverbs as you chart their ideas.

5 Point to one of the adverbs students brainstormed (for example, "happily"). Ask, "What about washing the dishes may look different if you are doing it happily?" Take several specific student ideas.

6 Students do the actions with happy movements and facial expressions.

7 If time allows, try doing the actions in a different manner (for example, angrily, nervously, sleepily).

VARIATION

■ Different adverbs will keep the actions fresh and fun, so keep ideas for every-day actions in a jar and reuse them with this activity throughout the year.

EXTENSION FOR A LATER LANGUAGE ARTS LESSON

■ During a read-aloud, stop and notice when characters act in a specific way (smile triumphantly, wave energetically). Have students dramatize what this looks, feels, and sounds like.

Lively Limericks

How to do it:

Language Arts Content

Limericks, rhyme

Common Core Standards

RL.3.5 Refer to parts of stories, dramas, and poems; describe how each part builds on earlier sections

RF.3.4b Read grade-level prose/poetry orally with accuracy, appropriate rate, and expression

W.3.4 Produce writing in which development and organization are appropriate to task and purpose

Materials Needed

Chart with limerick posted

Vocabulary

Limerick, rhyme, rhythm

1 Post a limerick like the following:

A Young Lady of Lynn
by Anonymous

There was a young lady of Lynn,
Who was so uncommonly thin
That when she essayed
To drink lemonade
She slipped through the straw and fell in.

2 Read through the limerick in unison.

3 Explain that the verbal rhythm and the rhyme are what make the limerick unique.

4 Reread the limerick, this time having students take one step forward for each syllable in the first line (eight steps), backward for each syllable in the second line (eight steps), and so on. Remind students about moving safely near others and model if necessary. (If space is tight, students can sit in the circle and tap the syllables on their palms or knees.)

EXTENSION FOR A LATER LANGUAGE ARTS LESSON

■ Have students create their own limericks. They can use movement to help reinforce the verbal rhythm.

Radio Hour

Language Arts Content

Fluency, expression

Common Core Standards

RL.3.1 Ask and answer questions to demonstrate understanding of a text

RF.3.4b Read grade-level prose/poetry orally with accuracy, appropriate rate, and expression

SL.3.1 Engage effectively in collaborative discussions on grade 3 topics and texts

SL.3.5 Create audio recordings that demonstrate fluid reading at an understandable pace

Materials Needed

Audio recorder

How to do it:

1 Post a poem that lends itself to an engaging performance (and one students are already familiar with), such as "Godfrey Gordon Gustavus Gore" by William Brighty Rands, "Happy Poem" by James Carter, or "Darkness Is My Friend" by Joanne Ryder.

2 Read through the poem together.

3 Take student suggestions about where to add sound effects, how to highlight certain words, and how to adjust the volume of voices. Note ideas on the poem itself to help students remember when performing.

4 Assign students to different lines or stanzas. Some stanzas might be best performed by the whole class; others might be best with one, two, or three voices.

5 Turn the recording device on and begin performing the poem.

6 Have students listen to the audio recording and share their reactions.

EXTENSION FOR A LATER LANGUAGE ARTS LESSON

■ Divide students into poetry discussion groups. Have students reflect on and discuss poetry, using guiding questions such as "What does the poem say to you? How did the poem make you feel? What did the poem make you think about? Did you especially like any words or phrases? Does the poem remind you of anything in your life?"

The Affix Effect

Language Arts Content

Understanding word parts

Common Core Standards

RF.3.3 Apply grade-level phonics and word analysis skills in decoding words

L.3.4 Determine or clarify the meaning of unknown words and phrases

L.3.4b Determine the meaning of new word formed when known affix is added to known word

Materials Needed

Affix cards

Vocabulary

Affix, prefix, suffix

How to do it:

1 Give everyone a moment to make enough space around themselves so they can act out the words you'll be reading. Remind students about staying in their space while moving arms, legs, and bodies safely; model if necessary.

2 Write on a chart a word the class knows, for example, "comfortable."

3 Ask students to dramatize what it looks, sounds, and feels like to be comfortable.

4 Place the affix card "un-" before "comfortable." Ask for volunteers to give the meaning of the new word.

5 Ask students to dramatize what it looks, sounds, and feels like to be uncomfortable.

6 Repeat steps 2–5 for stem words and affixes such as "agreeable" (paired with "dis-"), "care" (paired with "-less" and "-ful"), and "do" (paired with "un-" and "re-").

VARIATION

■ Focus on one type of affix at a time instead of mixing prefixes and suffixes together.

EXTENSIONS FOR A LATER LANGUAGE ARTS LESSON

■ As a class, sort new words by affix (for example, words with "-ful" or "-less"). Then have students investigate the meanings of these affixes and note them on a class chart.

■ Have students go on an "Affix Hunt" in their independent books, writing words with the affixes they're studying on a sticky note and adding them to the class chart.

Big Ideas, Small Details

Language Arts Content

Identifying parts of text

Common Core Standards

RI.3.1 Ask and answer questions to demonstrate understanding of a text

RI.3.2 Determine main idea; recount key details, explain how they support main idea

SL.3.2 Determine main ideas and supporting details of text read aloud

Materials Needed

None

Vocabulary

Main idea, supporting details, topic

How to do it:

1 Display a message like the following:

Dear _____ Thinkers,

Lately we've practiced stopping to think about what we're reading. Stopping to think can lead to great questions and predictions about the text. Readers who stop to think about the text can also visualize better what is happening.

Today we'll work in pairs to stop and think about some news we'll be reading in a periodical.

Thinking questions: What is the topic of this message? What is the main idea? Can you spot the supporting details?

Be ready to share your ideas at our meeting.

2 Read through the message as a class.

3 Invite students to brainstorm possible words to describe "Thinkers."

4 Ask, "What is the topic of this message?" Repeat the question for the main idea and supporting details. Using different colored markers for each, highlight the topic, main idea, and supporting details in the message.

5 Promote discussion around all three aspects of the message. You might say, "In this passage, how can you tell the difference between the topic and the main idea?" or "What, specifically, did I want you to know about stopping to think?"

VARIATIONS

■ Continue locating topic, main idea, and supporting details with a similar message on a different topic and main idea that you want to reinforce for students. For example, your message could focus on the importance of showing your work in mathematics or the benefits of following classroom rules.

■ Sometimes students find it easier to name the supporting details first, followed by the main idea, so invite them to locate any of the three parts of the message in any order.

EXTENSION FOR A LATER LANGUAGE ARTS LESSON

■ Students work with a number of different informational texts to distinguish between the topic, main idea, and supporting details.

Comma Hunt

Language Arts Content

Using commas

Common Core Standards

RF.3.4b Read grade-level prose/poetry orally with accuracy, appropriate rate, and expression

SL.3.1a Come to discussions prepared; explicitly draw on that preparation to explore ideas

L.3.2 Demonstrate command of standard English capitalization, punctuation, and spelling when writing

L.3.2c Use commas and quotation marks in dialogue

Materials Needed

None

Vocabulary

Comma

How to do it:

1 Display a message like the following:

> October 21, _____
>
> Dear Considerate Students,
>
> Yesterday Ms. Thompson said to me, "Your students walk so quietly in the hallways." I responded, "Thank you for noticing."
>
> Other people are observing your effort, kindness, and respect for others' learning. How can we maintain that consideration every day?

2 Read through the message together.

3 Ask for student volunteers to help locate and circle commas in the message.

4 Have students read through the message again, this time acting out the commas (using one hand to make the shape of the comma) each time the class comes to one in the message.

5 Invite students to focus even further on commas: "Commas are useful punctuation marks. When and where are they necessary?" Take student responses.

VARIATION

■ When students become confident locating commas in different texts, write a morning message without commas. Invite students to place the commas where they're needed.

EXTENSION FOR A LATER LANGUAGE ARTS LESSON

■ Send your students on a "Comma Hunt" during reading time. Make copies of different pages of various texts and have students circle or highlight all the commas they see. As a class, chart when commas are used in text (separating items in a list, setting off dialogue in a story, after a salutation in a letter, etc.).

Multisyllabic Madness

Language Arts Content

Multisyllabic words

Common Core Standards

RF.3.3 Apply grade-level phonics and word analysis skills in decoding words

RF.3.3c Decode multisyllable words

Materials Needed

None

Vocabulary

Multisyllabic, decode, syllabicate

How to do it:

1 Display a message like the following:

> Dear _____ Decoders,
>
> You've been decoding multisyllabic words with a great deal of confidence. You are discovering how knowing syllabication rules can help you. The more you practice these strategies, the more you will succeed when decoding three- and four-syllable words.
>
> Today we'll practice decoding multisyllabic words in isolation.
>
> P.S. This message contains a number of multisyllabic words. How many do you count in all? Write your total below.

2 As a class, brainstorm an adjective that would describe "Decoders." Write it in the blank space in the message.

3 Read through the message together.

4 Look over student responses at the bottom of the message chart and ask for volunteers to share the multisyllabic words they found, underlining or circling the multisyllabic words as you go.

5 Call on student volunteers until you've marked all the words.

VARIATION

■ Have students put a hand under their chins when they come to a multisyllabic word.

EXTENSION FOR A LATER LANGUAGE ARTS LESSON

■ Using your morning message as the text, scoop the multisyllabic words—that is, draw a semicircle under each syllable in the word. Then label the syllables "closed," "open," "VCe," etc.

What's the Motive?

Language Arts Content

Understanding character

Common Core Standards

RL.3.1 Ask and answer questions to demonstrate understanding of a text

RL.3.3 Describe characters; explain how their actions contribute to the sequence of events

SL.3.1a Come to discussions prepared; explicitly draw on that preparation to explore ideas

SL.3.1d Explain their own ideas and understanding

Materials Needed

None

Vocabulary

Evidence, motive

How to do it:

1 Display a message like the following:

> Dear Sleuthing Students,
>
> Yesterday we got to a very exciting part in *Sleepover Sleuths*. Hollywood Heather has gone missing, and we've got a number of suspects on our list. What we're trying to understand is **why** any one of these characters would have taken her.
>
> On a sticky note, name one person who might have taken Hollywood Heather, his or her motive, and one piece of evidence. Place your idea in the space below.

2 Read through the message. For each mystery-themed word, make a physical gesture, such as pantomiming moving a magnifying glass up to your eye.

3 Share some of the ideas students posted.

VARIATION

- Although mystery is a natural genre to use when exploring motive, you can expand your students' thinking about motivation by using different genres in your messages. For example, for nonfiction you might ask, "Why do you think explorers would choose to go to challenging places like the polar regions? If you decided to go, what would be your reasons?" For poetry, you might ask, "What do you think made our poet for today decide to write this poem? Does the poem give you any clues?"

EXTENSION FOR A LATER LANGUAGE ARTS LESSON

- Students can discuss character motivation during book clubs. Post questions such as "Why did _____ act in this way?" and "What makes _____ say/do this?" to help students begin a conversation.

Wonderful Words

Language Arts Content

Using context clues

Common Core Standards

RI.3.4 Determine the meaning of academic and domain-specific words and phrases

RF.3.4c Use context to confirm or self-correct word recognition and understanding

L.3.4a Use sentence-level context as a clue to the meaning of a word or phrase

Materials Needed

None

Vocabulary

Context clues

How to do it:

1 Display a message like the following:

> Dear Wordsmiths,
>
> Spring is finally upon us. Yesterday I was able to go outside without a coat! Unfortunately, the forecast calls for snow on Wednesday, even though the weather is quite warm today.
>
> Considering the paragraph above, how would you define "forecast"? Use context clues, and be ready to share your idea during our meeting.

2 Have students read through the message silently.

3 Take a few ideas about the meaning of "forecast." Highlight students' use of context clues to decipher the meaning.

EXTENSION FOR A LATER LANGUAGE ARTS LESSON

■ Have students add new words and definitions to their personal vocabulary lists.

Hi-Definition

Language Arts Content

Vocabulary development

Common Core Standards

RF.4.4c Use context to confirm or self-correct word recognition and understanding

SL.4.1 Engage effectively in collaborative discussions on grade 4 topics and texts

L.4.4a Use context as a clue to the meaning of a word or phrase

Materials Needed

Index card pairs (one card with a vocabulary word, the other with the word used in a sentence)

Vocabulary

Context clues

How to do it:

1 Give each student a card on which you've written a word (from a vocabulary list, read-aloud, informational text, etc.) or a sentence using that word.

2 Students mingle, trying to find the student with the matching card.

3 When students find their match, they greet each other with a friendly "Hello!" and then sit down together to try to decode the meaning of their word by using the context clues in the sentence.

4 After a minute or so, invite a few pairs to explain what they think their word means and how they used context clues to figure it out.

EXTENSION FOR A LATER LANGUAGE ARTS LESSON

■ Have students work in pairs to add the new words from this greeting to a class dictionary. They can include the word, its definition, an illustration, synonyms, antonyms, and two or three sentences that use the word in context.

The Root of It

How to do it:

Language Arts Content

Vocabulary development

Common Core Standards

SL.4.1 Engage effectively in collaborative discussions on grade 4 topics and texts

L.4.4b Use Greek and Latin affixes and roots as clues to the meaning of a word

Materials Needed

Groups of three cards with words that contain the same Greek or Latin root (for example, autograph, photograph, telegraph; homophone, homonym, homogeneous)

Vocabulary

Root

1 Give each student a card and introduce the greeting: "We're going to use these cards for our greeting today. The word on your card contains a common Latin or Greek root. Two other students will have words with the same root. You'll find them and greet them. For example, if I'm holding a card that says 'audience' [hold up the card], I'll look for a classmate who also has a word with 'aud' in it, such as 'audition,' and we'll greet each other with a "Good morning" and a handshake. Then the two of us will find the third person with an 'aud' word, greet him or her, and stand together. Let's try it."

2 Students start searching for and greeting all members of their root group while you coach as needed.

3 After all students are in their root groups, signal for attention and explain the next part of the greeting: "Now use your three words to try and figure out the meaning of your root."

4 Root groups share out what they think their root means. Chart all roots represented during today's greeting.

VARIATIONS

- Students greet one another in Greek ("Kalimera") or Latin ("Salve").

- After students have become comfortable with roots, try Greek and Latin affixes.

EXTENSION FOR A LATER LANGUAGE ARTS LESSON

- Challenge students to think of as many words as they can with a certain root. Try common roots such as -aud (Latin, "hear or listen"), -ject (Latin, "throw"), and -graph (Latin, "write").

What Are You Doing?

Language Arts Content:

Dramatizing

Common Core Standards:

RL.4.3 Describe in depth a character, setting, or event, drawing on details in the text

W.4.3b Use dialogue and description to develop experiences and events or show responses of characters

SL.4.1b Follow agreed-upon rules for discussions; carry out assigned roles

Materials Needed:

None

Vocabulary:

Pantomime

How to do it:

Before the meeting, practice modeling the greeting with a student volunteer.

1 Introduce and model the greeting: "This is a pantomime greeting. Remember that pantomiming means showing without speaking or making any sounds. The tricky part today is that when you greet your partner and ask what she's doing, she won't name the action she's actually pantomiming; she'll name another action instead. You'll then pantomime the action she named as you greet her back. You'll greet each other several times, doing different actions each time. Watch as Micah and I show you."

2 Model with Micah:

You: Pantomime brushing your teeth.

Micah: "Good morning, Mr. M. What are you doing?"

You: Continue pantomiming brushing your teeth, but say, "Good morning, Micah. I'm wrapping a present."

Micah: Begins pantomiming wrapping a present.

You: "What are you doing, Micah?"

Micah: Continues to pantomime wrapping a present, but says, "I'm combing my hair."

You: Begin pantomiming combing your hair.

Micah: "What are you doing, Mr. M?" and so forth for a few rounds.

3 After the modeling, students pair up and spread themselves around the room. On your signal, they start the greeting and do several rounds.

VARIATION

■ Students stay in the meeting circle; partners take turns stepping to the center to greet each other while classmates watch and listen attentively.

EXTENSION FOR A LATER LANGUAGE ARTS LESSON

■ Have students pantomime characters' actions when reading realistic fiction, to better comprehend the characters and the story, and when writing realistic fiction, to create fuller characters and more specific actions.

What's Your Scoop?

Language Arts Content:

Questioning

Common Core Standards:

W.4.4 Produce writing in which development and organization are appropriate to task, purpose, and audience

W.4.7 Conduct short research projects

SL.4.1b Follow agreed-upon rules for discussions; carry out assigned roles

SL.4.4 Report on a topic or text, tell a story, or recount an experience

Materials Needed:

Interview sheet, clipboard (or other hard surface to write on), and pen or pencil for each student

How to do it:

One partner plays the role of the journalist and the other the role of the interviewee. The interview sheet could list questions like these:

➤ What is your full name?

➤ What is your favorite subject?

➤ What is something you like to do after school?

1 Students sit facing a partner and decide who'll take the first turn being the journalist. The journalist greets her partner and then asks the questions, writing down the response to each: "Good Morning, Waylon! What is your full name?" and so on.

2 Partners switch roles and repeat step 1.

3 When all partners have completed steps 1 and 2, students report on their partners' responses.

VARIATION

■ As students become more comfortable with one another, vary the questions. Students could ask each other, "What is your greatest fear?" or "What do you look forward to doing when you grow up?"

EXTENSION FOR A LATER LANGUAGE ARTS LESSON

■ Staying with their partners from this activity, students complete a few more rounds of "What's Your Scoop?" with different questions each time. Each student then writes a detailed piece on their partners.

Answering As …

Language Arts Content

Character analysis

Common Core Standards

RL.4.1 Refer to details and examples in a text when explaining and drawing inferences

RL.4.3 Describe in depth a character, setting, or event, drawing on details in the text

W.4.9 Draw evidence from literary or informational texts to support analysis, reflection, and research

SL.4.1b Follow agreed-upon rules for discussions; carry out assigned roles

Materials Needed

None

How to do it:

Keep your questions broad so they'll apply to any of the characters students might choose to represent for this greeting.

1 Tell students they'll be answering a question as a literary character of their choice—one they know well from a series or a longer chapter book. Give them a moment to think of a character.

2 Ask a broad question, such as "What makes you smile?" or "What do you fear?"

3 Students think for a few moments and silently put a thumb on their knee when they're ready to respond.

4 Taking turns around the circle, students respond "in character." For example, a student who chose Opal from *Because of Winn-Dixie* might say, "I fear being all alone in the world."

5 Go around the circle until all students have had the opportunity to share.

VARIATION

■ Weave a greeting into this sharing by adding, "Hello, I'm _____ and _____ makes me smile." For example, "Hello, I'm Opal, and being with my dog, Winn-Dixie, makes me smile."

EXTENSION FOR A LATER LANGUAGE ARTS LESSON

■ As students read independently, have them practice drawing inferences about characters based on the characters' thoughts and feelings. Guide students in creating graphic organizers to record their inferences and the evidence to support them.

A Time of Change

How to do it:

Language Arts Content

Storytelling

Common Core Standards

W.4.3 Write narratives to develop real or imagined experiences or events using effective technique, descriptive details, and clear event sequences

SL.4.1 Engage effectively in collaborative discussions on grade 4 topics and texts

SL.4.4 Report on a topic or text, tell a story, or recount an experience

Materials Needed

None

Vocabulary

Narrative, sequence

Have one or two students sign up to share each day. Brainstorm together about times of change that students might share about (becoming a big sister or brother, moving, learning something new) and suggest they plan their sharing the night before.

1 Introduce the sharing: "This week, we'll be taking turns sharing brief stories about a time in our lives when we experienced a big change. As you tell your story, remember to use what we've learned about narrative sequence, and include details to help listeners picture what happened."

2 Post a list of possible sentence starters ("One big change in my life was when . . ." "Things really changed for me when . . .") and model the sharing to help students understand the kind and number of details to include.

3 The first sharer tells about a time of change and ends by saying, "I'm ready for questions."

4 The sharer takes questions from three to five classmates; after answering all of the questions, she says, "Thank you."

5 Repeat steps 3 and 4 for the next sharer.

VARIATIONS

- Change the theme of the sharing, depending on student interest or curriculum. Themes could include "A Surprising Time" or "A Time of Frustration." Encourage students to think of details that make their sharing unique.

- As students learn to offer comments (not just questions) to sharers, have sharers say, "I'm ready for questions and comments."

EXTENSION FOR A LATER LANGUAGE ARTS LESSON

- Use this sharing as a launching pad for a narrative writing piece. Have students draft the piece using details such as dialogue, specific action, and internal thought to expand on the ideas and details they shared during Morning Meeting.

Author as Character

How to do it:

Language Arts Content

Character development

Common Core Standards

RL.4.3 Describe in depth a character, setting, or event, drawing on details in the text

W.4.3a Orient reader by establishing a situation and introducing narrator/ characters; organize an event sequence

W.4.3b Use dialogue and description to develop experiences and events or show responses of characters

Materials Needed

None

Vocabulary

Realistic fiction

This sharing works best when students are creating imaginary characters in realistic fiction. Set aside a week for around-the-circle sharings focused on these characters.

1 Ask students to respond to the following questions as a character they are creating: "What is your name and where do you live?"

2 Students respond as their imaginary character, for example, "My name is Lily and I live in Manitoba, Canada."

3 When all students have answered the first question, ask another question, for example, "What's your biggest problem?"

4 Continue for a few more rounds.

EXTENSION FOR A LATER LANGUAGE ARTS LESSON

■ To help students create realistic three-dimensional characters, have them jot down ideas from these sharings and from their reading of realistic fiction in their writing notebooks.

Of Utmost Importance

How to do it:

This sharing takes time, so plan to do it over a few weeks, with one or two students sharing each day. Suggest that students plan their sharing the night before.

1 Let students know that they will each have a turn sharing about an important event in their life, and then take questions and comments from classmates.

2 Post a list of possible sentence starters ("Something important that's happening in my life is . . ." "This is important because . . ." "I feel _____ about this . . ."). Also post reminders about the structure of the sharing. Model first to reinforce students' understanding of appropriate topics, number of details, and length of sharing.

3 The first sharer talks about something important in her life that has recently happened, is currently happening, or will happen in the near future. For example, a student might share about a trip, a special achievement, or a change at home, such as the arrival of a new pet. She includes a few details about the important event, why it is important, and how it makes her feel.

4 After concluding, the sharer takes three to five questions and comments from the class.

5 Continue with the second sharer.

EXTENSION FOR A LATER LANGUAGE ARTS LESSON

■ Create an "Important Events" bulletin. Then, each time you do this sharing, invite students to act as journalists and write up brief news flashes about what their classmates shared.

Language Arts Content

Organizing personal narratives

Common Core Standards

W.4.3 Write narratives to develop real or imagined experiences or events using effective technique, descriptive details, and clear event sequences

W.4.8 Recall relevant information from experiences or gather relevant information

SL.4.1 Engage effectively in collaborative discussions on grade 4 topics and texts

SL.4.1b Follow agreed-upon rules for discussions; carry out assigned roles

Materials Needed

None

Seconds to Respond

Language Arts Content

Paraphrasing

Common Core Standards

W.4.4 Produce writing
in which development
and organization are
appropriate to task,
purpose, audience

SL.4.1 Engage effectively
in collaborative discussions
on grade 4 topics and texts

SL.4.2 Paraphrase text read
aloud or information pre-
sented in diverse media

L.4.3a Choose words and
phrases to convey ideas
precisely

Materials Needed

2 to 4 sticky notes and a pen
for each student

Vocabulary

Key ideas, paraphrase

How to do it:

This sharing takes time, so plan to do it over a few weeks, with one or two students sharing each day. Suggest that students plan their sharing the night before.

1 Let students know that they will each have a turn sharing a piece of news,
after which the rest of the class will paraphrase.

2 Post a list of possible sentence starters ("The news I want to share is . . ."
"I'd like to tell you about . . .") and reminders about the structure of the sharing. Model being a sharer to reinforce students' understanding of appropriate
topics, number of details, and length of sharing.

3 Next, model paraphrasing what the sharer said to reinforce what a paraphrase
is: Have a student volunteer tell a piece of news while you pretend to be an
audience member. After hearing what the student said, pause a moment to
think, write your paraphrase on a sticky note, and read it aloud to the class.

4 To start the sharing, say, "Today, Cate is going to share some news with us.
As she shares, listen closely for her key ideas. When she finishes, quickly
paraphrase what she said with a few precise words of your own." Cate shares
some appropriate news (for example, her first soccer practice, a new puppy,
or her grandfather's upcoming visit).

5 The class takes 15 to 30 seconds to write their paraphrase on a sticky note.

6 Invite a few students to read their paraphrase aloud, and then move on to the
next sharer.

VARIATION

■ Students respond to the sharing verbally. For example, they might turn to a
partner and share one word or image that stood out to them.

EXTENSIONS FOR A LATER LANGUAGE ARTS LESSON

■ Post a written version of the sharer's news. Place students' sticky note responses
around the sharing. Then have students discuss what stands out to them about
the sharing and the paraphrases, and why.

■ Read aloud part of an informational text, and then have students write their
paraphrase of it in their reading notebooks.

Book Talk

How to do it:

1 Create an inner and an outer circle, with each student in the inner circle facing a classmate in the outer circle, to form partners.

2 Explain the activity: "For today's activity, you'll get to share your ideas and opinions about the read-aloud we just finished. I'll ask a question about the book, and then you'll chat with your circle partner. Let's try it."

3 Ask an open-ended question, such as "Who was a favorite character for you and why?"

4 Give pairs an allotted time to talk (30 seconds to a minute).

5 On your signal, students say "Goodbye!" to their partner; inner circle students move one step to their right to face a new partner.

6 Repeat steps 2–5 with a new open-ended question about the read-aloud.

7 Continue with two or three more questions.

VARIATION

■ Have students discuss their own independent reading books. Be sure you ask open-ended questions that will apply to the various books students may choose: "Would you recommend this book? Why or why not?" or "Did you find yourself focused or distracted while reading? Why?"

EXTENSION FOR A LATER LANGUAGE ARTS LESSON

■ Ask students for phrases or questions they used during this activity that helped keep their conversations lively (for example, "Not only that, but . . ." "That reminds me of . . ." "That's interesting. Can you say more?"). Post these on a chart. Have students refer to this chart during book club conversations.

Language Arts Content

Reading comprehension

Common Core Standards

RF.4.4a Read grade-level text with purpose and understanding

SL.4.1 Engage effectively in collaborative discussions on grade 4 topics and texts

Materials Needed

None

On My Back

Language Arts Content

Vocabulary development

Common Core Standards

RL.4.3 Describe in depth a character, setting, or event, drawing on details in the text

RF.4.4c Use context to confirm or self-correct word recognition and understanding

L.4.4a Use context as a clue to the meaning of a word or phrase

Materials Needed

Sticky notes (one per round)

How to do it:

1 On a sticky note, write a word relating to something the class is studying. For example, if the class is studying persuasive writing, the sticky note might say, "opinion."

2 Ask a volunteer to come to the center of the circle, and place the sticky note on his back without him seeing the word. The volunteer walks one time around the circle, turning so that all students get a good look at the word.

3 Model how the class can offer clues to help the student guess the word—a broader first clue followed by more specific ones that build on it. For example, for the word "opinion," a first clue might be "You are something we've focused on during writing" and a follow-up might be "You are not always based on fact."

4 Classmates signal when they have a clue, and the student calls on them. After three to five clues, the student says, "Am I _____?" If he's correct, move on to the next round with a new word and new guesser. If he's incorrect, he asks for one or two additional clues.

5 Stop the round before the guesser becomes frustrated or embarrassed. You can say, for example, "OK, that was a tough one. The word was _____."

VARIATION

■ Use the names of characters from favorite stories or words that have to do with specific genres; for example, for fiction try words such as "theme," "character," and "plot."

EXTENSION FOR A LATER LANGUAGE ARTS LESSON

■ Jot down the clues students offer and display them along with the sticky-note words. Have students add other ideas for clues, helping to solidify their understanding of the words.

Say It!

Language Arts Content

Vocabulary development

Common Core Standards

SL.4.1b Follow agreed-upon rules for discussions; carry out assigned roles

L.4.5 Understand figurative language, word relation-ships, and nuances in word meanings

Materials Needed

None

Vocabulary

Association, associate

How to do it:

Briefly review word association.

1 Begin by saying one word, for example, "Tree."

2 The student to your right says a word he associates with the word *tree*, perhaps "Brown."

3 The next student in the circle says a word she associates with the word *brown*, such as "Chocolate."

4 Continue this pattern around the circle.

5 Invite observations from the class. Possible responses: "A lot of us came up with food words!" "Our last word was really different from our first word." "I wonder what would happen if we did another round with the same starting word."

VARIATIONS

- Try different parts of speech for the starting word: common and proper nouns, verbs, adjectives, adverbs.

- Increase the challenge by requiring all the words, including the first one, to be nouns, adjectives, or some other part of speech.

EXTENSION FOR A LATER LANGUAGE ARTS LESSON

- Keep track of all of the words spoken during one round of "Say It!" and have students analyze the parts of speech. How many adjectives were used? How many nouns? Do students notice any trends?

Scrambled Sentence

Language Arts Content

Revising for clarity

Common Core Standards

W.4.5 Develop and strengthen writing by planning, revising, and editing

L.4.1 Demonstrate command of standard English grammar and usage

L.4.2 Demonstrate command of standard English capitalization, punctuation, and spelling

Materials Needed

Pocket chart and index cards (one word per index card). This activity works well on an interactive whiteboard, if available.

Vocabulary

Revise, clarity, grammar, punctuation

How to do it:

1 Explain that the goal of this activity is to revise a sentence for clarity. Ask for a volunteer to be the reviser—the person who will take student suggestions and move the cards on the pocket chart.

2 Display the pocket chart in which you've placed words and punctuation out of order. For example, the pocket chart might read: "not car. The red but win fast, fast race drove to enough"

3 The reviser asks for a command from a student, who might say, "Put 'The' at the beginning of the sentence."

4 The reviser follows the command and asks for another.

5 When the class believes they have the sentence revised correctly, they signal (thumb on knee or arms crossed).

6 Write the sentence in its correct form on a chart or whiteboard and invite students to compare and contrast the two sentences.

VARIATION

■ Vary what you include in the sentence to reflect your current grammar studies. For example, you might insert progressive verb tenses, relative pronouns and adverbs, or prepositional phrases.

EXTENSION FOR A LATER LANGUAGE ARTS LESSON

■ Include this type of activity in a grammar center. Have partners work together to unscramble mixed-up sentences and check their work against the correct sentence.

Sparkle

How to do it:

One student will be the spelling word list holder.

1 The list holder chooses a word from the list and says it aloud.

2 A volunteer from the meeting circle begins spelling the word by saying its first letter.

3 The next student in the circle says the second letter, the next student says the third letter, and so forth. The list holder keeps an eye on the word list to make sure the word is being spelled correctly.

4 If anyone makes a mistake, the list holder calls out "Check!" (If the list holder misses the mistake, anyone else in the circle can say "Check.") The student who made the mistake either corrects it or asks for a "lifeline"—help from the group.

5 When the entire word has been spelled correctly, the next student in the circle says "Sparkle" to indicate that the whole word has been spelled correctly.

6 Repeat steps 1–5 for four or five more words.

VARIATIONS

- Ask a volunteer to write the letters on a whiteboard as students say them aloud. This will help students visualize the word as it is spelled.

- If a classmate makes a mistake during his turn, students respectfully make a silent signal, such as wiggling their fingers, to let him know he needs to revise his thinking.

EXTENSION FOR A LATER LANGUAGE ARTS LESSON

- To help students practice spelling words during word study, break the class into smaller groups of five or six, each doing the "Sparkle" activity.

Language Arts Content

Spelling

Common Core Standards

L.4.2 Demonstrate command of standard English capitalization, punctuation, and spelling

L.4.2d Spell grade-appropriate words correctly, consulting references as needed

Materials Needed

Fourth grade spelling word list

Spoken Duet

Language Arts Content

Understanding point of view

Common Core Standards

RL.4.1 Refer to details and examples in a text when explaining and drawing inferences

RL.4.2 Determine a theme of a story, drama, or poem; summarize the text

RF.4.4 Read with sufficient accuracy and fluency to support comprehension

W.4.4 Produce writing in which development and organization are appropriate to task, purpose, and audience

SL.4.1 Engage effectively in collaborative discussions on grade 4 topics and texts

Materials Needed

Poem for two voices, such as "Honeybees" by Paul Fleischman

Vocabulary:

Perspective

How to do it:

1 Make a chart of the poem, with the words for each voice in side-by-side columns, and place the chart where everyone can see it. In your morning message, direct students to read the poem before coming to Morning Meeting.

2 Introduce the activity: "Today we are going to look at a poem written in a unique way. This poem is meant to be read by two voices instead of one. It's a poem that looks at the life of a bee from two perspectives: that of the queen bee and that of the worker bee."

3 Split the class into two sections: Section A will read the first stanza of the left-hand column (worker bee); then Section B will read the first stanza of the right-hand column (queen bee), and so on.

4 Invite students to share opinions about how the two types of bees feel about their lives: "How do you think the worker bee feels about life as a bee? How do you know?" "How about the queen bee? What does the poem say that makes you think so?"

5 Switch parts and read through the poem once again, inviting students to reflect their bee's feelings in their voices as they read.

EXTENSION FOR A LATER LANGUAGE ARTS LESSON

■ Just as "Honeybees" tells about the life of a bee from two different perspectives, challenge students to take on a subject (perhaps school) from two different perspectives (for example, teacher and student or student and parent) and write a poem for two voices.

Ten-Line Scene

Language Arts Content

Dramatizing

Common Core Standards

RL.4.5 Refer to structural elements of poems and drama when writing or speaking about a text

RL.4.7 Make connections between the text and a visual or oral presentation of the text

W.4.4 Produce writing in which development and organization are appropriate to task, purpose, and audience

SL.4.1 Engage effectively in collaborative discussions on grade 4 topics and texts

Materials Needed

A ten-line scene (as shown in step 1) posted on a chart or photocopied so that each student has a copy

Vocabulary

Interpretation, setting, theme

How to do it:

1 Post the ten-line scene shown below and ask two student volunteers to come to the front of the room to act it out. Give the volunteers the setting and the theme; for example, the setting is a pool, and the theme is that Character 1 wants to jump off the diving board but isn't sure how to do it.

Example scene:

Character 1: *(performs action)* I don't think I'm going to get it.

Character 2: If you try harder, you will.

Character 1: But it's impossible.

Character 2: Try this. *(performs action)*

Character 1: Really?

Character 2: Trust me.

Character 1: Okay, I'll try it. *(performs action)*

Character 2: AHHHHH!!

Character 1: It's working!

Character 2: See? I told you.

2 Take student suggestions for the relationship the actors will play (friends, parent and child, etc.).

3 Take student suggestions for the actions each character will do.

4 The student actors act out the scene.

5 Repeat with new volunteers and a new setting as time allows.

VARIATION

■ Have students pair up and rehearse the same scene at the same time, in different parts of the classroom. After partners perform their scenes, discuss differences in interpretation.

EXTENSION FOR A LATER LANGUAGE ARTS LESSON

■ Have students team up to write their own ten-line scenes.

Precious Paragraphs

Language Arts Content

Organizing information

Common Core Standards

RI.4.5 Describe the overall structure of events, ideas, concepts, or information

W.4.3 Write narratives to develop real or imagined experiences or events using effective technique, descriptive details, and clear event sequences

W.4.5 Develop and strengthen writing by planning, revising, and editing

Materials Needed

None

How to do it:

1 Post a chart like the following:

> Dear Fabulous Fourth Graders,
>
> Today is going to be a busy day. This morning, we will have a visitor from the theater. After our theater visitor, we will have our latest dictation and time to plan for our projects. Our morning will also include work on our science projects. This afternoon, we'll host our reading buddies for partner reading. It will take a lot of energy to get through our day. We'll end our day with a closing circle. What are you looking forward to most? Write your thoughts below in complete sentences.
>
> P.S. All of the information in this message is bunched together. How would you separate it into paragraphs? What seems to go together? Be ready to share your ideas during our meeting.

2 Read through the message aloud as students follow along.

3 Ask students to help you edit the message: "What parts of the message should be grouped together?"

4 Using markers, circle the main topic sentence in one color, the sentences for the "This morning" paragraph in another color, and so on for the afternoon paragraph, conclusion, and question.

5 As a class, read the message again, this time saying "New paragraph" at the start of a new paragraph.

6 Share a few of the sentences about what students are looking forward to.

VARIATION

- Instead of bunching all the sentences together in one long paragraph, break them up, but awkwardly, with paragraph breaks coming at inappropriate spots. Have students suggest better paragraph breaks.

EXTENSION FOR A LATER LANGUAGE ARTS LESSON

- Have students rewrite the message independently, inserting all paragraph edits (including indents).

Problem Solvers to the Rescue

How to do it:

Language Arts Content

Forming opinions

Common Core Standards

RF.4.4b Read grade-level prose and poetry orally with accuracy, appropriate rate, and expression

W.4.1 Write opinion pieces, supporting a point of view with reasons and information

SL.4.1 Engage effectively in collaborative discussions on grade 4 topics and texts

Materials Needed

None

1 Post a chart like the following:

> Dear Problem Solvers,
>
> A lot of you have been coming to me saying the same thing: "Our classroom doesn't have enough books!" This is, most definitely, a problem. If we don't have enough books, I fear you'll lose your love of reading!
>
> What ideas do you have to solve this problem? Write one idea for a solution below.

2 Invite students to read the message aloud chorally.

3 Before reading through some of the solutions, ask students to elaborate more fully about the problem. For example, a student might say, "I'm really getting into *Tales of a Fourth Grade Nothing*, but I notice we don't have *Superfudge* or *Double Fudge*" or "We have a lot of books about animals, but I'm really interested in sea mammals, and we don't have any books about them."

4 Choose one or two suggestions from student responses on the chart to implement; explain your choices.

VARIATION

■ Keep an eye and ear out for language arts–related problems that arise as the year goes on (students feel rushed when revising their writing, they want more read-aloud time, they don't have enough opportunity to illustrate their writing, etc.) and see what solutions students can come up with.

EXTENSIONS FOR A LATER LANGUAGE ARTS LESSON

■ Have students write opinion pieces that incorporate problems classmates have noticed along with solutions.

■ Invite students to create petitions, write letters or speeches, or make posters and videos about a problem and their proposed solutions.

Sophisticated Synonyms

Language Arts Content

Vocabulary development

Common Core Standards

RI.4.4 Determine the meaning of general academic and domain-specific words or phrases

RF.4.4 Read with sufficient accuracy and fluency to support comprehension

L.4.4 Determine or clarify the meaning of words and phrases, choosing flexibly from a range of strategies

L.4.5 Understand figurative language, word relationships, and nuances in word meanings

Materials Needed

None

Vocabulary

Synonym, sophisticated

How to do it:

1 Post a chart like the following:

> Dear Shrewd Scholars,
>
> Your analysis of the publication *Rules* has led me to believe that you presume a being has the capacity to evolve.
>
> Do you presume something comparable for mortal youngsters?
>
> Construct a viewpoint to communicate during our gathering.

2 Ask students, "What words in this message seem a bit out of the ordinary or sophisticated to you?" Circle those words with a marker.

3 Make sure students can decode the circled words. For example, reviewing the pronunciation of "shrewd" in isolation might be helpful before reading the word in context.

4 Read through the message in unison.

5 Students work with partners to decipher the meaning of each sentence by looking for synonyms of the more sophisticated words (for example, "think" is a simpler way to say "presume" and "book" is a synonym for "publication").

6 Students share out ideas about the question posed in the message.

VARIATION

■ Write the message with simpler vocabulary. Circle words that you'd like the class to make more sophisticated. As a class, work to find synonyms for those words.

EXTENSIONS FOR A LATER LANGUAGE ARTS LESSON

■ Begin a synonym chart with adjectives such as "smart" and verbs such as "think." When students come across words in their independent reading that are synonyms for these words, have them write each word on a sticky note and post it underneath the original word.

■ Have students use a thesaurus to rewrite a simple sentence using more sophisticated synonyms.

Too Many Twos

How to do it:

1 Post a chart like the following:

> Dear Energetic Editors,
>
> Yesterday, we held _____ sessions of read-aloud because our book was _____ exciting to put down. We had _____ find out what happened because we were _____ curious _____ wait.
> I suppose we'll have _____ have _____ sessions of word study _____ make up for lost time.

2 Ask, "What do you notice about the blank spaces?" A student might say, "There's a lot of missing two/to/too's!" Now explain the activity: "Yes, that's right. Sometimes people get confused about the correct usage of these words and choose the incorrect word. Let's revisit the meanings of each and see if we can correct our message."

3 Briefly review the meanings of the three different words.

4 Fill in the blank spaces as a class.

VARIATIONS

- Elicit ideas from students about a simple gesture for "two," "to," and "too" (for example, both forefingers coming together to make a plus sign for "too"). Then read through the message chorally, making the appropriate gestures for each of the three words.

- Create a message that incorporates there/their/they're or for/four/fore.

EXTENSION FOR A LATER LANGUAGE ARTS LESSON

- During word study, create reminder spelling/meaning charts for the three words. Include the word, an illustration or symbol of the word, its definition, and an example of the word in context. Post these charts so students can refer to them during writing time.

Language Arts Content

Usage

Common Core Standards

RF.4.4c Use context to confirm or self-correct word recognition and understanding

W.4.5 Develop and strengthen writing by planning, revising, and editing

SL.4.1c Pose and respond to questions; make comments that contribute to the discussion

L.4.1g Correctly use frequently confused words (e.g., to, too, two; there, their)

Materials Needed

None

Vocabulary

Usage

Blink 1-2-4

Language Arts Content

Communication skills

Common Core Standard

SL.5.1b Follow agreed-upon rules for discussions; carry out assigned roles

Note: This greeting's objective is to playfully ease students into making appropriate eye contact when greeting or speaking with each other. If it's inappropriate to require eye contact for your students because of their home cultures or other circumstances, offer an alternative, such as looking at the person's forehead just above the eyes.

Materials Needed

None

How to do it:

Use this greeting on a day when you want the next part of Morning Meeting—sharing—to be done in small groups. By the end of the greeting, the students will be in groups of four, ready for the sharing component.

1 Before the meeting, choose a student and practice modeling the greeting with her.

2 With students seated in the meeting circle, introduce the greeting: "Today's greeting is wordless. Watch as I greet a classmate by using a blink as a way to say 'Hello.'" Model by silently walking over to the student you practiced with, turning to face her, and then blinking. The student blinks back and stands to join you.

3 Explain, "Neva and I are now partners." You and the student silently walk over to a pair of students in the circle and each greets the two with a blink. Once the blinks are returned, the four of you stand in a clump and wait.

4 Select a new student to greet someone still sitting in the circle. This pair will become two and will then greet two more to make another group of four. Continue until everyone is in a group of four and standing silently together. (If you have an odd number of students, help one group form a group of three or five.)

5 Once everyone has been greeted, students can move right into a small-group sharing.

VARIATION

- Sitting in a circle, assign a code to the blinking. For example, one blink means "Hi," two blinks means "Hello," three blinks means "Good morning," etc. Send the greeting around the circle, allowing each child to select which blink to pass along.

EXTENSION FOR A LATER LANGUAGE ARTS LESSON

- When students work in pairs or small groups, remind them to practice looking at the speaker as a way to show interest and respect.

Broadcast Views

Language Arts Content

Using figurative language

Common Core Standards

RL.5.1 Quote accurately from a text when explaining and drawing inferences

W.5.4 Produce clear and coherent writing appropriate to task, purpose, and audience

SL.5.1 Engage effectively in collaborative discussions on grade 5 topics and texts

L.5.5b Recognize and explain the meaning of common idioms

Materials Needed

Chart of figures of speech used to convey emotions, such as: like a pig in clover, feeling blue, pleased as punch, over the moon, hot under the collar. Include some from students' current or upcoming reading.

Vocabulary

Metaphor, simile, idiom, figurative language

How to do it:

1 Introduce the greeting: "Today we'll combine our greeting with our sharing. You'll get a chance to talk to a classmate and find out how he or she is feeling. Each of you will pick an example of figurative language from this list and explain why you feel that way. Then you'll share what your partner said with the class."

2 Model with a student you have prepared in advance. Walk toward each other with your right hands up in front of you, gently give each other a high five or fist bump, and begin your greeting:

Student: "Good morning, Mrs. Lundgren. How are you doing today?"

Teacher: "Hello, Joanna. I have ants in my pants because I can't wait to hear you all in the concert. How are you feeling today?"

Student: "I am feeling down in the dumps because my brother is sick."

3 Return to your places in the circle. All students mingle until you say, "Hand up, and find a partner."

4 After partners have conversed, they return to the circle and sit next to each other. When all students are seated, go around the circle with students sharing what their partner said.

5 If time allows, ask for a question or comment about someone's sharing.

VARIATION

■ Do this greeting/sharing combination as a group activity but have students use the figurative language to explain how characters from a familiar book are feeling.

EXTENSIONS FOR A LATER LANGUAGE ARTS LESSON

■ Keep a running class list of figurative expressions and have students add to it when they discover them in their reading.

■ Invite students to choose a figurative expression and write a piece detailing what is causing them to feel that way.

Heeeeeeere's Johnny!

Language Arts Content

Summarizing

Common Core Standards

SL.5.1 Engage effectively in collaborative discussions on grade 5 topics and texts

SL.5.4 Report on a topic or text or present an opinion; speak clearly at an understandable pace

Materials Needed

Index cards (optional)

How to do it:

Students will interview each other in this combined greeting and sharing, so if you think they'll need to jot notes on index cards, pass the cards out before you begin. You may also want to preselect partners and model a round to remind students what respectful conversation looks and sounds like.

1 Students stand up and find someone they don't know well, say "Good morning," and take turns sharing things they'd like others to know about them. They then return to their places in the circle.

2 Select a volunteer to stand up and use their best announcer voice to introduce their partner using the information they just learned, leaving their partner's name for last. For example: "I am pleased to say we have a talented basketball player with us today! She is also an expert in Pokémon, and likes to draw animals, and in her spare she time enjoys gobbling up *Harry Potter* books. Heeeeeeere's Izzie!"

3 The person introduced stands up and takes a bow as the group applauds.

4 Continue until everyone has been introduced.

EXTENSION FOR A LATER LANGUAGE ARTS LESSON

■ Challenge students to write a short, intriguing introduction for a fictional character or a historical figure and then introduce him or her to the class.

I'm Speaking Greek and Latin!

Language Arts Content

Understanding Greek and Latin affixes

Common Core Standards

RF.5.3a Use knowledge of morphology (e.g., roots and affixes) to read accurately multisyllabic words

SL.5.6 Adapt speech to a variety of contexts and tasks

L.5.4b Use common Greek and Latin affixes and roots as clues to the meaning of a word

Materials Needed

A chart or whiteboard listing Greek and Latin affixes. Examples:

tele- (Greek, "far")

photo- (Greek, "light")

-ology (Greek, "study of")

trans- (Latin, "across")

co- (Latin, "together")

-able or -ible (Latin, "capable" or "worthy of")

Vocabulary:

Affix

How to do it:

It's fine for several students to use the same affix; the challenge is to think of different words using a repeated affix. Students who are stuck can ask a classmate for help.

1 Have everyone stand up. Model the greeting:

➤ Select an affix from the list and say it aloud in this format: "_____. It's all Greek [or Latin] to me." For example: "-ology. It's all Greek to me."

➤ Invite students who can make a complete word using –ology to raise their hands.

➤ Choose one of these students to greet: "Good Morning, Denise." Denise returns the greeting followed by a definition of the word she thought of: "Good Morning, Ms. Nelson. Biology is the study of life." You and Denise sit down to show you have been greeted.

2 Now start the greeting by having the student to your left choose an affix and say, "_____. It's all's Greek [or Latin] to me" and then having the class continue with the greeting as modeled.

3 Continue until everyone has been greeted.

VARIATION

■ Use Greek and Latin root words.

EXTENSIONS FOR A LATER LANGUAGE ARTS LESSON

■ Give each student an index card on which to write a word that contains Greek or Latin affixes, such as "contradiction." Then have students cut the card between the root and the affixes to create puzzle pieces: contra/dict/ion. Collect cards and store for independent practice.

■ Give each student four to six index cards. Challenge them to notice Greek and Latin words in their reading and record one word on each card and the matching meaning on a second card (using dictionary sources as needed). Make a class collection to use for a matching game.

You Can Call Me

Language Arts Content

Using conjunctions

Common Core Standards

SL.5.1b Follow agreed-upon rules for discussions; carry out assigned roles

L.5.1e Use correlative conjunctions (e.g., either/or, neither/nor)

Materials Needed

Chart of call-and-response sequence shown in step 2

How to do it:

1 Before beginning, invite students to call out appropriate, respectful words they would use to describe themselves, such as "artist," "musician," "gamer," "athlete," "reader," etc. Record these on a chart. Each student will soon see words in the list that apply to themselves as well as words that don't. For example, Charlene may see herself as a musician and athlete, but not a gamer.

2 Introduce the greeting: "Today's greeting is a call-and-response. Each person will call out these three sentences about themselves you see on the chart [point out the three "call" sentences on the chart] and we'll respond as a class with these three sentences [point out the three "response" sentences on the chart]." Then start the greeting yourself:

Speaker: "You can call me either Ms. Lyle or Ms. L."
(Choose two appropriate names for yourself.)

Crowd: "Hello, _____."
(Each person selects one of the names.)

Speaker: "I am a/an _____."
(Choose one noun to describe yourself or your talent or interest, using words from the list if you'd like.)

Crowd: "Hello, _____."
(Repeats word in unison.)

Speaker: "I am neither a/an _____ nor a/an _____."
(Choose two nouns, again referring to the list for ideas if you'd like.)

Crowd: "You are a/an _____."
(Repeats the noun the speaker chose to describe him- or herself.)

3 Continue the call-and-response around the circle until each person has been greeted.

VARIATION

■ The speaker speaks as a character in a book or a person from history that the class is studying.

EXTENSION FOR A LATER LANGUAGE ARTS LESSON

■ Make "either/or" and "neither/nor" charts and have students add example sentences from their reading. Occasionally review and reflect on the charts: "Are these grammatical structures used more often in certain kinds of books?" "Do some authors tend to use them frequently?" "Do they make the piece or passage harder or easier to understand?"

Say What?!

Language Arts Content

Using interjections

Common Core Standards

RF.5.4a Read grade-level text with purpose and understanding

W.5.5 Develop and strengthen writing by revising and editing

W.5.7 Conduct short research projects

SL.5.1c Pose and respond to questions

L.5.1a Explain the function of interjections

Materials Needed

A chart with common interjections such as "Really?" "Wow!" "Yikes!" "Gee!" "Amazing!" "What?"

Vocabulary

Interjection

How to do it:

Tell students in advance to come to Morning Meeting prepared to share about a research project they are working on.

1 Introduce the sharing: "Our sharing today is about your research project. You'll each share a fact about your research that you think will have an impact on your audience. Remember that 'impact' means the audience feels an emotion such as awe or sorrow, or feels compelled to take some action."

2 Explain the job of the listener: "Listeners, while you are actively listening, think of an appropriate interjection that corresponds to the fact you hear. For example, you could say 'Wow! I didn't know that Martin Luther King, Jr., entered college at age 15' or 'Yikes! That's so sad that viral infections and fungus killed so many okapi.'"

3 Ask two to four volunteers to share. Have each sharer call on three classmates to make a comment preceded by an interjection and then, if they wish, ask the sharer a question.

VARIATION

■ In the meeting circle, students practice using interjections as they create a class story. One student begins by using an interjection, such as "Wow!" The next student adds to the story: "I can't believe . . ." The third student adds on to complete the sentence: "the kangaroo slipped on a banana!" The next student begins again with a new interjection and so on around the circle.

EXTENSIONS FOR A LATER LANGUAGE ARTS LESSON

■ During reading time, ask students to notice interjections in their reading and jot down why they believe the author chose to use them. Students can pair up to discuss what they found, or share at Morning Meeting the next day.

■ Have students revise their current writing to include several appropriate interjections.

Take a Stand

Language Arts Content

Forming opinions

Common Core Standards

RI.5.2 Determine main ideas of a text and explain how they are supported by key details

W.5.1 Write opinion pieces on topics or texts, supporting a point of view with reasons and information

SL.5.1 Engage effectively in collaborative discussions on grade 5 topics and texts

SL.5.4 Report on a topic or text or present an opinion; speak clearly at an understandable pace

Materials Needed

None

How to do it:

Before beginning, remind students how to agree or disagree respectfully with a partner.

1 Think of a controversial opinion about an issue that the class has read about in an informational text and that students might be particularly interested in. For example, if the class is studying nutrition, the opinion might be that no junk food is allowed at school.

2 Name this opinion. Give students a moment to think about whether they agree or disagree, and to come up with three supporting reasons from their reading.

3 Students share with the classmate next to them. Each student responds to their partner's sharing by asking one question or making one comment.

4 Invite two volunteers to share with the whole class.

VARIATION

■ Students brainstorm a list of "hot topics" they'd like to research and have a Take a Stand sharing once a month.

EXTENSION FOR A LATER LANGUAGE ARTS LESSON

■ Have students practice crafting arguments by working with partners to plan and draft essays on high-interest topics, such as "Dogs are smarter than cats" or "Watching TV harms children's brains."

Tell Me About It

Language Arts Content

Understanding character

Common Core Standards

RL.5.1 and RI.5.1 Quote accurately from a text when explaining and drawing inferences

W.5.4 Produce clear and coherent writing appropriate to task, purpose, and audience

SL.5.1 Engage effectively in collaborative discussions on grade 5 topics and texts

L.5.5b Recognize and explain the meaning of common idioms

Materials Needed

A chart displaying figurative expressions (idioms, similes, metaphors, etc.) your class is already familiar with, such as tickled pink, has egg on her face, mad as a wet hen, has a chip on his shoulder, left high and dry

Vocabulary:

Idiom

How to do it:

1 Explain today's sharing: "We've been talking about how characters in books have many feelings, just as we do. In today's sharing, you'll pick a character from either our read-aloud or your independent reading and share how the character is feeling by using one example of figurative language from our list."

2 Model for students: "In the book *Hatchet*, Brian has a chip on his shoulder because he thinks his mother caused the divorce."

3 Have students share with a classmate next to them.

4 When everyone has shared, invite two volunteers to tell the whole class what they and their partner said.

VARIATION

■ Use historical or modern public figures from a social studies unit instead of book characters.

EXTENSION FOR A LATER LANGUAGE ARTS LESSON

■ During writing workshop, challenge students to use figurative expressions from Morning Meeting when they write about how characters are feeling.

You Don't Say

Language Arts Content

Using punctuation

Common Core Standards

W.5.5 Develop and strengthen writing by editing

SL.5.1 Engage effectively in collaborative discussions on grade 5 topics and texts

L.5.2d Use quotation marks, underlining, or italics to indicate titles of works

Materials Needed

None

Vocabulary

Pantomime

How to do it:

In your morning message, tell students to think of a favorite poem, song, or book before coming to Morning Meeting.

1 Explain today's sharing: "We have been practicing using the correct punctuation when writing the title of a poem, song, or book. For today's sharing, you'll tell us the title of your favorite poem, song, or book and pantomime the correct punctuation."

2 Model for students how to show punctuation in titles:

Poem or song in quotes: Make "air quotes" with your fingers as you say the title; for example, "My favorite song is [make air quotes] 'I Get By With a Little Help From My Friends' [make air quotes]."

Book underlined: Pantomime underlining by drawing a horizontal line in the air as you say the title; for example, "My favorite book is [pantomime under-lining] Charlie and the Chocolate Factory."

Book italicized: Pantomime italicizing by holding your hands parallel to each other and slanted to the right, and moving them while saying the title; for example, "My favorite book is [pantomime italicizing] *Charlie and the Chocolate Factory*."

3 Students share one at a time around the circle.

4 Invite several students to ask a question about someone else's favorite poem, song, or book. For example: "Who is your favorite character and why?" "What do you think the songwriter's message is in that song?" "What about the poem makes it your favorite?" "Do you have a special memory attached to your favorite book?"

VARIATION

■ Alert students before everyone starts sharing that you will ask questions to challenge their active listening, such as "Who remembers someone who shared a favorite poem?"

EXTENSION FOR A LATER LANGUAGE ARTS LESSON

■ Have students edit their current writing for correct punctuation of titles.

Cascading Characteristics

Language Arts Content

Understanding character

Common Core Standards

RL.5.3 Compare and contrast two or more characters

RI.5.3 Explain relationships or interactions between two or more individuals

W.5.9 Draw evidence from literary or informational texts to support analysis and reflection

SL.5.4 Report on a topic/ text or present an opinion; speak clearly at an understandable pace

Materials Needed

None

Vocabulary

Character trait, protagonist, contrasting

How to do it:

1 From a book the class has been reading, name two characters that interact with each other, such as the protagonists Doon and Lina in *City of Ember*.

2 Designate one side of the classroom for a character trait, perhaps "optimistic," and the other side for another trait, say "curious." The middle of the room represents both character traits. Be sure to choose traits that one could arguably say is present in some way in at least one character.

3 Students choose one of the two characters. When you say "Go," they walk to the side of the room that represents the trait they think best describes their character, or to the center if they think both traits describe the character.

4 Students partner up with someone near them (it's fine to form groups of three if necessary to include everyone), tell each other which character they chose, and explain why they think that character has that trait (or both traits), using examples from the text to support their reasoning.

5 Invite volunteers to briefly recap their partner or trio discussions for the whole class.

VARIATIONS

- Use characters from different books or historical figures the class is studying.

- Invite students to pick two character traits for the activity.

EXTENSIONS FOR A LATER LANGUAGE ARTS LESSON

- Students write a journal entry from their character's point of view that demonstrates the character's trait.

- Students complete a character attribute grid, noting different characters and one trait for each. Invite reflections on which characters share similar and contrasting qualities.

Character Traits

Language Arts Content

Understanding character

Common Core Standards

RL.5.1 and RI.5.1 Quote accurately from a text when explaining and drawing inferences

RF.5.4 Read with sufficient accuracy and fluency to support comprehension

SL.5.4 Report on a topic or text or present an opinion; speak clearly at an understandable pace

L.5.4 Determine or clarify the meaning of unknown and multiple-meaning words and phrases

Materials Needed

Four character traits (such as optimistic, callous, humble, tenacious), each written on a piece of paper

Vocabulary

Character trait, defining trait

How to do it:

1 Post the four character traits, one in each corner of the room.

2 Introduce the character traits and review the meaning of each.

3 Announce a character from a book the whole class knows.

4 At your signal, students walk to the corner for the character trait that they think best fits the character.

5 Students discuss with a partner why they feel this character trait is appropriate, using evidence from the text to support their argument. Remind the class that they're sharing opinions, so there are no right or wrong answers.

6 Invite one volunteer from each corner to explain his or her reasoning. If time allows, call out a different character's name and do another round.

VARIATION

■ Use historical figures.

EXTENSION FOR A LATER LANGUAGE ARTS LESSON

■ Students look through the book they're reading to find examples of a character's actions and words, the narrator's use of figurative language, and other methods the author has used to develop a character. In pairs or small groups, students discuss what they think the author meant to convey about the character, using context clues to support their positions.

Eeek, It's a …

Language Arts Content

Vocabulary development

Common Core Standards

RF.5.3a Use knowledge of morphology (e.g., roots and affixes) to read accurately multisyllabic words

SL.5.1 Engage effectively in collaborative discussions on grade 5 topics and texts

L.5.4 Determine or clarify the meaning of unknown and multiple-meaning words and phrases

L.5.4b Use common Greek and Latin affixes and roots as clues to the meaning of a word

Materials Needed

Index cards, each with one phobia and its meaning written on it. Possibilities:

Acrophobia—fear of heights

Aquaphobia—fear of water

Arachnophobia—fear of spiders

Dentophobia—fear of dentists

Nyctophobia—fear of the dark

Phasmophobia—fear of ghosts

Pyrophobia—fear of fire

Scoptophobia—fear of being stared at

Sophophobia—fear of learning

Trypanophobia—fear of needles

How to do it:

1 Divide the class into groups of four to six, then introduce the activity: "In today's activity, each group will receive a card with a type of phobia written on it. You'll work with your group to come up with a pantomime for that phobia. Remember, 'phobia' is the Greek word for an abnormal fear, and 'pantomime' means to act out without speaking, making sounds, or using props."

2 Model the activity: Say to your groupmates, "We have 'alektorophobia,' a fear of chickens. First, we could pantomime a chicken by flapping our arms like this." Tuck your thumbs under your armpits and move bent elbows up and down. "Then, if no one guesses, we could hop around and bob our heads as if we're pecking at grain."

3 Remind students to follow class rules for working respectfully in groups. Also remind them to speak quietly with their group so the rest of the class doesn't hear them.

4 Give each group a card and several minutes to work on their pantomime.

5 Each group acts out their phobia and calls on classmates to guess. Allow several guesses, but end the guessing before students become frustrated or embarrassed: "This is a tough one! Group two, tell us your phobia."

EXTENSIONS FOR A LATER LANGUAGE ARTS LESSON

■ Invite students to illustrate the phobia words.

■ Students can write about their own phobia or that of a character in their reading book.

■ Using additional phobia words, have students create matching game cards by writing the phobia word on one index card and its meaning on another. Then they can invent games using the cards.

Human Slide Show

Language Arts Content

Dramatizing poetry

Common Core Standards

RL.5.2 Determine a theme of a story, drama, or poem; summarize the text

RL.5.5 Explain how a series of chapters, scenes, or stanzas fits together

RF.5.4b Read grade-level prose and poetry orally with accuracy, appropriate rate, and expression

SL.5.5 Include multimedia/ visual displays to enhance development of main ideas or themes

Materials Needed

Chart with a grade-level poem

Vocabulary

Stanza, structure, theme

How to do it:

For a long poem, consider doing this activity over two days, covering half of the poem each day.

1 Introduce the activity: "In today's group activity, you will create a human slide show to illustrate a stanza in one of the poems we've been reading."

2 Create as many small groups as there are stanzas in the poem; assign a stanza to each group.

3 Each group chooses one person to be the narrator and discusses how the rest of the group will use their bodies to create a motionless image (a "freeze-frame photo") that represents their stanza.

4 Each group shows their freeze-frame photo in turn while the narrator reads the stanza, so that the class creates a human slide show of the poem.

5 Discuss how each stanza and human slide contributes to the poem overall, especially the poem's structure and theme.

VARIATION

- Create human slide shows to illustrate a series of historical events or a series of chapters in a book.

EXTENSIONS FOR A LATER LANGUAGE ARTS LESSON

- Invite students to illustrate stanzas of a poem to create a visual story line.

- Have pairs read a poem together and discuss how the stanzas create an image or message and support the poem's structure and theme.

Human Tic Tac Toe

Language Arts Content

Spelling

Common Core Standards

L.5.2e Spell grade-appropriate words correctly, consulting references as needed

L.5.5 Understand figurative language, word relationships, and nuances in word meanings

Materials Needed

Carpet tape (or yarn and masking tape) to create an easily removable, human-sized tic-tac-toe board on the floor

How to do it:

Before starting this activity, remind students about being good sports and what to say and do if a teammate makes a mistake.

1 Divide the class into two teams, the X's and the O's, and have them stand on either side of the tic-tac-toe board.

2 Give one student from the X team a current spelling word to spell aloud. If she spells the word correctly, she goes to stand in a spot on the tic-tac-toe board. If she spells it incorrectly, any teammate can try to spell the word and earn a place on the board. If the teammate makes a mistake, no one moves to the board and it's the O team's turn.

3 Give one student from the O team either a new spelling word or the word the X team missed.

4 Play continues until one team gets three players in a row diagonally, horizontally, or vertically.

VARIATION

■ Use synonyms or antonyms as the words.

EXTENSION FOR A LATER LANGUAGE ARTS LESSON

■ Instead of spelling, have students give their own definitions for vocabulary words or use the words correctly in a sentence.

Read. Rinse. Repeat.

Language Arts Content

Reading fluency

Common Core Standards

RF.5.4b Read grade-level prose and poetry orally with accuracy, appropriate rate, and expression

SL.5.1 Engage effectively in collaborative discussions on grade 5 topics and texts

SL.5.6 Adapt speech to a variety of contexts and tasks, using formal English when appropriate

Materials Needed

A chart with the same sentence written multiple times but with a different word underlined each time (see step 1)

Vocabulary

Fluency, pace, intonation, expression, implied

How to do it:

1 On a chart, write a sentence multiple times and underline a different word each time. For example:

<u>When</u> you know better you do better.

When <u>you</u> know better you do better.

When you <u>know</u> better you do better.

When you know <u>better</u> you do better.

When you know better you <u>do</u> better.

2 Explain the activity and model for students: "We've been practicing reading aloud with expression and intonation, and we've seen how stressing a specific word can change the meaning of a sentence. Today we're going to try it together. Let's see how different this one sentence can be, depending on how we read it. Listen while I read the first sentence with stress on the underlined word."

3 Ask students what they noticed about how you read the sentence. If necessary, draw their attention to how you stressed the underlined word by saying it louder, with more force, with rising intonation, etc.

4 Invite students' thoughts on the meaning implied when the underlined word is stressed.

5 Continue having the class read each sentence in unison and then discuss the meaning implied by each reading.

VARIATION

■ Use a sentence drawn from a current unit of study in literature, history, science, or another content area.

EXTENSIONS FOR A LATER LANGUAGE ARTS LESSON

■ Have students practice what they learned about applying appropriate emphasis to different words by reading various texts aloud. For example, students could:

• Pose as news anchors, reading a passage from a nonfiction magazine or a piece of their own writing about a topic they're researching.

• Report the latest community or national sports news.

• Select a section from a book they're reading and read it aloud to a partner.

Check That Verb Past

Language Arts Content

Verb tense

Common Core Standards

RF.5.4 Read with sufficient accuracy and fluency to support comprehension

W.5.3 Write narratives to develop real or imagined experiences or events

L.5.1c Use verb tense to convey various times, sequences, states, and conditions

L.5.1d Recognize and correct inappropriate shifts in verb tense

Materials Needed

None

How to do it:

1 Display a message like this:

> Salutations, Editors.
>
> I've notice many writers remembering to check their verbs for the correct tense. Let's practice using a piece of my writing. If you see a verb in need of revision, be prepare to share.
>
> **It was a gloomy and fearful situation. She scream and yell for help but the wind is swallowing her cry.**

2 Have students echo-read the message (one student reads a sentence, and then the rest of the class reads the same sentence).

3 Ask students, "What did you notice about the verb tenses? How can we edit the verbs that are out of sync with the rest of the piece?"

4 Reinforce students' efforts: "You're paying careful attention to the editing process. Correcting errors in your own rough drafts will allow readers to better understand your interesting tales."

VARIATIONS

■ Read the chart chorally after students have edited it.

■ Ask students what they notice about the elements of writer's craft, such as personification and strong word choices, in the passage embedded in the message.

EXTENSION FOR A LATER LANGUAGE ARTS LESSON

■ Invite students to write a narrative story using the embedded passage as a prompt.

Consult as Needed

Language Arts Content

Vocabulary development

Common Core Standards

RI.5.10 By the end of the year, read and comprehend informational texts at high end of grades 4–5 text complexity band

RF.5.4b Read grade-level prose and poetry orally with accuracy, appropriate rate, and expression

SL.5.1c Pose and respond to questions by making comments that contribute to the discussion

L.5.4c Consult reference materials to find pronunciation and determine meaning

Materials Needed

Several dictionaries or school-approved dictionary websites

How to do it:

1 Display a message like this:

Dear Diligent Researchers,

Your tenacity for fact-finding is really paying off! One source researchers use to comprehend new words is the dictionary. While investigating okapis, I have found the following words: ruminant, solitary, prehensile, susceptibility. With a partner and a dictionary, pick one unfamiliar word in this message and try to come to agreement on either its meaning in this message or its pronunciation. Be prepared to share your idea with the class.

Teamwork counts,

Mr. R.

2 Ask for a few volunteers who looked up the pronunciation of a word to share first. Have the class repeat the correct pronunciation.

3 Ask for a volunteer to take the challenge of reading a hard word in the message that no one has called attention to.

4 Invite partners who worked on the meaning of a word to share what they discovered.

5 As a class, read the message aloud.

EXTENSIONS FOR A LATER LANGUAGE ARTS LESSON

■ Give students blank bingo boards. Have them fill in the squares with grade-level vocabulary words. Play bingo as a class with students practicing pronouncing the words as they play.

■ Students create a growing personal dictionary by recording new words and their meanings from their independent reading of various informational texts.

Say What You Mean to Say

Language Arts Content

Punctuation, spelling

Common Core Standards

W.5.5 Develop and strengthen writing by planning and editing

SL.5.1b Follow agreed-upon rules for discussions; carry out assigned roles

L.5.2 Demonstrate command of standard English capitalization, punctuation, and spelling

L.5.4 Determine or clarify the meaning of unknown and multiple-meaning words and phrases

Materials Needed

None

How to do it:

To adjust this activity to students' needs, consider teaching and practicing sound effects before reading the message chorally, or consider limiting the number of sound effects.

1 Display a message like this:

> Good Morning, Wonderful Writers!
>
> wow you our ready to publish your persuasive essays. how does it feel! Watching your tenacious editing thoughtful revision collaborative conferring and resolve to succeed was breathtaking? Can you help apply those skills to this letter.
>
> Your number won fan
>
> Mrs Zuckerman

2 Read the message chorally, using sound effects for the punctuation displayed. Some suggestions:

➤ "Ba-zinga" for an exclamation point

➤ A sigh for a comma

➤ "Huh?" for a question mark

➤ "Errrr" for a period

3 Ask for volunteers to correct the spelling, capitalization, and punctuation errors. Challenge students to explain the grammar rule behind their correction; for example, they might say, "A comma separates items in a series."

EXTENSIONS FOR A LATER LANGUAGE ARTS LESSON

■ Students can write a short paragraph with omitted commas for others to correct.

■ Have students look up unfamiliar vocabulary used in the morning message.

■ Return to the message and discuss strategies for figuring out unfamiliar words. Brainstorm synonyms and antonyms for those words.

Where's That Thesaurus?

Language Arts Content

Vocabulary development

Common Core Standards

RF.5.4c Use context to confirm or self-correct word recognition and understanding

W.5.5 Develop and strengthen writing by planning, revising, editing, rewriting, or trying new approach

L.5.4c Consult reference materials to find pronunciation and determine meaning

L.5.6 Accurately use grade-appropriate academic and domain-specific words and phrases

Materials Needed

Grade-level thesauruses or approved thesaurus websites

Vocabulary

Synonym, thesaurus

How to do it:

1 Display a message like this:

> Greetings, <u>Wordsmiths!</u>
>
> We've been working hard on synonyms! Synonyms are an author's <u>friends</u>. When we <u>craft</u> poems, <u>tell</u> a story, or read a <u>book</u>, it might be easiest to use <u>common</u> words over and over. However, <u>obtaining</u> new words <u>allows</u> your world to grow. Take this <u>challenge</u> and find a synonym for one of the underlined words. <u>Write</u> yours in the space below. Use a thesaurus for ideas.
>
> Sincerely,
>
> Ms. Henry

2 Read the message together as is.

3 Ask for several volunteers to "upgrade" one of the underlined words by crossing it out and writing a synonym in its place. Encourage students to use context clues to choose appropriate synonyms.

4 Reread the upgraded chart.

EXTENSIONS FOR A LATER LANGUAGE ARTS LESSON

- Have students revisit a piece of writing they're working on and use a thesaurus to find upgrades for three words.

- Invite students to create a pocket-size writer's resource of common words, such as "said," "very," "went," "asked," and "stuff," that they'd like to upgrade.

Witch Won?

How to do it:

1 Display a message like this:

> Deer Spectacular Spellers,
>
> We no that spelling is a skill kneaded to communicate. Witch word you choose is important! Their our several errors in this letter. Sea if you can find won. Than circle it and right the correct spelling. If your in need of assistance, consult a reference or ask a friend.
>
> You're teacher,
>
> Mrs. Thorvald

Language Arts Content

Spelling homophones

Common Core Standards

RF.5.3 Apply grade-level phonics and word analysis skills in decoding words

W.5.5 Develop and strengthen writing by revising, editing, and rewriting

SL.5.1 Engage effectively in collaborative discussions on grade 5 topics and texts

L.5.2e Spell grade-appropriate words correctly, consulting references as needed

Materials Needed

Dictionaries, word walls, class spelling list

2 Ask students to count the number of errors included in the message (there are twelve).

3 Discuss the meanings of several homophone pairs at play in this message—such as won–one and kneaded–needed. Brainstorm strategies for avoiding misspelling such words.

EXTENSIONS FOR A LATER LANGUAGE ARTS LESSON

- Have the class keep a running list of homophones and their meanings. They can compile these into a class homophone dictionary to use when writing and editing their work.

- Challenge students to create an acrostic poem using the word "homophone."

Idiomatic Handshakes

Language Arts Content

Understanding idioms

Common Core Standards

RL.6.4 Determine the meaning of words and phrases as they are used in a text, including figurative and connotative meanings

SL.6.4 Use appropriate eye contact, adequate volume, and clear pronunciation

L.6.5 Understand figurative language, word relationships, and nuances in word meanings

Materials Needed

A chart with idioms from books the class has read or is about to read

How to do it:

1 Explain that in today's greeting, students will greet each other in ways that illustrate certain idioms.

2 Model with a student you've practiced with ahead of time. For example:

➤ Like a fish out of water: Extend your hand past your partner's hand. Both of you lightly flop your hand against each other's forearm while exchanging greetings: "Good morning, Kat." "Good morning, Ms. Glenn."

➤ Look on the bright side: Face your partner and, with a large grin, pantomime putting on sunglasses and say, "Good morning, Kat!" Kat copies the gesture and replies, "Good morning, Ms. Glenn!"

➤ Weak in the knees: While standing, shake hands while wobbling your knees and say, "Good morning, Kat." Kat returns the greeting in the same manner.

➤ All wound up: Grasp your partner's hand as for a standard handshake, then circle your arm toward her three times (while still holding her hand) and say, "Good morning, Kat." Kat replies using the same gesture.

3 At your signal, students walk around and greet as many classmates as they can in one minute using these handshakes. When they find a partner, the two decide together which handshake to do. (If it's early in the year and you feel your class may not be comfortable yet with a walk-around greeting, do it as an around-the-circle greeting instead.)

VARIATION

■ Invite students to create handshakes for other idioms, such as walking on eggs, get off your high horse, and skating on thin ice.

EXTENSIONS FOR A LATER LANGUAGE ARTS LESSON

■ Have students illustrate different idioms and write their meanings below the drawings. Compile these into a classroom book or display them on the wall.

■ Keep a running chart of idioms and their meanings and invite students to add to it as they encounter more idioms in their reading or conversations.

In the Voice Of

Language Arts Content

Reading comprehension

Common Core Standards

SL.6.4 Use appropriate eye contact, adequate volume, and clear pronunciation

SL.6.6 Adapt speech to a variety of contexts and tasks

Materials Needed

Chart listing three or four characters from the current class read-aloud

Vocabulary

Dialect, accent, intonation, expression

How to do it:

1 Introduce the greeting: "Today's greeting is a chance to explore character voices. When we use a character's voice in our minds or out loud, we understand both the character and the story better. We'll use *Skellig*, our read-aloud, and think of voices that go with the traits and emotions of Michael, Mina, and Skellig in that scene where Michael and Mina visit Skellig in the garage and realize he's much younger than they thought."

2 Read the scene aloud.

3 As a class, brainstorm voices that would reflect the characters' traits and emotions during the scene. Remind students that to come up with voices, they can use the author's descriptions (Mina's eyes are "burning with astonishment and joy," Skellig "winces with pain") as well as their knowledge of the characters (Mina is bold and self-confident, Michael tends to worry).

4 To show students how this greeting will go, take your turn first by greeting the student next to you in the voice of the character you've chosen to impersonate: In a bold voice, say, "Good morning, _____. I'm Mina." The student replies in a worried voice, "Good morning, Mina. I'm Michael."

5 Continue the greeting around the circle, with each student choosing a character to impersonate. A student uncomfortable speaking in a character voice may select another student to supply the voiceover while they lip-sync.

EXTENSION FOR A LATER LANGUAGE ARTS LESSON

■ Invite students to pair up and take turns reading aloud a passage from a book they're currently reading, changing their voices as different characters speak. Have them chat about how this kind of reading helps them better understand the characters and the story.

Superhero Greeting

Language Arts Content

Developing character

Common Core Standards

W.6.3a Engage and orient the reader by establishing a context and introducing a narrator/characters; organize an event sequence that unfolds naturally and logically

W.6.3b Use narrative techniques to develop experiences, events, and characters

SL.6.1b Follow rules for discussions, set specific goals and deadlines, and define individual roles

SL.6.4 Use appropriate eye contact, adequate volume, and clear pronunciation

Materials Needed

A chart with a list of words often used to name superheroes, such as Super, Wonder, Captain, Boy, Girl, Doctor, General, Professor

How to do it:

1 Have students stand. Let them know that in today's greeting they'll invent a superhero and introduce themselves as that superhero by acting out their special power. Refer to the chart and ask students for any more words to add.

2 Model for students how to choose a word from the list to use in their superhero name and a special skill or power they wish they had. Use a think-aloud to show how to decide: "I love yoga and I'd like to be really strong and brave so I could be Yoga Woman and lunge across the circle in a Warrior Pose. I've always wanted to be invisible, too, so I could be Professor Hide and Seek. Hmm, I've got a good idea for acting that one out, so I'll go with Professor Hide and Seek."

3 Continue the modeling: Stealthily tiptoe over toward Enzo and "hide" behind a student next to him. Poke your arm out from behind that student to shake hands with Enzo, greeting him: "Good morning, Enzo. I am Professor Hide and Seek." Have Enzo step forward to be the next greeter while you sit down in Enzo's spot to show you've been greeted.

4 Give students a moment to think of a superhero and then start the greeting. A student may ask the group for a suggestion or say, "All superheroes are off today" and offer a standard greeting—for example, a simple "Good morning, _____" with a friendly handshake.

5 Continue until everyone has been greeted.

EXTENSIONS FOR A LATER LANGUAGE ARTS LESSON

■ Students write a story in which their superhero saves the day.

■ Students create a comic strip starring their superhero.

Thinking Themes

Language Arts Content

Understanding themes

Common Core Standards

RL.6.2 Determine a theme or central idea of a text and how it is conveyed

RL.6.9 Compare and contrast texts in terms of their approaches to similar themes and topics

W.6.4 Produce clear and coherent writing appropriate to task, purpose, and audience

SL.6.1 Engage effectively in collaborative discussions on grade 6 topics, texts, and issues

Materials Needed

None

Vocabulary

Theme

How to do it:

1 Name a theme that could easily apply to the different books students have been reading, such as "Family is important" or "Things aren't always what they seem."

2 Students walk around looking for a partner. Partners greet each other (along with a handshake, elbow shake, or high five) and chat using the following format. (Model this with a student you've practiced with ahead of time.)

Student 1: "Good morning, Davis."

Student 2: "Good morning, Tony."

Student 1: "What did you read that had the importance of family as a theme?"

Student 2: "I read some *A Series of Unfortunate Events* books, and even though Violet, Klaus, and Sunny's parents are dead, they rely on each other to escape Count Olaf. Family is important to them."

Student 1: "Yeah, those kids stick together. I read *The Gold Cadillac*, and when the father is arrested for a crime he didn't commit, Lois wants to protect her family so she sleeps with a knife in her hand. Their family is very important, too."

3 As students chat, walk around and listen in. If anyone is stymied, help them by reminding them of a text that you know they are familiar with (such as the class read-aloud) and asking some prompting questions.

4 If time permits, have students find new partners and repeat the greeting and sharing, using the same theme or a new one you name. (If it's early in the year and your class isn't comfortable yet with this type of greeting, they can do this in a circle, greeting and sharing with the classmates on their left and right.)

VARIATION

■ Display a chart of various themes, such as "Life goes on," "Life is short," "Don't prejudge," "Determination helps you succeed," "Jealousy is harmful." Allow partners to pick a theme and find evidence in a book each of them is reading that supports that theme.

EXTENSIONS FOR A LATER LANGUAGE ARTS LESSON

■ Students write a poem or a song about their book, conveying the theme they talked about in the morning's greeting and sharing combination.

■ In writing, students compare and contrast two pieces of literature with the same theme.

■ Students create a picture that illustrates the theme of a book they've read.

Headline News

Language Arts Content

Recognizing the main idea

Common Core Standards

RI.6.2 Determine a central idea and how it is conveyed through details; provide a summary

W.6.4 Produce clear and coherent writing appropriate to task, purpose, and audience

SL.6.1 Engage effectively in collaborative discussions on grade 6 topics, texts, and issues

Materials Needed

None

Vocabulary

Headline, concise

How to do it:

1 Introduce the sharing: "In today's sharing you will report one bit of information about yourself in the form of a news headline. Remember, effective headlines state the main idea of a news story. They're true, clear, and concise, yet leave readers wanting to read more."

2 Model for students: "For my sharing, I might say, 'Teacher Cleans Home in Record Time' or 'Teacher Detours on Way Home, Sees Rare Sight.'"

3 Give students a moment to think of a headline for something important or exciting in their lives, such as a family member visiting, a book or movie that struck a chord in them, or the celebration of an upcoming family event.

4 Students take turns sharing their headlines.

5 After every student has stated a headline, invite three or four students to ask a question to gain more details from a classmate's sharing. For example: "Ruby, why do you think you were able to score so many points in that game?"

VARIATIONS

▪ Instead of headlines about themselves, have student create and share headlines about:

- Their current research topics

- Current events at school or in the community

EXTENSIONS FOR A LATER LANGUAGE ARTS LESSON

▪ Have students write a magazine or newspaper article to go with their headline.

▪ Give students grade-level newspaper articles without the headlines. Have them read and summarize their article and create a headline for it.

Lend Me Your Ear

Language Arts Content

Forming opinions

Common Core Standards

RI.6.8 Trace and evaluate the argument in a text

W.6.1 Write arguments to support claims with clear reasons and relevant evidence

SL.6.1 Engage effectively in collaborative discussions on grade 6 topics, texts, and issues

SL.6.3 Delineate a speaker's argument

Materials Needed

None

Vocabulary

Point of view, reasoning, perspective

How to do it:

1 Name a hypothetical issue related to the class's studies and alert the class in advance to think about it. For example, if the class is doing a unit on human interactions with the environment, the issue could be that a road is being planned that would start in an urban center and cut through adjacent farmland.

2 Organize students into groups of four or five. Assign each group a population of people who will be affected by the issue. For example:

a. Farmers whose fields will be destroyed by the new road

b. City developers who must decide where to build the road

c. Unemployed people who will be hired as construction workers

d. Politicians who want to be re-elected

3 Taking on the role of their assigned population, each group discusses what their opinion on the issue would be and comes up with three supporting reasons. (With students you prepared in advance, model this, showing the thinking and speaking involved: "Our group is farmers whose fields will be destroyed by the road. I think we would be against it because if our fields are destroyed we won't be able to grow food for the community. What do you all think?")

4 Give groups five minutes for discussion. Then have one representative from each group share out.

5 Students in other groups may ask a question, make a comment, or briefly share the reasoning behind having a different position.

VARIATION

■ Students work in pairs instead of small groups. Partners assume the roles of people likely to have opposing opinions about the issue, and share their opinions and underlying reasoning.

EXTENSIONS FOR A LATER LANGUAGE ARTS LESSON

■ Using the issue debated in the morning, students could:

• Write a diary entry from the point of view of the role they took.

• Research the issue and write an essay arguing for or against it.

• Conduct a mock trial or mock protest about the issue.

Picture This

How to do it:

Language Arts Content

Understanding point of view

Common Core Standards

RI.6.6 Determine an author's point of view and explain how it is conveyed

RI.6.7 Integrate information presented in different media to develop a coherent understanding of a topic or issue

SL.6.2 Interpret information presented in diverse media and explain how it contributes to a text under study

SL.6.5 Include multimedia components and visual displays in presentations

RH.6–8.7 Integrate visual and other information in print and digital texts

Materials Needed

Copies of a photo or illustration depicting an event from current studies or reading

Vocabulary

Point of view

1 Introduce the sharing: "We've been talking about how characters in both fiction and nonfiction can have very different points of view about the same events. Today, you'll have a chance to take the point of view of someone from the nonfiction piece we've been reading, about the whaling ships that became stuck in Arctic ice back in 1871. I'm going to pass around copies of an illustration from that time that shows the captain, sailors, and passengers from one of the ships. Take a moment to choose one person who interests you and think about this event from his or her point of view."

2 Explain the sharing: "As we go around the circle, you'll share a thought or a question that you think fits the point of view of the character you've chosen. For example, if I chose one of the children in the drawing who seems to be smiling, I might think, 'Hmm . . . I know from our reading that some of the children thought at first that getting shipwrecked was a big adventure. This girl is sort of smiling.' Then, for my sharing, I might say, 'It's cold, but it's so beautiful. Maybe they'll let us off the ship to explore.'"

3 Invite a volunteer to begin and continue until everyone has had a turn.

VARIATION

■ After students share from their chosen point of view, go around the circle again with students taking a different point of view.

EXTENSION FOR A LATER LANGUAGE ARTS LESSON

■ Have students develop a short presentation that includes multimedia components to convey the perspective of one person shared about in Morning Meeting. Afterward, discuss how the presentations helped them understand the author's point of view.

Character Interrogation

How to do it:

1 Introduce the activity: "In today's activity, one student will pose as a special guest—a character from literature we've been reading. The rest of us will ask this guest specific questions to gain a deeper understanding of their life and decision making."

2 Model the activity with students you've practiced with ahead of time. For example, pose as the White Witch from *The Lion, the Witch, and the Wardrobe* while the students ask you preselected questions, such as "What was your motivation in grammar school, White Witch?" "What are your hobbies?" "How do you compare with other witches, like the Wicked Witch in *The Wizard of Oz*?" Answer each question while staying in character.

3 Now start the activity. Name a character from a book the entire class is familiar with, such as your read-aloud. Brainstorm questions that could be posed to gain a deeper understanding of the character, for example, "Who is your best friend?" "Whom do you admire most?" "What are you most afraid of?"

4 Now invite a student to pose as that character and answer questions from several classmates while staying in character.

5 Repeat with a different character and student volunteer.

EXTENSION FOR A LATER LANGUAGE ARTS LESSON

■ Students choose a character from a book they're reading, research major events that occurred or are occurring during the character's time period, and write a journal entry showing their character's response to several of the events.

Language Arts Content

Understanding character

Common Core Standards

RI.6.1 Cite textual evidence to support analysis as well as inferences

W.6.7 Conduct short research projects to answer a question

SL.6.1a Come to discussions prepared

SL.6.1c Pose and respond to specific questions with elaboration and detail

Materials Needed

None

Character Timeline

How to do it:

Language Arts Content

Understanding character

Common Core Standards

RL.6.3 Describe how a plot unfolds as well as how the characters respond or change

W.6.4 Produce clear and coherent writing appropriate to task, purpose, and audience

W.6.7 Conduct short research projects to answer a question, drawing on several sources

SL.6.1 Engage effectively in collaborative discussions on grade 6 topics, texts, and issues

Materials Needed

None

1 Choose a main character from a book the class has been reading, for example, Brian in *Hatchet* by Gary Paulsen.

2 Designate one side of the classroom as the beginning of the book, the other side as the end of the book, and the center as the middle of the book.

3 Name a response Brian had in the story, such as "Brian was filled with self-pity."

4 When you say "Go," students walk to the part of the room that represents when in the story they think Brian responded in that way and then discuss their reasoning with a nearby classmate, using the text to support their ideas. (Tell students to form groups of three if necessary to include everyone.)

5 Invite one pair or trio from each section to briefly share their discussion with the whole class.

6 Repeat a few more times using different statements about the same character, such as "Brian was depressed" or "Brian was confident."

VARIATION

■ Do the activity using a minor character from the book.

EXTENSIONS FOR A LATER LANGUAGE ARTS LESSON

■ Students write several journal entries as the character they focused on in this morning's activity—one from early in the story, one from the middle of the story, and one from the end of the story.

■ Students research tips for solving problems the character faces in the course of the book and then create a pocket survival guide for him or her.

Creating Commercials

Language Arts Content

Persuasive writing

Common Core Standards

W.6.4 Produce clear and coherent writing appropriate to task, purpose, and audience

SL.6.1 Engage effectively in collaborative discussions on grade 6 topics, texts, and issues

SL.6.5 Include multimedia components and visual displays in presentations

Materials Needed

None

Vocabulary

Persuasive

How to do it:

1 Introduce the activity: "We've been talking about what makes an author's writing persuasive—able to convince others to think a certain way or to do something. In today's activity, you'll form teams to create a short commercial for a product that I name. Your commercial must be 15 to 30 seconds long, and you may not use any props."

2 Before starting the activity, brainstorm phrases that grab audiences' attention, such as "Because you're worth it," "Accept no substitute," "Happiness is ————."

3 Organize students into groups of five or six. Assign each group a product that has to do with a topic in your curriculum, such as a barrel (if studying colonial America), a simple machine (if studying machines in science), or a specific food (related to your cultural studies). Give the groups five minutes to plan and act out their commercials.

4 Each group presents their short commercial to the class. If time is tight, have some groups present the next day.

EXTENSIONS FOR A LATER LANGUAGE ARTS LESSON

■ Students write a commercial for their favorite book.

■ Imagining that their favorite book has been made into a movie, students create a persuasive movie poster for it.

■ Students use the persuasive-writing skills they're learning to create and read aloud a 15-second public service announcement about an issue facing your school or community.

Fact or Fiction

Language Arts Content

Distinguishing fact from fiction

Common Core Standards

RI.6.1 Cite textual evidence to support analysis as well as inferences drawn from the text

W.6.9 Draw evidence from literary or informational texts to support analysis, reflection, and research

SL.6.4 Present claims and findings, sequencing ideas logically and using pertinent descriptions, facts, and details; use appropriate eye contact, adequate volume, and clear pronunciation

RH.6–8.8 Distinguish among fact, opinion, and reasoned judgment in a text

Materials Needed

None

Vocabulary

Fact, fiction, factual, fictional

How to do it:

1 Students come to Morning Meeting with three written statements about their current research topic or social studies curriculum. Two of the statements should be factual, and one should be fictional. For example:

➢ One: The most fertile land in Africa is the Congo Basin. (factual)

➢ Two: Zebras and elephants graze in the rain forest. (fictional)

➢ Three: Millions of people live along the boundaries of deserts in Africa. (factual)

2 One student volunteer begins the activity by announcing her research topic and reading her statements out loud.

3 Using their fingers to indicate one, two, or three, the rest of the class guesses which statement is fictional. After everyone has guessed, the student reveals the fictional statement and explains why it's fictional. For example: "The fictional statement is 'Zebras and elephants graze in the rain forest.' Zebras and elephants graze on the savannah."

4 Repeat with other students as time allows, and continue with the remaining students over the next few days.

VARIATION

■ Instead of bringing two facts and a fictional statement to the meeting, students bring a fact, an opinion, and a fictional statement. They then select which type of statement they would like their classmates to identify.

EXTENSION FOR A LATER LANGUAGE ARTS LESSON

■ Have students use the statements they brought to the meeting in writing about their research topic.

Go Figure

How to do it:

1 Display a list of idioms, similes, metaphors, and other figurative expressions, such as solid as a rock, like a fish out of water, bare your soul, money doesn't grow on trees, busy as a bee, let the cat out of the bag, raining cats and dogs, couldn't give a hoot. Include several that students have encountered in recent readings.

2 Form groups of four to six students and give each team an expression to act out without using words, sounds, or props.

3 Model how to share ideas with teammates:

➤ "If I were on the team that got 'Like a fish out of water,' I might say, 'We have to show a fish first, so we could start by pantomiming a fish swimming, like this.'"

➤ Pantomime a fish swimming; then ask your pretend teammates, "What do you guys think we could do to show the 'out of water' part?"

➤ Remind students to follow class rules for safe movement and respectful group work.

4 Give each group a card and allow a few minutes of planning time.

5 Groups take turns acting out their expression and calling on classmates to guess what it is.

6 Invite students to share their ideas about the literal and figurative meanings of the expressions.

VARIATIONS

■ Do the activity using:

• Famous quotes from literature or history

• Proverbs

• Vocabulary words that have multiple meanings (each group acts out all the possible meanings of their word)

EXTENSION FOR A LATER LANGUAGE ARTS LESSON

■ Students find examples of figurative language in their current reading, illustrate the literal meaning of the language, and then write what the author was trying to convey by using the language. For example, "The author used the expression 'like a fish out of water' to show that Jem felt really uncomfortable in his new school; he didn't know how to act or how to talk to the other kids."

Language Arts Content

Understanding figurative language

Common Core Standards

RL.6.4 Determine the meaning of words and phrases, including figurative and connotative meanings

SL.6.1 Engage effectively in collaborative discussions on grade 6 topics, texts, and issues

L.6.4 Determine or clarify the meaning of unknown and multiple-meaning words and phrases

L.6.5 Understand figurative language, word relationships, and nuances in word meanings

Materials Needed

A chart listing several figurative expressions; index cards, each with one of the expressions

Vocabulary

Idiom, simile, metaphor, figurative language

Mood Orchestra

Language Arts Content

Understanding character

Common Core Standards

RL.6.3 Describe how a plot unfolds as well as how the characters respond or change

W.6.3 Write narratives to develop real or imagined experiences or events using effective technique

SL.6.4 Present claims and findings, using pertinent descriptions, facts, and details; use appropriate eye contact, adequate volume, and clear pronunciation

Materials Needed

None

Vocabulary

Mood, emotion

How to do it:

1 Introduce the activity: "We've been paying attention to how characters' moods drive or are driven by the plot of a story. Today's activity will be a warmup for thinking more about characters' moods. We'll form an orchestra section but instead of making the sounds of instruments, we'll make the sound of an emotion."

2 Create sections of three or four students and have them stand, kneel, and sit in an orchestra-like arrangement. Assign each section an emotion, using rich vocabulary words such as melancholic, ecstatic, terrified, jubilant, timid, bewildered, and irate.

3 Give each section a moment to think of one sound to convey the emotion assigned.

4 Now conduct your orchestra:

➤ When you point to a section, that section makes the sound of their assigned emotion.

➤ When you raise your hand higher, that section gets louder; when you lower your hand, they get softer.

➤ When you point to a different section, the previous section falls silent. When you point to more than one section at a time, all those sections chime in with their sounds.

EXTENSIONS FOR A LATER LANGUAGE ARTS LESSON

■ Ask students to name the mood that the author is creating in a story, drama, or poem they're reading, citing evidence from the text. Then have them focus on how the characters' moods change as they encounter different situations in the story.

■ Challenge students in their own narrative writing to show, not tell, how their characters are feeling.

Quadrilateral Quandary

Language Arts Content:

Domain-specific vocabulary development

Common Core Standards:

L.6.4b Use Greek or Latin affixes and roots as clues to the meaning of a word

L.6.5 Understand figurative language, word relationships, and nuances in word meanings

L.6.6 Accurately use grade-appropriate academic and domain-specific words and phrases

Materials Needed:

Chart with words to a song that will help students learn domain-specific vocabulary

How to do it:

1 Using a familiar tune that your students can get a little playful with, create lyrics and accompanying motions to help students remember domain-specific vocabulary—in this example, terms associated with quadrilaterals.

2 Direct students' attention to the chart. Echo sing (sing the first few lines and have the students sing back) and then sing again with the motions.

The Quadrilateral Song
by Jodie Luongo
(Sung to the tune of "The Wheels on the Bus")

Quadrilaterals have four sides *(hold up four fingers)*
Have four sides, have four sides
Quadrilaterals have four sides
And that's what makes a quadrilateral, a quadrilateral

Parallelograms have parallel sides *(hold forearms parallel to each other vertically)*
Parallel sides, parallel sides
Parallelograms have parallel sides
And that's what makes a parallelogram, a parallelogram

The sides of a rhombus are ALL the same length *(make an equal sign with both index fingers)*
ALL the same length, ALL the same length
The sides of a rhombus are ALL the same length
And that's what makes the rhombus, a rhombus

But a trapezoid is NOT a parallelogram *(shake your index finger "no")*
NOT a parallelogram, NOT a parallelogram
But a trapezoid is NOT a parallelogram
Because it only has one set *(hold up one finger)* of parallel sides *(hold forearms parallel)*

A kite is NOT a parallelogram *(shake your index finger "no")*
NOT a parallelogram, NOT a parallelogram
A kite is NOT a parallelogram *(shake your index finger "no")*
Because it has ZERO parallel *(hold your forearms crossed to make an 'X')* sides!

EXTENSIONS FOR A LATER LANGUAGE ARTS LESSON

■ Ask for student ideas about the meanings of the root words from which the terms are formed; in this example, poly- (Greek, "many"), -gon (Latin and Greek, "angle"), para- (Greek, "on the side of").

■ Students write their own lyrics using a set of domain-specific terms.

Sound Symphony

Language Arts Content

Auditory recognition

Common Core Standards

SL.6.4 Use appropriate eye contact, adequate volume, and clear pronunciation

L.6.2b Spell correctly

L.6.3 Use knowledge of language and its conventions when writing, speaking, reading, or listening

L.6.4 Determine or clarify the meaning of unknown and multiple-meaning words and phrases

Materials Needed

None

Vocabulary

Syllable, multisyllabic

How to do it:

1 Introduce the activity: "Today's activity challenges the wordsmith—the guesser in this activity—to listen for and identify the vocabulary word being sung by the Sound Symphony." Invite one volunteer to be the wordsmith and leave the room.

2 The class selects a vocabulary word related to a current classroom curriculum topic. The word must have three or more syllables. For example, if the class is studying colonial America, the word could be "democracy."

3 Going around the circle, each person takes one syllable. For example, the first person is "de," the second "moc," the third "ra," the fourth "cy." The fifth person starts over with "de," and so forth.

4 Using a familiar tune such as "Happy Birthday" or "Row, Row, Row, Your Boat," explain that each person will sing his or her syllable sound to the tune. Model this: "For example, I would sing 'de, de, de' the whole time; Maria would sing 'moc, moc, moc'; Ezra would sing 'ra, ra, ra'; and Bikram would sing 'cy, cy, cy.'"

5 The wordsmith returns, and the whole group sings simultaneously.

6 The wordsmith listens carefully, trying to decipher the word. Once the word is declared, review its meaning and then challenge a student to spell it correctly.

VARIATION

■ To make the activity even more challenging, have the Sound Symphony mill about the room as the wordsmith listens.

EXTENSIONS FOR A LATER LANGUAGE ARTS LESSON

■ Keep a class chart of multisyllabic words that students discover during their reading. Encourage students to incorporate these vocabulary words into their writing.

■ Make a class dictionary of favorite words; for each word, students provide a pronunciation key, word origin, word used correctly in a sentence, and an illustration.

■ Provide grid paper so students can create crossword puzzles using multisyllabic words.

Finish This

How to do it:

1 Display a message like this about a topic the class is studying:

Dear Persuasive Writers,

Judging from yesterday's class discussion, it seems many of you are concerned about how orcas are treated in captivity. Here's a way to capture your main points:

Orcas may suffer in captivity. Taken from their deep oceanic homes and from their families, orcas have to live in shallow tanks. Isolated, these animals may become confused and depressed and may even kill themselves.

Be prepared to share a concluding statement for this paragraph.

Ms. P.

2 Students read the message silently.

3 Ask for volunteers to state what they think the author's point of view or purpose for writing is, and why.

4 Have students share ideas for a concluding sentence that is in keeping with the paragraph's formal style.

VARIATION

■ Have students add transitional phrases to the paragraph.

EXTENSION FOR A LATER LANGUAGE ARTS LESSON

■ Students research a topic of interest and craft a one-paragraph persuasive argument in the style of the one used in the message.

Language Arts Content

Persuasive writing

Common Core Standards

RI.6.6 Determine an author's point of view or purpose and explain how it is conveyed

W.6.1 Write arguments to support claims with clear reasons and relevant evidence

W.6.1e Provide a concluding statement or section that follows from the argument presented

SL.6.1 Engage effectively in collaborative discussions on grade 6 topics, texts, and issues

Materials Needed

None

Vocabulary

Concluding statement, point of view

List and Tell

Language Arts Content

Recognizing topic-related ideas

Common Core Standards

W.6.2a Introduce a topic; organize ideas, concepts, and information, using strategies such as classification; include formatting, graphics, and multimedia when useful

W.6.7 Conduct short research projects to answer a question, drawing on several sources

SL.6.1 Engage effectively in collaborative discussions on grade 6 topics, texts, and issues

RH.6–8.1 Cite specific textual evidence to support analysis

Materials Needed

None

How to do it:

1 Drawing on content students are currently studying, display a message like this:

Dear Social Scientists,

We are about to begin our study of the United States government and its branches. Using your prior knowledge about the government, write a related word or short phrase below, next to the letter it begins with. Challenge: No repeats.

A	J	S
B	K	T
C—Congress	L—Laws	U
D	M—Money	V
E	N	W
F	O	X
G	P	Y
H	Q	Z
I	R—Road building	

Be prepared to share your input.
Mr. Diaz

2 Students turn and talk with a partner about what they added to the message.

3 Several volunteers share two or three sentences about their word or phrase.

4 Ask students what questions they have about the U.S. government (or the topic your class is studying).

5 Tell students you will keep this chart so they can revisit it after their unit of study to see how much they've learned.

VARIATION

■ Challenge students to group or classify the ideas entered on the message.

EXTENSION FOR A LATER LANGUAGE ARTS LESSON

■ Students research a question that was asked about the topic during this activity and prepare brief reports, citing their sources. Reports can include graphics or multimedia elements. Students then present their work to the class and field questions and comments.

What's Your Perspective?

Language Arts Content

Understanding narrative

Common Core Standards

RL.6.5 Analyze how a sentence, chapter, scene, or stanza fits into the overall structure and contributes to theme, setting, or plot

RI.6.3 Analyze how a key individual, event, or idea is introduced, illustrated, and elaborated

W.6.9 Draw evidence from literary or informational texts to support analysis, reflection, and research

SL.6.1 Engage effectively in collaborative discussions on grade 6 topics, texts, and issues

Materials Needed

None

Vocabulary

Perspective, opinion

How to do it:

1 Display a message like this about a current book your class is familiar with:

Dear Literary Critics,

What ups and downs the characters in our book are enduring! From your perspective as a critical reader, ponder whether the snowstorm in *Julie of the Wolves* was positive or negative for Julie. Use a tally mark to indicate your opinion and be prepared to defend it.

Positive:

Negative:

With bated breath,

Ms. Schermer

2 Challenge a student volunteer to paraphrase the message.

3 Have students pair up with someone who has a different opinion about the snowstorm and discuss their differing perspectives. If there aren't enough students with differing opinions to do this, simply ask for three or four volunteers to share their opinions and reasoning with the whole class.

VARIATION

- Instead of a fictional character, use a famous historical figure and an event they endured in real life.

EXTENSIONS FOR A LATER LANGUAGE ARTS LESSON

- Students select a theme from the book discussed in the morning and write a paragraph explaining how the book asserts this theme.

- Have students write a journal entry about the event discussed in the meeting from the character's point of view.

What's Your Point?

Language Arts Content

Interpreting visual information

Common Core Standards

RI.6.7 Integrate information in different media or formats to develop understanding of a topic or issue

SL.6.1a Come to discussions prepared, having read or studied required material

SL.6.5 Include multimedia components and visual displays in presentations

RH.6–8.5 Describe how a text presents information

RH.6–8.7 Integrate visual information with other information in print and digital texts

Materials Needed

Graph or chart of information on a topic of class interest

Vocabulary

Chart, graph, title, mean, mode, maximum, data, analyze, ascertain

How to do it:

1 Display a message like this:

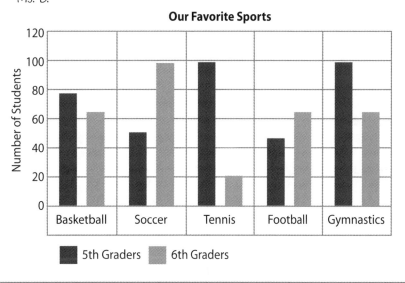

Dear Data Analysts,

I've been amazed by your progress in learning to use graphs to analyze data across several of our subject areas. Take a look at the data in this graph. It's from a survey done by last year's class.

What information can you ascertain from this graph? Be prepared to share.

Ms. D.

Our Favorite Sports

■ 5th Graders   ■ 6th Graders

2 Ask students what information they learned from the graph.

3 Ask students what questions they have after digesting the graph.

VARIATION

■ Use a graph or table from your current curriculum materials or a newspaper or current events magazine used in your class.

EXTENSIONS FOR A LATER LANGUAGE ARTS LESSON

■ Students look in their science, social studies, and math texts for statistics such as maximum, minimum, range, mode, mean, and median and explain how the statistics help them better understand the topic.

■ Have students conduct a survey about the class's interests, opinions on a hot issue, family makeup, or another topic and then construct a graph to present and display the results.

Worlds Apart?

How to do it:

Language Arts Content

Understanding figurative language

Common Core Standards

RI.6.1 Cite textual evidence to support analysis as well as inferences drawn from the text

RI.6.4 Determine the meaning of words and phrases as they are used in a text

W.6.4 Produce clear and coherent writing appropriate to task, purpose, and audience

SL.6.1 Engage effectively in collaborative discussions on grade 6 topics, texts, and issues

Materials Needed

None

Vocabulary

Metaphor, personification

1 Display a message like this:

Dear Historians,

As we study ancient India, we contemplate ancient quotes. Read, digest, and be prepared to share how the following quote relates to today's world:

"There is nothing more dreadful than the habit of doubt. Doubt separates people. It is a poison that disintegrates friendships and breaks up pleasant relations. It is a thorn that irritates and hurts; it is a sword that kills."

—Gautama Buddha

Chewing on this also,

Ms. W.

2 Discuss the imagery created by the metaphors and the impact of those images.

3 Have a volunteer underline the personification in the quote.

VARIATION

■ Use a quote from a current text or famous person within your curriculum.

EXTENSIONS FOR A LATER LANGUAGE ARTS LESSON

■ Students choose a word from the quote and then use it to create an acrostic poem.

■ From a book they're reading, students choose a character and write from that character's perspective about how the quote relates to his or her world.

■ Students reread the message to themselves and then turn and talk to a partner about how they think it relates to our lives today.

10 Complete Meeting Ideas

Focusing an entire Morning Meeting on a particular language arts theme can build extra excitement for this learning. It can also allow you to build even more language arts learning into your students' day—without having to cut anything out or shorten any other content you teach.

In this section, you'll find ten language arts themed Morning Meetings—meetings in which all four components (greeting, sharing, group activity, and morning message) cover the same language arts theme. Here are some tips for using them:

Adapt as needed ■ All ten of these meetings can be adapted to fit grades beyond the ones indicated. If your students have a deeper knowledge about any of these topics, you may need to add complexity. Conversely, if a topic is unfamiliar to students, you may need to simplify. And you will want to tailor the morning messages to your students' reading levels.

Create your own themed meetings ■ Use the ideas included in this book to come up with combinations of language arts themed greetings, sharings, group activities, and morning messages that fit your students and curriculum.

Consider the overall flow of the meeting ■ When you start creating your own themed meetings, balance the energy level of the components. In general, these meetings should have an ebb and flow to them. An active greeting should generally be followed by a relatively calm sharing. If the meeting has a complicated group activity, keep the reading and use of the message fairly simple and straightforward.

Let students help ■ Students love coming up with a variation for a greeting, sharing, group activity, or morning message. If you want to plan a meeting on a given topic, consider asking for students' ideas several days beforehand.

Remember to focus on community ■ A primary purpose of Morning Meeting is for students to begin the day on a positive note and build community. Reinforce friendly words and tone of voice, inclusiveness, and cooperation rather than competition.

Language Arts Content: Syllables

Materials Needed: None

Vocabulary: Syllable, segment

Common Core Standards:

KINDERGARTEN

RF.K.2b Count, pronounce, blend, and segment syllables in spoken words

RF.K.4 Read emergent-reader texts with purpose and understanding

SL.K.2 Confirm understanding by asking and answering questions

L.K.1f Produce complete sentences in shared language activities

L.K.4 Determine or clarify the meaning of unknown and multiple-meaning words/phases

FIRST GRADE

RF.1.2 Demonstrate understanding of spoken words, syllables, and sounds

RF.1.3d Know that every syllable must have a vowel sound

RF.1.4 Read with sufficient accuracy and fluency to support comprehension

SL.1.2 Ask/answer questions about key details in a text read aloud/ information presented orally

L.1.1j Produce complete simple/compound declarative, interrogative, imperative, and exclamatory sentences

L.1.4 Determine or clarify the meaning of unknown and multiple-meaning words/phases

Syllable Sense

Display a message like the following:

Salutations, syllable counters!

Today is _____.

We will segment words into syllables.

How many syllables are in your name?

Write the number below.

4   1   2

Hickety Pickety Bumble Bee
(RF.K.2b ▪ RF.1.2)

1 Post the following chant and read it aloud for students:

Hickety Pickety Bumble Bee

Won't you say your name for me?

Let's all say it.

Let's all clap it.

2 Explain how the greeting will work: "We'll start by greeting Allyson. She'll say her name, we'll say it back to her all together, and then we'll all say it again while we clap the syllables. Then we'll greet the next person in the circle in the same way."

3 Begin the greeting:

Hickety Pickety Bumble Bee

Won't you say your name for me?
  "Allyson" (*student says her name*)

Let's all say it.
  "Allyson" (*whole class says name*)

Let's all clap it.
  "All-y-son" (*whole class says name while clapping the syllables*)

Syllables in Names
(RF.K.2b, SL.K.2, L.K.1f ▪ RF.1.2, SL.1.2, L.1.1j)

1 Around the circle, students share their name and something they like to do, for example: "My name is Isaiah. It has three syllables. I like to play soccer. Soccer has two syllables."

2 If you have time after everyone has shared, ask, "Can anyone name a student who has just one syllable in his name?" "Who has the most number of syllables in her name?" "Who liked to do something that has two syllables?"

Syllable Drama
(RF.K.2b, L.K.4 ▪ RF.1.2, RF.1.3d, L.1.4)

1 Introduce the activity: "Our activity has a lot of movement, so you'll need to show self-control. Stay in your spots and move your hands and feet in safe ways, just as we've talked about and practiced."

2 State a verb and have the class clap out the syllables and then act out the verb. (You may need to define some of the words and get or give suggestions for ways to act them out.)

Some verbs to get you started:

1 syllable	2 syllables	3 syllables
jump, jog, dance, march, bow, waltz, hop, stroll, drive, sway, freeze, tap, strut	wiggle, gallop, curtsey, giggle, shuffle, tiptoe, waddle, zigzag, moonwalk, balance, dribble, saunter	exercise, meander, concentrate, celebrate, irritate, decorate, unfasten

For first graders, after stating the verb and clapping out the syllables, write the verb on a chart. Segment the word into syllables and point out the vowel in each syllable.

Syllable Count
(RF.K.2b, RF.K.4 ▪ RF.1.2, RF.1.3d, RF.1.4)

1 Have students with one syllable in their names read the first sentence in the message, students with two syllables in their names read the second sentence, and students with three or more syllables in their names read the third sentence.

2 Challenge students to tell you words from the message that have one syllable, two syllables, etc.

Grade Level
K–2

Language Arts Themed Meeting

Language Arts Content: Fluency, expression

Materials Needed: A chart with the words to "Humpty Dumpty" or other familiar text

Vocabulary: Expression, fluently, gesture

Common Core Standards:

KINDERGARTEN

RL.K.10 and RI.K.10 Engage in group reading activities with purpose and understanding

RF.K.1 Understand the organization and basic features of print

SL.K.1 Participate in collaborative conversations about kindergarten topics and texts

SL.K.6 Speak audibly and express thoughts, feelings, and ideas clearly

L.K.2b Recognize and name end punctuation

L.K.6 Use words acquired through conversation/reading/being read to/responding to text

FIRST GRADE

RL.1.10 Read prose/poetry of appropriate complexity

RI.1.10 Read informational texts appropriately complex for grade 1

RF.1.4b Read with accuracy, appropriate rate, and expression

SL.1.1 Participate in collaborative conversations about grade 1 topics and texts

SL.1.6 Produce complete sentences

L.1.2b Use end punctuation

L.1.6 Use words and phrases, including conjunctions to signal simple relationships

SECOND GRADE

RL.2.10 Read and comprehend literature in the grades 2–3 text complexity band

RI.2.10 Read and comprehend informational texts in the grades 2–3 text complexity band

RF.2.4b Read with accuracy, appropriate rate, and expression

SL.2.1 Participate in collaborative conversations about grade 2 topics and texts

SL.2.6 Produce complete sentences

L.2.3 Use knowledge of language and conventions when writing, speaking, reading, listening

L.2.6 Use words and phrases, including adjectives and adverbs to describe

154

Express Yourself

Display a message like one of the following:

K–1

Good Morning, Rootin' Tootin' Readers!

Today is Thursday, _____.

We will practice reading smoothly.

Find a classmate. Act out one of these faces with each other:

Happy   Sad   Worried

1–2

Good Morning, Rootin' Tootin' Readers!

At reader's workshop today, we will focus on reading fluently. What helps you read fluently? Be prepared to share your ideas during our meeting.

We will also read with expression.

Write an emotion below.

Happy   sad   EXCITED

How to do it:

Let's Get Emotional

(SL.K.6, L.K.6 ■ SL.1.6, L.1.6 ■ SL.2.6, L.2.6)

1 With students standing in a circle, introduce the greeting: "We will choose an emotion and greet a classmate using our voices, facial expressions, and gestures to show that emotion."

2 Read the list of emotions written on the morning message. Act out a few with the class.

3 Invite students to choose an emotion and put a thumb up when they have an idea for how to act out that emotion.

4 Model the greeting with a student you've practiced with beforehand:

➤ Turn to the student volunteer and say, "Good morning, William!" in an excited way while jumping gently up and down.

➤ William replies, "Good morning, Mr. Hunt. How are you feeling today?"

➤ You reply, "I'm feeling excited!" in a lively voice.

5 Tell students, "Now we'll start the greeting. William will greet Chelsea on his right, and then Chelsea will greet Darius, and so on." Turning to Chelsea, William says, "Good morning, Chelsea" in a sad voice while pretending to wipe tears from his eyes.

6 Continue around the circle, each student showing their chosen emotion, until everyone has been greeted.

SHARING

Fluency Matters

(SL.K.1, SL.K.6 ■ SL.1.1, SL.1.6 ■ SL.2.1, SL.2.6)

1 Introduce the sharing: "Today, we are going to share what helps us read fluently. For example, I read fluently when I recognize most of the words.

Who has another idea about what helps them read fluently?" Take a few ideas.

2 Have students pair up and share their ideas with each other.

GROUP ACTIVITY

Reading Rates

(RL.K.10, RF.K.1 ■ RL.1.10, RF.1.4b ■ RL.2.10, RF.2.4b)

1 Display the chart with the words to "Humpty Dumpty" (or another familiar grade-level text).

2 Read the poem with the class.

3 Explain that students are now going to reread parts of the poem too fast, too slow, or just right.

4 Choose one student volunteer to read the first line in the poem and another to tell him how to read it: Too fast, too slow, or just right.

5 Continue taking volunteers to set the rate and read lines in the poem.

MORNING MESSAGE

Punctuation Play

(RI.K.10, L.K.2b ■ RI.1.10, RF.1.4b, L.1.2b ■ RI.2.10, RF.2.4b, L.2.3)

1 Read the morning message to the class.

2 Invite a student to circle the end punctuation that shows when to read with enthusiasm (in this example, the exclamation point in "Good Morning, Rootin' Tootin' Readers!").

3 Change the exclamation point to a question mark, and invite another student to read the salutation in a way that reflects the new punctuation.

4 Continue changing other types of punctuation in the message, and asking for volunteers to read the sentence with the new punctuation.

K–3

Language Arts Themed Meeting

Language Arts Content: Sharing facts from nonfiction reading

Materials Needed: None

Vocabulary: Fact, nonfiction

Common Core Standards:

KINDERGARTEN

RI.K.1 Ask and answer questions about key details in a text

W.K.2 Compose informative/explanatory texts; supply some information about the topic

W.K.8 Recall information from experiences or gather information from provided sources to answer a question

SL.K.1 Participate in collaborative conversations about kindergarten topics and texts

FIRST GRADE

RI.1.1 Ask and answer questions about key details in a text

W.1.2 Write informative/explanatory texts; supply facts about topic, provide sense of closure

W.1.8 Recall information or gather information to answer a question

SL.1.1 Participate in collaborative conversations about grade 1 topics and texts

SECOND GRADE

RI.2.1 Ask and answer questions to demonstrate understanding of key details

W.2.2 Write informative/explanatory texts; use facts and definitions, provide concluding statement/section

W.2.8 Recall information from experiences or gather information from sources to answer a question

SL.2.1 Participate in collaborative conversations about grade 2 topics and texts

THIRD GRADE

RI.3.1 Ask and answer questions to demonstrate understanding of a text

W.3.2 Write informative/explanatory texts and convey ideas and information clearly

W.3.8 Recall information from experiences/gather information from sources; take brief notes and sort evidence

SL.3.1 Engage effectively in collaborative discussions on grade 3 topics and texts

Is That a Fact?

Display a message like one of the following:

Dear Fact Finders,

Today is Tuesday, March 9, 20 _ _.

We will keep working on our nonfiction books.

Have you started revising your work yet? Answer with a tally mark.

Yes	No
(l l	(l l

2–3

Felicitations, Fact Finders.

You have been finding interesting facts to use in your writing. Be ready to share one of these facts at Morning Meeting.

Where are you in the writing process?

Answer with a tally mark.

Taking notes	Writing a draft	Publishing
(l l	⊬⊬⊬ l l l l	(l l

156

Fountain of Knowledge

(RI.K.1, W.K.2, SL.K.1 ■ RI.1.1, W.1.2, SL.1.1 ■ RI.2.1, W.2.2, SL.2.1 ■ RL.3.1, W.3.2, SL.3.1)

1 As partners stand facing each other, introduce the greeting: "Today we are going to greet each other in a way that celebrates the information we know—our knowledge. We are going to call each other 'fountain of knowledge,' which means we are overflowing with information and ideas the way a fountain overflows with water."

2 Model the greeting (rehearse ahead of time with your partner):

➤ As you and your partner face each other, tell her one fact you know based on your research about your writing topic. "Hi, Juniper. I know that polar bears have black skin to absorb the sun."

➤ Your partner responds, "Hi, Ms. Kupferman. You are a fountain of knowledge." As she responds, she makes a motion to imitate a fountain: With palms together, she raises her hands to head height, then separates her palms and lowers her hands while gently wiggling her fingers to simulate falling water.

➤ Your partner then shares her fact and you offer the "fountain of knowledge" response.

3 Now invite all partners to share facts with each other and respond as demonstrated. Switch partners once or twice as time allows.

Nifty Nonfiction

(RI.K.1, W.K.2, SL.K.1 ■ RI.1.1, W.1.2, SL.1.1 ■ RI.2.1, W.2.2, SL.2.1 ■ RI.3.1, W.3.2, SL.3.1)

1 Students go around the circle, sharing one thing they like about nonfiction reading or writing. Model first: "I like nonfiction books because sometimes they have close-up photographs and they show me things I've never seen before."

For kindergartners, offer a simple question and let them answer without giving a reason. If you ask, "Which do you like better—fiction or nonfiction?" a student might reply, "I like fiction best" or "Nonfiction is my favorite."

2 After everyone has shared, invite students to ask a few questions. For example, Will might say, "Sid, you said you like writing nonfiction because you get to learn new facts. What is one interesting fact you've learned from your research?"

A kindergartner might ask, "Kai, what is your favorite fiction book?" or "Della, what nonfiction book are you reading now?"

News Anchor Antics

(RI.K.1, W.K.2, SL.K.1 ■ RI.1.1, W.1.2, SL.1.1 ■ RI.2.1, W.2.2, SL.2.1 ■ RI.3.1, W.3.2, SL.3.1)

1 Introduce this group activity. (Model steps first.)

➤ One student (the guesser) covers her eyes and you choose a student to pretend to be a news anchor.

➤ All students except the guesser move to new places in the circle.

➤ The news anchor states a fact about her research in a clear, confident, news-anchor-like voice.

➤ The guesser tries to guess who the news anchor is.

2 Continue with different guessers and news anchors as time allows.

Writing Preview

(W.K.8, SL.K.1 ■ W.1.8, SL.1.1 ■ W.2.8, SL.2.1 ■ W.3.8, SL.3.1)

1 Read the morning message to students.

2 Invite a few students to share where they are in the writing process and one step they'll be taking next in their writing today.

Language Arts Content: Spelling irregular words

Materials Needed: 15–20 cards with irregularly spelled words

Vocabulary: Irregular

Common Core Standards:

FIRST GRADE

RF.1.3g Recognize and read irregularly spelled words

RF.1.4b Read with accuracy, appropriate rate, and expression

SL.1.1 Participate in collaborative conversations about grade 1 topics and texts

L.1.1j Produce complete simple/compound declarative, interrogative, imperative, and exclamatory sentences

L.1.2d Use conventional spelling

SECOND GRADE

RF.2.3f Recognize and read irregularly spelled words

RF.2.4b Read with accuracy, appropriate rate, and expression

SL.2.1 Participate in collaborative conversations about grade 2 topics and texts

L.2.1f Produce complete simple and compound sentences

L.2.2d Generalize learned spelling patterns

THIRD GRADE

RF.3.3d Read irregularly spelled words

RF.3.4b Read with accuracy, appropriate rate, and expression

SL.3.1 Engage effectively in collaborative discussions on grade 3 topics and texts

L.3.1i Produce simple, compound, and complex sentences

L.3.2 Demonstrate command of standard spelling

Irregular? Who, Me?

Display a message like the following:

Dear Careful Spellers,

We have a spelling review today.

Find a partner and go over your words together one more time.

Those irregularly spelled words can be tricky!

One irregular word in this message is our secret word for the day.

What do you think it is? Write your guess below. (Hint: It is an irregularly spelled word and has four letters.)

What   Dear

Your

GREETING
An Irregular Handshake
(None)

1 Brainstorm ideas for ways to shake someone's hand that are irregular but still safe and kind (for example, a high handshake, a low handshake, a handshake under your other arm).

2 Model the greeting:

➤ Turn to the person on your left. Shake her hand in an irregular way and say, "Have an irregular day, Jhosseline."

➤ Jhosseline replies, "You too, Ms. Riordan."

3 Continue around the circle until everyone has been greeted.

SHARING
Irregular Thinking
(SL.1.1, L.1.1j ■ SL.2.1, L.2.1f ■ SL.3.1, L.3.1i)

1 Students go around the circle, sharing one unique or "irregular" strategy they have for learning new words. Model first: "When I have to learn new words, it helps if I repeat the word and the spelling a few times as I walk around."

2 After each student shares, classmates put a thumb up if they think the student's strategy might help them.

GROUP ACTIVITY
Step and Spell
(RF.1.3g, L.1.2d ■ RF.2.3f, L.2.2d ■ RF.3.3d, L.3.2)

1 With students standing in a circle, spread the irregularly spelled word cards on the floor inside the circle and choose a volunteer to go first.

2 State a word.

3 The class repeats the word, spells the word out together slowly, and repeats the word again.

4 The volunteer tries to find the word card and gently step on it before the class finishes spelling the word.

5 Repeat as time allows.

MORNING MESSAGE
What's the Word?
(RF.1.3g, RF.1.4b ■ RF.2.3f, RF.2.4b ■ RF.3.3d, RF.3.4b)

1 Ask for student volunteers to read the message one sentence at a time.

2 Choose students to underline a few of the irregularly spelled words in the message.

3 Call on a few students to share the word they wrote on the chart and why they think it's the secret word. Then reveal the secret word and why you chose it.

Language Arts Content: Collective nouns

Materials Needed: A list of collective nouns (optional)

Vocabulary: Collective noun

Common Core Standards:

SECOND GRADE

RF.2.4b Read with accuracy, appropriate rate, and expression

SL.2.1 Participate in collaborative conversations about grade 2 topics and texts

SL.2.1a Follow agreed-upon rules for discussions

L.2.1a Use collective nouns

L.2.5a Identify real-life connections between words and their use

THIRD GRADE

RF.3.4b Read on-level prose/poetry orally with accuracy, appropriate rate, and expression

SL.3.1 Engage effectively in collaborative discussions on grade 3 topics and texts

SL.3.1b Follow agreed-upon rules for discussions

L.3.1b Form and use regular and irregular plural nouns

L.3.5b Identify real-life connections between words and their use

Noun the Wiser

Display a message like the following:

Good morning, class.

Yesterday we had fun playing 20 Questions with nouns. We all know that a noun is a word that names a person, place, or thing. Today we are going to discuss collective nouns. A collective noun names a group. For example, a group of related people is a family. A group of lions is a pride.

Are you a member of any of the following groups? Answer with a tally mark.

team	club	troop	class or school committee
‖‖ ‖‖	‖	‖‖	‖

Hi, Group!

(SL.2.1a, L.2.1a, L.2.5a ▪ SL.3.1b, L.3.1b, L.3.5b)

1 Model the greeting:

> ➤ Turn to the student sitting next to you and say "Good morning, Ben. We're in class together."

> ➤ Ben responds, "Good morning, Mrs. Perry."

> ➤ Brainstorm with students other collective nouns to use in the sentence starter "We're _____ together" (on the baseball team, in student council, etc.).

2 Continue around the circle until everyone has been greeted.

VARIATION

Students walk up to any classmate in the circle and say the sentence starter. Continue until everyone is greeted. (Children can clasp their hands to show they've been greeted.)

SHARING
Gabbing About Groups

(SL.2.1, L.2.1a, L.2.5a ▪ SL.3.1, L.3.1b, L.3.5b)

Plan to have a few sharers each day throughout the week so everyone can have a turn.

1 Model a dialogue sharing that uses a collective noun: "This morning on the way to school, I saw a gaggle of geese. It was crossing the road. I'm ready for questions and comments." Call on a few students.

2 Brainstorm other ideas for collective nouns to use—for example, animals that live in groups (herd, pride, flock) or people who do things together (team, audience, family).

3 Ask for a few volunteers to share their own statements using a collective noun.

GROUP ACTIVITY
A Clutch of Clues

(SL.2.1a, L.2.1a, L.2.5a ▪ SL.3.1b, L.3.1b, L.3.5b)

1 Have a volunteer think of a collective noun, such as "swarm." You may want to refer to the brainstormed list from the sharing component.

2 The volunteer gives three clues to describe her noun. For example: "It includes a lot of creatures. It could hurt if you were in one. It makes a buzzing noise."

3 The volunteer then takes up to three guesses about which noun she's describing. If after three guesses the class hasn't figured out the noun, the volunteer reveals the answer.

4 Repeat with several more volunteers.

MORNING MESSAGE
Collective Nouns

(RF.2.4b, SL.2.1, L.2.1a, L.2.5a ▪ RF.3.4b, SL.3.1, L.3.1b, L.3.5b)

1 As a class, read the message chorally.

2 Invite volunteers to underline the collective nouns found in the message.

3 Count up the tally marks under each collective noun. Lead a discussion about this data: "Are more people in our class in teams, clubs, troops, or class or school committees? Why might this be?"

Language Arts Content: Modifiers

Materials Needed: A clean tissue

Vocabulary: Adjective, adverb

Common Core Standards:

THIRD GRADE

RF.3.4 Read with sufficient accuracy and fluency to support comprehension

SL.3.1 Engage effectively in collaborative discussions on grade 3 topics and texts

SL.3.1b Follow agreed-upon rules for discussions

L.3.1a Explain the function of adverbs

L.3.3a Choose words and phrases for effect

FOURTH GRADE

RF.4.4 Read with sufficient accuracy and fluency to support comprehension

SL.4.1 Engage effectively in collaborative discussions on grade 4 topics and texts

SL.4.1b Follow agreed-upon rules for discussions

L.4.1 Demonstrate command of standard English grammar and usage

L.4.3a Choose words and phrases to convey ideas precisely

Modify as We Go

Display a message like the following:

Howdy _____ Pupils,

What a _____ day! With _____ weather like this, you could get your hat whipped off _____. Inclement weather can cancel outdoor recess and make you feel _____.

What specific adjectives and adverbs could plug up these blanks? Be prepared to share at Morning Meeting.

Inquisitively,
Mr. R

Show, Don't Tell

(SL.3.1b ▪ SL.4.1b)

1 Introduce the greeting: "Today's greeting will show us how you are feeling. For example, you might be feeling excited, tired, or content. You will convey how you're feeling through your handshake. Watch and listen while I model."

➤ Turn to a student and, sleepily shaking his hand, say in a tired voice, "Good morning, Rohan." Rohan greets you back in the same way (sleepily).

➤ Then Rohan turns to greet Bob, conveying through his voice and handshake how he is feeling.

➤ Let students know that it's okay if their handshake is the same as someone else's and remind them that handshakes conveying emotions such as excitement or irritation still need to remain respectful and safe.

2 Continue greeting around the circle.

SHARING
Why, Oh Why?

(SL.3.1 ▪ SL.4.1)

1 Introduce the sharing by explaining to students, "For our sharing today, we will go around the circle again, each saying why we're feeling the way we're feeling. For example, in the greeting I showed I was tired. Now I might say, 'I am tired because I woke up early this morning to finish my homework. My homework was to finish grading your math tests so you can share them with your families tonight.' Then we'll each take one question from our audience."

2 Start the sharing around the circle. Encourage students to vary the feeling words they choose so as to express nuance, for example, "giddy" and "disappointed" rather than "happy" and "sad."

GROUP ACTIVITY
The Laughing Tissue

(SL.3.1, L.3.1a ▪ SL.4.1, L.4.1)

1 Introduce the group activity: "We're going to brainstorm several adverbs that we can act out. Remember that adverbs tell how an action is done—for example, 'slowly.' Each time I say an adverb, we'll all laugh in the manner of the adverb until the tissue that I'll drop hits the floor. Now, what adverbs could we use?"

2 As students generate a list of adverbs, chart them. Then announce an adverb from the list, such as "rapidly," while at the same time tossing a tissue into the air. Everyone laughs "rapidly" until the tissue hits the floor.

3 Repeat a few times with different adverbs.

VARIATIONS

▪ Change the action from laughing to marching, jumping, clapping, etc.

▪ Have students notice adverbs in their reading and keep a running list of them to use the next time they do this activity.

MORNING MESSAGE
Fill in the Modifier

(RF.3.4, SL.3.1, L.3.3a ▪ RF.4.4, SL.4.1, L.4.3a)

1 Give students time to reread the message silently and signal with a thumb up when they've finished.

2 Invite volunteers to share an adverb or adjective that could fill in a blank and explain why they chose that word.

3 Continue taking volunteers until all the message blanks are filled.

Language Arts Content: Story elements

Materials Needed: Chart paper showing list of synonyms for the word "detective"

Vocabulary: Synonym

Common Core Standards:

THIRD GRADE

SL.3.1 Engage effectively in collaborative discussions on grade 3 topics and texts

SL.3.1b Follow agreed-upon rules for discussions

SL3.4 Report on a topic or text with facts and relevant details, speaking clearly

FOURTH GRADE

SL.4.1 Engage effectively in collaborative discussions on grade 4 topics and texts

SL.4.1b Follow agreed-upon rules for discussions

SL.4.4 Report on a topic or text, tell a story, or recount an experience

FIFTH GRADE

SL.5.1 Engage effectively in collaborative discussions on grade 5 topics and texts

SL.5.1b Follow agreed-upon rules for discussions

SL.5.4 Report on a topic or text or present an opinion; speak clearly at an understandable pace

SIXTH GRADE

SL.6.1 Engage effectively in collaborative discussions on grade 6 topics, texts, and issues

SL.6.1b Follow rules for discussions

SL.6.4 Present claims and findings; use appropriate eye contact, adequate volume, and clear pronunciation

Who Dun It?

Display a message like the following:

Greetings Gumshoes,

Today we will continue reading mysteries, so get your detective minds ready! Solving a mystery takes a keen eye for details, clues, and character development. When you read a mystery, your job is to guess the culprit before the author reveals it. Remember, every character is a suspect!

Be prepared to share your experience with mysteries. Have you read or watched any? Do you have a favorite sleuth?

GREETING
On the Case

(SL.3.1b ▪ SL.4.1b ▪ SL.5.1b ▪ SL.6.1b)

1 Introduce the greeting: "For today's greeting, you'll get a chance to introduce yourself to the group as a detective. Choose a word from our list of synonyms for the word 'detective.'" Quickly review the pronunciation of any unfamiliar words.

2 Tell students they may use their first or last name with the title, and model for them: "Greetings, I am Private Eye Johnson and I am on the case." The entire class replies, "Hello, Private Eye Johnson."

3 Continue the greeting around the circle.

SHARING
Mysterious Experience

(SL.3.1, SL.3.4 ▪ SL.4.1, SL.4.4 ▪ SL.5.1, SL.5.4 ▪ SL.6.1, SL.6.4)

1 Half the class forms an inner circle, facing out. The rest of the class forms an outer circle and faces in, creating partnerships.

2 Pose the questions on the morning message again: "Have you read or watched any mysteries?" "Do you have a favorite sleuth?"

3 The inner circle students share their answers while their outer circle partners listen. Then the partners switch roles.

4 After a few minutes, signal for attention and tell the outer circle to take one step to the left to form new partnerships.

5 Repeat steps 3 and 4 until all students have shared with three or four classmates.

GROUP ACTIVITY
Mystery Winker

(None)

1 With students back to standing in one big circle, explain the activity: "We're going to have one 'Mystery Winker' and one 'detective.' The Mystery Winker's job is to wink at classmates without getting caught by the detective; the detective's job is to try to guess who the Mystery Winker is. Once you're winked at, you'll safely and quietly squat without giving away the identity of the Mystery Winker."

2 Ask for a volunteer to play the detective. The detective turns away from the group and covers his eyes.

3 Ask for a volunteer to be the Mystery Winker. Point to the Mystery Winker and have her confirm by putting a thumb up for all but the detective to see. The detective then comes to the center of the circle and gets three guesses to identify the Mystery Winker.

MORNING MESSAGE
Sneaking Suspicion

(SL.3.1, SL.3.4 ▪ SL.4.1, SL.4.4 ▪ SL.5.1, SL.5.4 ▪ SL.6.1, SL.6.4)

1 Have students silently read the message again.

2 Based on their mystery reading, ask students to share some "suspicious" behaviors a character might exhibit, such as changing the subject or speaking rapidly.

Language Arts Content: Using commas

Materials Needed: A chart of the song displayed near the circle area

Vocabulary: Punctuation

Common Core Standards:

FOURTH GRADE

SL.4.1 Engage effectively in collaborative discussions on grade 4 topics and texts

SL.4.6 Use formal English when appropriate

L.4.2 Demonstrate command of standard English capitalization, punctuation, and spelling

FIFTH GRADE

SL.5.1 Engage effectively in collaborative discussions on grade 5 topics and texts

SL.5.6 Adapt speech to a variety of contexts and tasks, using formal English when appropriate

L.5.2 Demonstrate command of standard English capitalization, punctuation, and spelling

L.5.2a Use punctuation to separate items in a series

L.5.2c Use a comma to set off yes and no, a tag question, and to indicate direct address

SIXTH GRADE

SL.6.1 Engage effectively in collaborative discussions on grade 6 topics, texts, and issues

SL.6.6 Adapt speech to a variety of contexts and tasks, demonstrating command of formal English when appropriate

L.6.2 Demonstrate command of standard English capitalization, punctuation, and spelling

Commas, Commas, Commas

Display a message like the following:

Yes, Writers, commas do count!

My, oh my, we've been learning so much about commas this week! When we use commas strategically, we help our readers understand our meaning. Look at the sentences below and put a tally mark next to the one you think uses the comma correctly.

His best friend, Teresa, was late.

His best friend Teresa, was late.

His, best friend, Teresa was late.

GREETING
Comma Commotion

(L.4.2 ■ L.5.2c ■ L.6.2)

1 Begin by reminding students about some uses for a comma: "A comma is a punctuation mark used to offset a name. It is also used to offset an answer such as, 'Yes, it is.' For today's greeting we are going to pantomime the correct placement of a comma as we greet each other."

2 Model the greeting with a student whom you have prepared ahead of time.

➤ "I'm going to model with Leroy how this pantomime will look." Look at Leroy and say, "Good morning. Is it you, Leroy?" After the word "you," use your hand to pantomime the curve of a comma.

➤ Leroy replies, mimicking the motion for the comma: "Yes, it is."

3 Continue the greeting around the circle.

SHARING
My To-Do List

(SL.4.6, L.4.2 ■ SL.5.6, L.5.2a ■ SL.6.6, L.6.2)

1 Students stand in two concentric circles, each student in the inner circle facing a partner in the outer circle.

2 On your signal, inner circle students share three things they need to do while outer circle students pantomime comma placement. For example: "I need to study for my test, [outer student pantomimes comma] take care of my little brother, [outer student pantomimes comma] and feed my hamsters." Then the outer student shares while the inner student pantomimes.

3 After each pair has shared, inner circle students take one step to their left to stand facing a new partner.

4 The sharing pattern continues until each student has shared with three or four classmates.

GROUP ACTIVITY
Where's the Comma?

(L.4.2 ■ L.5.2 ■ L.6.2)

1 Write the following lyrics by Jodie Luongo (sung to the tune of "Frère Jacques") on a chart and teach it ahead of time, perhaps during a language arts lesson.

Where's the comma? Where's the comma?
Separating. Separating.
The year and the date,
The city and the state,
A list of three. A list of three.

Where's the comma? Where's the comma?
Here I am. Here I am.
I follow a salutation,
Sit before a coordinating conjunction
In a compound sentence. In a compound sentence.

How will I remember? How will I remember?
The FAN BOYS. The FAN BOYS.
For, and, nor. But, or, yet.
So, so, so. So, so, so.
Commas give a pause. Commas give a pause.

Are you the comma? Are you the comma?
Yes, I am. Yes, I am.
After an introductory word
Or an appositive
Place a comma. Place a comma.

2 Bring the chart into your meeting circle and sing the song, or do it as a chant.

MORNING MESSAGE
Pause Accordingly!

(SL.4.1, L.4.2 ■ SL.5.1, L.5.2 ■ SL.6.1, L.6.2)

1 Read the message chorally using a comma sound effect, such as a sigh, each time a comma is used.

2 Talk about the data collected on the message chart. Ask a student who placed a tally mark next to the correct sentence to explain his or her reasoning.

Grade Level
4–6
Language Arts Themed Meeting

Language Arts Content: Onomatopoeia

Materials Needed: Words to the greeting posted on a chart

Vocabulary: Onomatopoeia

Common Core Standards:

FOURTH GRADE

RF.4.4b Read on-level prose orally with accuracy, appropriate rate, and expression

SL.4.1 Engage effectively in collaborative discussions on grade 4 topics

SL.4.1b Follow agreed-upon rules for discussions

SL.4.6 Differentiate formal English and informal discourse

L.4.5 Understand figurative language

FIFTH GRADE

RF.5.4b Read on-level prose orally with accuracy, appropriate rate, and expression

SL.5.1 Engage effectively in collaborative discussions on grade 5 topics

SL.5.1b Follow agreed-upon rules for discussions

SL.5.6 Adapt speech to a variety of contexts and tasks

L.5.5 Understand figurative language

SIXTH GRADE

SL.6.1 Engage effectively in collaborative discussions on grade 6 topics

SL.6.1b Follow rules for discussions

SL.6.6 Adapt speech to a variety of contexts and tasks

L.6.5 Understand figurative language

On-o-mat-o-what?

Display a message like the following:

R-i-i-i-ng, Morning Risers.

Yahoo! We have been capturing our readers' attention with specific word choices. Wham! Do you wish to energize your audience with a bold point of view or whisper a sense of calm in your essay? Below, write one example of onomatopoeia you've noticed in your reading or have used in your own writing.

GREETING

GREETING
Chugga-Chugga

(SL.4.1b ■ SL.5.1b ■ SL.6.1b)

1 Remind students to be safe: "In this greeting, we'll be walking around and moving our arms and bodies quite a bit. What will you need to do to follow our rule about safety as you greet each other?"

2 A volunteer begins the greeting by standing in front of a classmate seated in the circle and chanting:

Hey there, _____,

You're a real cool cat. *(greeter uses fingers to mimic whiskers under nose)*

You've got a little of this *(both students snap their fingers)*

And a little of that. *(both students snap their fingers)*

So don't be afraid

To boogie and jam.

Just stand up and chugga *(greeted student stands up)*

Fast as you can.

Chugga up, chugga, chugga, chugga, chugga. *(both students point up to sky)*

Chugga down, chugga, chugga, chugga, chugga. *(both students point to the floor)*

To the left, chugga, chugga, chugga, chugga. *(both students point to the left)*

To the right, chugga, chugga, chugga, chugga. *(both students point to the right)*

3 Each standing student then walks to another seated student and the greeting begins again; after this round, four students are standing.

4 Continue until everyone has been greeted.

SHARING
Bing Bang Boom

(SL.4.1, L.4.5 ■ SL.5.1, L.5.5 ■ SL.6.1, L.6.5)

1 Brainstorm a dozen or so examples of onomatopoeia. You can prompt students by giving them a category; for instance, for the category "machinery and gadgets," the class might come up with whiz, burble, fizz, zing, and ding.

2 Students take turns around the circle briefly sharing some news about themselves, followed by an onomatopoeia that they think fits their news: "My birthday was yesterday; *ding!*" or "I'm going skateboarding with my cousin this weekend; *whoosh!*"

GROUP ACTIVITY
The Onomatopoeia Machine

(SL.4.1, SL.4.6, L.4.5 ■ SL.5.1, SL.5.6, L.5.5 ■ SL.6.1, SL.6.6, L.6.5)

1 Tell students they'll be creating an "Onomatopoeia Machine" that produces sounds to match simple movements. Again, remind them of the need to keep everyone safe.

2 Start the activity by going into the center of the circle. Do a hammering motion and say "Bang" each time you lower your hand.

3 The student who was on your left steps in and joins you with a motion and an onomatopoeia of their own. Then the next student joins in, and so on.

4 Continue adding students until you think the machine is as big as possible while still remaining safe. Then signal the end of the round: "Machine, stop!"

5 Start another round; classmates who've already had a turn watch from their places in the circle as the new machine comes to life. Continue until all students have had a chance to be part of a machine.

MORNING MESSAGE
A Melody of Sounds!

(RF.4.4b, L.4.5 ■ RF.5.4b, L.5.5 ■ L.6.5)

1 Read the message chorally.

2 Invite several volunteers to circle the examples of onomatopoeia.

Language Arts Content: Alliteration

Materials Needed: None

Vocabulary: Alliteration

Common Core Standards:

FOURTH GRADE

RL.4.4 Determine the meaning of words/phrases as used in a text

RF.4.4b Read on-level prose and poetry orally with accuracy, appropriate rate, and expression

SL.4.1 Engage effectively in collaborative discussions on grade 4 topics and texts

SL.4.1a Come to discussions prepared

L.4.5 Understand figurative language

L.4.6 Accurately use grade-appropriate words/phrases

FIFTH GRADE

RL.5.4 Determine the meaning of words/phrases as used in a text

RF.5.4b Read on-level prose and poetry orally with accuracy, appropriate rate, and expression

SL.5.1 Engage effectively in collaborative discussions on grade 5 topics and texts

SL.5.1a Come to discussions prepared

L.5.5 Understand figurative language

L.5.6 Accurately use grade-appropriate words/phrases

SIXTH GRADE

RL.6.4 Determine the meaning of words and phrases as used in a text; analyze impact of word choice on meaning and tone

SL.6.1 Engage effectively in collaborative discussions on grade 6 topics, texts, and issues

SL.6.1a Come to discussions prepared

L.6.5 Understand figurative language

L.6.6 Accurately use grade-appropriate words/phrases

"Uh" is for Alliteration

Display a message like the following:

Welcome Wonderful Writers,

While reading, you have been thinking about the author's craft, especially the clever clustering of words. Today we will try it in our own writing.

Below, write one positive adjective to describe yourself. The adjective must begin with the same sound as your first name. For example: Jubilant Julia or Fabulous Fiona.

If you like, you can look through your independent reading book for an adjective to use. Make sure you know the meaning of your word!

How to do it:

GREETING
Alliterative Aloha

(SL.4.1a, L.4.5, L.4.6 ▪ SL.5.1a, L.5.5, L.5.6 ▪ SL.6.1a, L.6.5, L.6.6)

1 Introduce the greeting: "For today's greeting, you'll each use the alliterative adjective you wrote on the Morning Message. If you didn't write one, take a moment to think of one now."

2 Model by beginning the greeting yourself with a student you've practiced with ahead of time (have that student seated to your right):

➤ Turn to the student and say, "Pleasure to see you. I am Loquacious Ms. Lewis. 'Loquacious' means 'talkative.'"

➤ The student replies, "Nice to see you, Loquacious Ms. Lewis. I am Zealous Zarius."

➤ Zarius greets the next student: "Pleasure to see you. I'm Zealous Zarius. 'Zealous' means 'enthusiastic.'"

3 Continue the greeting around the circle.

SHARING
Noticing Author's Craft

(RL.4.4, RF.4.4b, SL.4.1, L.4.5 ▪ RL.5.4, RF.5.4b, SL.5.1, L.5.5 ▪ RL.6.4, SL.6.1, L.6.5)

1 The first sharer reads an example of alliteration from her independent reading book, and then shares what she visualized when she read the alliteration and its significance to the text.

2 The sharer calls on two or three classmates for questions or comments.

3 Repeat with the rest of the day's sharers.

GROUP ACTIVITY
Sound Says

(None)

1 Pick a beginning sound such as /t/. Ask students for four appropriate words that begin with this sound, such as "touch," "type," "tank," and "total." Write each word on a chart.

2 Have students stand in several rows with enough space between them so that each student can step to the right, left, forward, and backward. (If you have limited space, have students stagger themselves in the meeting circle, or use any other arrangement that allows for safe movement.)

3 Assign a direction to step in for each word, and have students practice stepping in each direction. For example, "When I say 'touch,' you will take one step your right. When I say 'type,' take one step to your left. When I say 'tank,' take one step forward. Finally, when I say 'total,' take one step backward." Practice these as a group before doing the activity "for real."

4 Remind students how to be respectful if anyone missteps: "It's OK if someone steps in the wrong direction; we can just smile or say, 'You'll be back in step soon' or 'Don't worry—you'll get it.'"

VARIATIONS

▪ To increase the challenge, ask the class for four more words and assign diagonal steps.

▪ Use words with beginning blend sounds such as /str/ or /ch/.

▪ Use vocabulary words or spelling words with the same beginning sounds.

MORNING MESSAGE
Circling Sounds

(SL.4.1, L.4.5 ▪ SL.5.1, L.5.5 ▪ SL.6.1, L.6.5)

1 Ask for volunteers to circle or highlight the alliterative parts of the morning message.

2 Prompt students to notice the difference between blends and single consonant sounds.

3 Challenge students to think deeply about the author's craft. For example: "What effect did the use of alliteration have on you when you were reading the message?" or "How might you apply this to your writing later?"

171

Kindergarten

Language Arts Content	Activity Title & Page	Morning Meeting Component	Common Core Standards
Alphabetical order	Everything's in Order, p. 11	Greeting	**SL.K.6** Speak audibly **RF.K.1d** Recognize upper- and lowercase letters **L.K.1a** Print upper- and lowercase letters
Beginning, middle, and ending sounds	What's That Sound? p. 26	Group activity	**RF.K.1b** Recognize that specific sequences of letters represent spoken words in writing **RF.K.2d** Pronounce initial, medial vowel, and final sounds
Capitalization	A Capital Idea, p. 27	Morning message	**RI.K.10** Engage in group reading activities **RF.K.1a** Follow words left to right and top to bottom **L.K.1a** Print many uppercase letters **L.K.2a** Capitalize the first word in a sentence **L.K.2b** Recognize and name end punctuation
Expression	Let's Get Emotional, p. 155	Greeting	**SL.K.6** Speak audibly **L.K.6** Use words and phrases
	Fluency Matters, p. 155	Sharing	**SL.K.1** Participate in collaborative conversations **SL.K.6** Speak audibly
	Reading Rates, p. 155	Group activity	**RL.K.10** Engage in group reading activities **RF.K.1** Understand organization and basic features of print
	Punctuation Play, p. 155	Morning message	**RI.K.10** Engage in group reading activities **L.K.2b** Recognize and name end punctuation
Fluency	Let's Get Emotional, p. 155	Greeting	**SL.K.6** Speak audibly **L.K.6** Use acquired words and phrases
	Fluency Matters, p. 155	Sharing	**SL.K.1** Participate in collaborative conversations **SL.K.6** Speak audibly
	Reading Rates, p. 155	Group activity	**RL.K.10** Engage in group reading activities **RF.K.1** Understand organization and basic features of print
	Punctuation Play, p. 155	Morning message	**RI.K.10** Engage in group reading activities **L.K.2b** Recognize and name end punctuation
Identifying topics and events	I See, p. 21	Group activity	**W.K.3** Narrate events **SL.K.4** Describe familiar people, places, things, and events **L.K.1f** Produce complete sentences **L.K.5c** Identify real-life connections between words and their use

Language Arts Content	Activity Title & Page	Morning Meeting Component	Common Core Standards
Interrogatives	Reading Inquiry, p. 17	Sharing	**W.K.8** Recall and gather information to answer questions **SL.K.3** Ask/answer questions **L.K.1d** Use question words **L.K.1f** Produce complete sentences
Letters and sounds	If Your Letter's on the Card, p. 20	Group activity	**RF.K.1d** Recognize upper- and lowercase letters **RF.K.3a** Demonstrate basic knowledge of one-to-one letter-sound correspondence **SL.K.6** Speak audibly **L.K.1a** Print many upper- and lowercase letters
Nonfiction	Fountain of Knowledge, p. 157	Greeting	**RI.K.1** Ask/answer questions about key text details **W.K.2** Compose informative/explanatory texts **SL.K.1** Participate in collaborative conversations
	Nifty Nonfiction, p. 157	Sharing	**RI.K.1** Ask/answer questions about key text details **W.K.2** Compose informative/explanatory texts **SL.K.1** Participate in collaborative conversations
	News Anchor Antics, p. 157	Group activity	**RI.K.1** Ask/answer questions about key text details **W.K.2** Compose informative/explanatory texts **SL.K.1** Participate in collaborative conversations
	Writing Preview, p. 157	Morning message	**W.K.8** Recall and gather information to answer questions **SL.K.1** Participate in collaborative conversations
Opposites	Let's All Do the Opposite, p. 22	Group activity	**RF.K.3c** Read high-frequency words by sight **L.K.5b** Relating verbs and adjectives to their opposites **L.K.6** Use words acquired through conversations, reading and being read to, and responding to texts
Parts of a book (informational texts)	The Bookey Pokey, p. 24	Group activity	**RI.K.5** Identify the front cover, back cover, and title page of a book **RF.K.1** Understand the organization and basic features of print **RF.K.4** Read emergent-reader texts **W.K.8** Recall and gather information to answer questions
Phonemic awareness	What's That Sound? p. 26	Group activity	**RF.K.1b** Recognize that specific sequences of written letters represent spoken words **RF.K.2d** Pronounce initial, medial vowel, and final sounds
Plural nouns	One Is Never Enough, p. 23	Group activity	**RF.K.2e** Add or substitute individual sounds to make new words **W.K.2** Compose informative/explanatory texts **L.K.1b** Use frequently occurring nouns **L.K.1c** Form regular plural nouns orally by adding /s/ or /es/

Language Arts Content	Activity Title & Page	Morning Meeting Component	Common Core Standards
Print concepts	Give Me Space, p. 28	Morning message	**RI.K.10** Engage in group reading activities **RF.K.1a** Follow words from left to right and top to bottom **RF.K.1c** Understand that words are separated by spaces in print
	Typewriter, p. 30	Morning message	**RI.K.10** Engage in group reading activities **RF.K.1a** Follow words from left to right and top to bottom
Punctuation	A Capital Idea, p. 27	Morning message	**RI.K.10** Engage in group reading activities **RF.K.1a** Follow words from left to right and top to bottom **L.K.1a** Print many uppercase letters **L.K.2a** Capitalize the first word in a sentence **L.K.2b** Recognize and name end punctuation
	That's the Point! p. 14	Greeting	**RF.K.4** Read emergent-reader texts with purpose and understanding **SL.K.1a** Follow discussion rules **L.K.1d** Use question words **L.K.2b** Recognize and name end punctuation
Reading behaviors	Hey Readers, p. 12	Greeting	**RF.K.1** Understand organization and basic features of print **RF.K.1a** Follow words from left to right **RF.K.2** Demonstrate understanding of spoken words, syllables, and sounds **SL.K.6** Speak audibly
Rhyming words	1, 2, 3, Rhyme With Me, p. 19	Group activity	**RF.K.2a** Recognize and produce rhyming words **RF.K.2e** Add or substitute individual sounds to make new words **RF.K.3d** Distinguish between similarly spelled words by identifying the sounds of the letters that differ
Role of authors and illustrators	Author? Illustrator? You Decide, p. 15	Sharing	**RL.K.6** Define the role of the author and illustrator in telling a story **W.K.2** Compose informative/explanatory texts **SL.K.1** Participate in collaborative conversations **L.K.1d** Use question words
Segmenting and blending sounds	Phoneme Fun, p. 29	Morning message	**RI.K.10** Engage in group reading activities **RF.K.1a** Follow words from left to right and top to bottom **RF.K.2** Demonstrate understanding of spoken words, syllables, and sounds **RF.K.3** Apply grade-level phonics and word analysis skills **L.K.2d** Spell simple words phonetically
Sight words	Set Your Sights on a Word, p. 13	Greeting	**RF.K.1b** Recognize that specific sequences of written letters represent spoken words **RF.K.3c** Read high-frequency words by sight **SL.K.1a** Follow discussion rules

Language Arts Content	Activity Title & Page	Morning Meeting Component	Common Core Standards
Speaking about a topic	Talking in Circles, p. 18	Sharing	**RF.K.4** Read emergent-reader texts **W.K.2** Compose informative/explanatory texts **SL.K.1** Participate in collaborative conversations **SL.K.3** Ask/answer questions **SL.K.6** Speak audibly
Stating opinions	Book Share, p. 16	Sharing	**RL.K.1** Ask/answer questions about text details **RL.K.10** Engage in group reading activities **W.K.1** Compose opinion pieces **SL.K.1** Participate in collaborative conversations **L.K.1d** Use question words
Syllables	Hickety Pickety Bumble Bee, p. 153	Greeting	**RF.K.2b** Syllabicate spoken words
	Syllables in Names, p. 153	Sharing	**RF.K.2b** Syllabicate spoken words **SL.K.2** Ask/answer questions about information presented orally **L.K.1f** Produce complete sentences
	Syllable Drama, p. 153	Group activity	**RF.K.2b** Syllabicate spoken words **L.K.4** Determine word meaning
	Syllable Count, p. 153	Morning message	**RF.K.2b** Syllabicate spoken words **RF.K.4** Read emergent-reader texts
Vowel sounds	The Long and Short of It, p. 25	Group activity	**RF.K.2d** Pronounce initial, medial vowel, and final sounds **RF.K.3b** Associate long and short sounds with major vowels

First Grade

Activities Listed by Language Arts Content

Language Arts Content	Activity Title & Page	Morning Meeting Component	Common Core Standards
Adjectives	If You're Jovial and You Know It, p. 41	Group activity	**W.1.3** Write narratives **L.1.1f** Use frequently occurring adjectives **L.1.5c** Identify real-life connections between words and their use **L.1.5d** Distinguish shades of meaning among verbs and adjectives
Capitalization	Sentence Structure Models, p. 49	Morning message	**RF.1.1a** Recognize the distinguishing features of a sentence **L.1.2a** Capitalize dates and names of people **L.1.2b** Use end punctuation **L.1.2c** Use commas in dates and series
Categories	I'm Thinking Of, p. 42	Group activity	**SL.1.1a** Follow discussion rules **SL.1.4** Describe people, places, things, and events with relevant details **L.1.5b** Define words by category and key attributes **L.1.6** Use words and phrases to signal simple relationships
	My Son John, p. 45	Group Activity	**RL.1.7** Use illustrations and details to describe a story **RL.1.10** Read prose and poetry of appropriate complexity **W.1.8** Recall or gather information to answer questions **L.1.5a** Sort words into categories
Character	Are You Curious, George? p. 31	Greeting	**RL.1.3** Describe characters using key details **RL.1.7** Use illustrations and details to describe a story **W.1.1** Write opinion pieces
	Character Comparisons, p. 35	Sharing	**RL.1.3** Describe characters using key details **RL.1.9** Compare and contrast characters **W.1.1** Write opinion pieces **SL.1.2** Ask/answer questions about information presented orally **SL.1.3** Ask/answer questions about what a speaker says
Conjunctions	And, But, Because, p. 38	Group activity	**SL.1.1b** Build on others' talk **L.1.1g** Use frequently occurring conjunctions **L.1.1j** Produce complete sentences
Consonant blends	Greetings, Digraph Detectives, p. 48	Morning message	**RI.1.5** Use text features to locate information **RF.1.2b** Blend sounds to produce single-syllable words **RF.1.3a** Know spelling-sound correspondences for consonant digraphs **SL.1.1** Participate in collaborative conversations
Context clues	What Do You Mean? p. 50	Morning message	**RI.1.4** Ask/answer questions to determine word meaning **SL.1.1** Participate in collaborative conversations **L.1.4** Determine meaning of unknown words **L.1.4a** Use sentence-level context as clue to word meaning

Language Arts Content	Activity Title & Page	Morning Meeting Component	Common Core Standards
Digraphs	Greetings, Digraph Detectives, p. 48	Morning message	**RI.1.5** Use text features to locate information **RF.1.2b** Blend sounds to produce single-syllable words **RF.1.3a** Know spelling-sound correspondences for consonant digraphs **SL.1.1** Participate in collaborative conversations
Expression	Let's Get Emotional, p. 155	Greeting	**SL.1.6** Produce complete sentences **L.1.6** Use words and phrases to signal simple relationships
	Fluency Matters, p. 155	Sharing	**SL.1.1** Participate in collaborative conversations **SL.1.6** Produce complete sentences
	Reading Rates, p. 155	Group activity	**RL.1.10** Read prose and poetry **RF.1.4b** Read prose and poetry
	Punctuation Play, p. 155	Morning message	**RI.1.10** Read informational text **RF.1.4b** Read prose and poetry **L.1.2b** Use end punctuation
Final -e	Final-E Decoded, p. 32	Greeting	**RF.1.2** Demonstrate understanding of spoken words, syllables, and sounds **RF.1.3b** Decode regularly spelled one-syllable words **RF.1.3c** Know final -e for representing long vowel sounds **SL.1.1a** Follow discussion rules **L.1.4** Determine meaning of unknown words
Fluency	Let's Get Emotional, p. 155	Greeting	**SL.1.6** Produce complete sentences **L.1.6** Use words and phrases to signal simple relationships
	Fluency Matters, p. 155	Sharing	**SL.1.1** Participate in collaborative conversations **SL.1.6** Produce complete sentences
	Reading Rates, p. 155	Group activity	**RL.1.10** Read prose and poetry **RF.1.4b** Read prose and poetry
	Punctuation Play, p. 155	Morning message	**RI.1.10** Read informational text **RF.1.4b** Read prose and poetry **L.1.2b** Use end punctuation
Irregular words	An Irregular Handshake, p. 159	Greeting	None
	Irregular Thinking, p. 159	Sharing	**SL.1.1** Participate in collaborative conversations **L.1.1j** Produce complete sentences
	Step and Spell, p. 159	Group activity	**RF.1.3g** Recognize and read irregularly spelled words **L.1.2d** Use conventional spelling
	What's the Word? p. 159	Morning message	**RF.1.3g** Recognize and read irregularly spelled words **RF.1.4b** Read prose and poetry

Language Arts Content	Activity Title & Page	Morning Meeting Component	Common Core Standards
Nonfiction (informational texts)	Fact Finding, p. 36	Sharing	**RI.1.1** Ask/answer questions about key text details **RI.1.2** Retell key details of a text **RI.1.5** Use text features to locate information **W.1.7** Participate in shared research and writing projects **SL.1.1** Participate in collaborative conversations
	Fountain of Knowledge, p. 157	Greeting	**RI.1.1** Ask/answer questions about key text details **W.1.2** Write informative/explanatory texts **SL.1.1** Participate in collaborative conversations
	Nifty Nonfiction, p. 157	Sharing	**RI.1.1** Ask/answer questions about key text details **W.1.2** Write informative/explanatory texts **SL.1.1** Participate in collaborative conversations
	News Anchor Antics, p. 157	Group activity	**RI.1.1** Ask/answer questions about key text details **W.1.2** Write informative/explanatory texts **SL.1.1** Participate in collaborative conversations
	Writing Preview, p. 157	Morning message	**W.1.8** Recall or gather information to answer questions **SL.1.1** Participate in collaborative conversations
Opinions	Proud Publishers, p. 37	Sharing	**W.1.1** Write opinion pieces **SL.1.1** Participate in collaborative conversations **L.1.1j** Produce complete sentences **L.1.6** Use words and phrases to signal simple relationships
Point of view	Lazy Mary, p. 44	Group activity	**RL.1.4** Identify "feeling" and "sense" words and phrases **RL.1.6** Identify who is telling the story at various points in a text **RL.1.9** Compare/contrast characters **RF.1.4** Read accurately and fluently **W.1.8** Recall or gather information to answer questions
Prepositions	Have I Got a Preposition for You! p. 40	Group activity	**RF.1.4a** Read grade-level text with purpose and understanding **W.1.6** Use digital tools for writing **L.1.1i** Use frequently occurring prepositions **L.1.6** Use words and phrases to signal simple relationships
Pronouns	Me, Myself, and I, p. 33	Greeting	**W.1.7** Participate in shared research and writing projects **L.1.1d** Use personal, possessive, and indefinite pronouns **L.1.6** Use words and phrases to signal simple relationships
Proper and possessive nouns	That's Not Nellie's, p. 34	Greeting	**W.1.3** Write narratives **SL.1.1** Participate in collaborative conversations **L.1.1b** Use proper and possessive nouns **L.1.1e** Use verbs to convey past, present, and future
Punctuation	Sentence Structure Models, p. 49	Morning message	**RF.1.1a** Recognize the distinguishing features of a sentence **L.1.2a** Capitalize dates and names of people **L.1.2b** Use end punctuation **L.1.2c** Use commas in dates and series

Language Arts Content	Activity Title & Page	Morning Meeting Component	Common Core Standards
Sequencing	First, Next, Last, p. 39	Group activity	**W.1.3** Write narratives **W.1.7** Participate in shared research and writing projects **L.1.1** Demonstrate command of standard English grammar and usage
Sight words	Just Say the Word, p. 43	Group activity	**RF.1.3** Use phonics and word analysis to decode words **RF.1.3g** Recognize and read irregularly spelled words **L.1.2d** Use conventional spelling
Syllables	Hickety Pickety Bumble Bee, p. 153	Greeting	**RF.1.2** Demonstrate understanding of spoken words, syllables, and sounds
	Syllables in Names, p. 153	Sharing	**RF.1.2** Demonstrate understanding of spoken words, syllables, and sounds **SL.1.2** Ask/answer questions about information presented orally **L.1.1j** Produce complete sentences
	Syllable Drama, p. 153	Group activity	**RF.1.2** Demonstrate understanding of spoken words, syllables, and sounds **RF.1.3d** Decode words with prefixes and suffixes **L.1.4** Determine meaning of unknown words
	Syllable Count, p. 153	Morning message	**RF.1.2** Demonstrate understanding of spoken words, syllables, and sounds **RF.1.3d** Decode words with prefixes and suffixes **RF.1.4** Read accurately and fluently
Temporal words	First, Next, Last, p. 39	Group activity	**W.1.3** Write narratives **W.1.7** Participate in shared research and writing projects **L.1.1** Demonstrate command of standard English grammar and usage
Verb tenses	What's Going On? p. 47	Group activity	**SL.1.1a** Follow discussion rules **L.1.1e** Use verbs to convey past, present, and future **L.1.4c** Identify frequently occurring root words and their inflectional forms
Vocabulary development	Shades of Meaning, p. 46	Group activity	**RF.1.4c** Use context to confirm or self-correct word recognition and understanding **SL.1.1** Participate in collaborative conversations **L.1.5d** Distinguish shades of meaning among verbs and adjectives **L.1.6** Use words and phrases to signal simple relationships
Vowel sounds	Final-E Decoded, p. 32	Greeting	**RF.1.2** Demonstrate understanding of spoken words, syllables, and sounds **RF.1.3b** Decode regularly spelled one-syllable words **RF.1.3c** Know final -e for representing long vowel sounds **SL.1.1a** Follow discussion rules **L.1.4** Determine meaning of unknown words

Second Grade

Activities Listed by Language Arts Content

Language Arts Content	Activity Title & Page	Morning Meeting Component	Common Core Standards
Adverbs	In the Manner of the Adverb, p. 53	Greeting	**RF.2.4** Read accurately and fluently **L.2.1e** Use adjectives and adverbs **L.2.5** Demonstrate understanding of word relationships and meanings
Character	Commonalities, p. 60	Group activity	**RL.2.3** Describe characters' response to major events/challenges **RL.2.6** Acknowledge differences in characters' points of views **RL.2.7** Use information from illustrations/words to demonstrate story understanding **SL.2.1** Participate in collaborative conversations **SL.2.6** Produce complete sentences
	ReACT! p. 63	Group activity	**RL.2.1** Ask/answer questions to demonstrate understanding of key details **RL.2.3** Describe characters' response to major events/challenges **RL.2.7** Use information from illustrations/words to demonstrate story understanding **W.2.8** Recall or gather information to answer questions
	What a Charac-ter! p. 64	Group activity	**RL.2.3** Describe characters' response to major events/challenges **RL.2.6** Acknowledge differences in characters' points of view **W.2.8** Recall or gather information to answer questions
Comparing and contrasting	Just Say Venn! p. 66	Morning message	**RL.2.2** Recount stories from diverse cultures **RL.2.9** Compare and contrast two or more versions of the same story **RF.2.4** Read accurately and fluently **SL.2.2** Recount or describe key ideas/details from text
Compound words	Compound Charades, p. 61	Group activity	**RF.2.3** Apply phonics and word analysis skills to decode words **L.2.4d** Use knowledge of individual words to predict meaning of compound words **L.2.6** Use words and phrases, including using adjectives and adverbs to describe
Decoding	Syllable Hunt, p. 67	Morning message	**RF.2.3** Apply phonics and word analysis skills to decode words **RF.2.3c** Decode regularly spelled two-syllable words with long vowels **L.2.2d** Generalize spelling patterns
Describing	Describe It! p. 62	Group activity	**W.2.8** Recall or gather information to answer questions **SL.2.1a** Follow discussion rules **SL.2.1b** Build on others' talk **SL.2.6** Produce complete sentences
Expression	Let's Get Emo-tional, p. 155	Greeting	**SL.2.6** Produce complete sentences **L.2.6** Use acquired words and phrases

181

continued

Language Arts Content	Activity Title & Page	Morning Meeting Component	Common Core Standards
Expression (continued)	Fluency Matters, p. 155	Sharing	**SL.2.1** Participate in collaborative conversations **SL.2.6** Produce complete sentences
	Reading Rates, p. 155	Group activity	**RL.2.10** Read stories and poetry **RF.2.4b** Read orally
	Punctuation Play, p. 155	Morning message	**RI.2.10** Read informational text **RF.2.4b** Read orally **L.2.3** Use language knowledge when writing, speaking, reading, or listening
Fluency	Let's Get Emotional, p. 155	Greeting	**SL.2.6** Produce complete sentences **L.2.6** Use acquired words and phrases
	Fluency Matters, p. 155	Sharing	**SL.2.1** Participate in collaborative conversations **SL.2.6** Produce complete sentences
	Reading Rates, p. 155	Group activity	**RL.2.10** Read stories and poetry **RF.2.4b** Read orally
	Punctuation Play, p. 155	Morning message	**RI.2.10** Read informational texts **RF.2.4b** Read orally
Headings	Heading Hello, p. 52	Greeting	**RI.2.5** Know and use various text features to locate key facts or information **L.2.2e** Consult reference materials to check and correct spelling
Illustrations	Worth a Thousand Words, p. 70	Morning message	**RL.2.7** Use information from illustrations/words to demonstrate story understanding **RI.2.7** Explain how specific images contribute to and clarify a text **SL.2.1** Participate in collaborative conversations **SL.2.3** Ask/answer questions about what a speaker says
Inflection	Emphatic Exclamations, p. 51	Greeting	**RF.2.4b** Read orally **L.2.2** Demonstrate command of standard capitalization, punctuation, and spelling **L.2.3** Use language knowledge when writing, speaking, reading, or listening
Irregular words	An Irregular Handshake, p. 159	Greeting	None
	Irregular Thinking, p. 159	Sharing	**SL.2.1** Participate in collaborative conversations **L.2.1f** Produce complete sentences
	Step and Spell, p. 159	Group activity	**RF.2.3f** Read irregularly spelled words **L.2.2d** Generalize spelling patterns

Language Arts Content	Activity Title & Page	Morning Meeting Component	Common Core Standards
Irregular words (continued)	What's the Word? p. 159	Morning message	**RF.2.3f** Read irregularly spelled words **RF.2.4b** Read orally
Letter formation	Alphabet Aerobics, p. 59	Group activity	**L.2.1** Demonstrate command of standard grammar and usage **L.2.2** Demonstrate command of standard capitalization, punctuation, and spelling
Main topic	What's It All About? p. 69	Morning message	**RI.2.2** Identify the main topic of a text as well as the focus of specific paragraphs **RI.2.8** Describe how reasons support points the author makes **W.2.8** Recall or gather information to answer questions **SL.2.2** Recount or describe key ideas/details from text
Nonfiction	Fountain of Knowledge, p. 157	Greeting	**RI.2.1** Ask/answer questions about text details **W.2.2** Write informative/explanatory texts **SL.2.1** Participate in collaborative conversations
	Nifty Nonfiction, p. 157	Sharing	**RI.2.1** Ask/answer questions about text details **W.2.2** Write informative/explanatory texts **SL.2.1** Participate in collaborative conversations
	News Anchor Antics, p. 157	Group activity	**RI.2.1** Ask/answer questions about text details **W.2.2** Write informative/explanatory texts **SL.2.1** Participate in collaborative conversations
	Writing Preview, p. 157	Morning message	**W.2.8** Recall or gather information to answer questions **SL.2.1** Participate in collaborative conversations
Nouns	Irregular Plural Hello, p. 54	Greeting	**RF.2.3** Apply phonics and word analysis skills to decode words **L.2.1** Demonstrate command of standard grammar and usage **L.2.1b** Form and use frequently occurring irregular plural nouns **L.2.2d** Generalize spelling patterns
	Hi, Group! p. 161	Greeting	**SL.2.1a** Follow discussion rules **L.2.1a** Use collective nouns **L.2.5a** Connect words to real-life uses
	Gabbing About Groups, p. 161	Sharing	**SL.2.1** Participate in collaborative conversations **L.2.1a** Use collective nouns **L.2.5a** Connect words to real-life uses
	A Clutch of Clues, p. 161	Group activity	**SL.2.1a** Follow discussion rules **L.2.1a** Use collective nouns **L.2.5a** Connect words to real-life uses
	Collective Nouns, p. 161	Morning message	**RF.2.4b** Read orally **SL.2.1** Participate in collaborative conversations **L.2.1a** Use collective nouns **L.2.5a** Connect words to real-life uses

Language Arts Content	Activity Title & Page	Morning Meeting Component	Common Core Standards
Opinions	Readers Recommend, p. 57	Sharing	**RL.2.1** Ask/answer questions to demonstrate understanding of key details **W.2.1** Write opinion pieces **W.2.5** Focus on a topic and strengthen writing by revising and editing **SL.2.1** Participate in collaborative conversations **SL.2.3** Ask/answer questions about what a speaker says
	Would You Rather? p. 65	Group activity	**SL.2.1c** Ask for clarification about topics under discussion **SL.2.3** Ask/answer questions **W.2.1** Write opinion pieces
Punctuation	Emphatic Exclamations, p. 51	Greeting	**RF.2.4b** Read orally **L.2.2** Demonstrate command of standard capitalization, punctuation, and spelling **L.2.3** Use language knowledge when writing, speaking, reading, or listening
Questioning	It's All in the Details, p. 56	Group activity	**W.2.3** Write narratives **W.2.8** Recall or gather information to answer questions **SL.2.3** Ask/answer questions about what a speaker says **SL.2.4** Tell a story/recount an experience **SL.2.6** Produce complete sentences
Spelling	Alphabet Aerobics, p. 59	Morning message	**L.2.1** Demonstrate command of standard grammar and usage **L.2.2** Demonstrate command of standard capitalization, punctuation, and spelling
Story elements	Question Quest, p. 68	Morning message	**RL.2.1** Ask/answer questions to demonstrate understanding of key details **RL.2.7** Use information from illustrations/words to demonstrate story understanding **RF.2.4c** Use context to confirm/self-correct word recognition and understanding **SL.2.2** Recount or describe key ideas/details from text
Syllables	Syllable Hunt, p. 67	Morning message	**RF.2.3** Apply phonics and word analysis skills to decode words **RF.2.3c** Decode regularly spelled two-syllable words with long vowels **L.2.2d** Generalize spelling patterns
	Syllable Sharing, p. 58	Sharing	**RF.2.3** Apply phonics and word analysis skills to decode words **SL.2.1a** Follow discussion rules
Vowel sounds	What's in a Name? p. 55	Greeting	**RF.2.3a** Distinguish long/short vowels in regularly spelled one-syllable words **RF.2.3b** Know spelling–sound correspondences for common vowel teams

Third Grade

Activities Listed by Language Arts Content

Language Arts Content	Activity Title & Page	Morning Meeting Component	Common Core Standards
Adjectives	How Are You Feeling Today? p. 72	Greeting	**RL.3.3** Describe characters, explain their actions **SL.3.1c** Ask questions to check understanding, stay on topic, and link comments **SL.3.3** Ask/answer questions about information from a speaker **L.3.1a** Explain the function of nouns, pronouns, verbs, adjectives, and adverbs
Adverbs	It's *How* You Do It, p. 82	Group activity	**RL.3.3** Describe characters in a story **SL.3.1** Engage in collaborative discussions **L.3.1a** Explain the function of nouns, pronouns, verbs, adjectives, and adverbs
Character	Character Corners, p. 78	Group activity	**RL.3.1** Ask/answer questions to demonstrate understanding of a text **RL.3.3** Describe characters in a story **SL.3.1a** Come to discussions prepared
	What's the Motive? p. 89	Morning message	**RL.3.1** Ask/answer questions to demonstrate understanding of a text **RL.3.3** Describe characters, explain their actions **SL.3.1a** Come to discussions prepared **SL.3.1d** Explain ideas and understanding
Commas	Comma Hunt, p. 87	Morning message	**F.3.4b** Read prose and poetry orally **SL.3.1a** Come to discussions prepared **L.3.2** Demonstrate command of standard capitalization, punctuation, and spelling **L.3.2c** Use commas and quotation marks in dialogue
Comparison	Comparatively Speaking, p. 71	Greeting	**RF.3.3** Use phonics and word analysis skills to decode words **L.3.1g** Form and use comparative or superlative adjectives
Context clues	Wonderful Words, p. 90	Morning message	**RI.3.4** Determine word meaning **RF.3.4c** Use context to confirm/self-correct word recognition and understanding **L.3.4a** Use sentence-level context as a clue to word meaning
Elaboration	If I Were, p. 74	Sharing	**W.3.1** Write opinion pieces with supporting reasons **W.3.1a** Introduce topic or text, state opinion, create organizational structure that lists reasons **W.3.1b** Provide reasons that support an opinion **W.3.1c** Use linking words and phrases to connect opinion and reasons **SL.3.1d** Explain ideas and understanding

Language Arts Content	Activity Title & Page	Morning Meeting Component	Common Core Standards
Expression	Radio Hour, p. 84	Group activity	**RL.3.1** Ask/answer questions to demonstrate understanding of a text **RF.3.4b** Read prose and poetry orally **SL.3.1** Engage in collaborative discussions **SL.3.5** Create fluid audio recordings
Figurative language	Idiom-ania, p. 80	Group activity	**RL.3.4** Determine literal and nonliteral meanings of words in text **RF.3.4c** Use context to confirm/self-correct word recognition and understanding **L.3.5a** Distinguish literal from nonliteral meanings of words/phrases in context
Fluency	Radio Hour, p. 84	Group activity	**RL.3.1** Ask/answer questions to demonstrate understanding of a text **RF.3.4b** Read prose and poetry orally **SL.3.1** Engage in collaborative discussions **SL.3.5** Create fluid audio recordings
Informational text	Five-Minute Sleuths, p. 79	Group activity	**RI.3.5** Use text features and search tools to locate information efficiently **RI.3.7** Use information gained from illustrations/words to demonstrate understanding **W.3.7** Conduct short research projects **W.3.8** Recall/gather information; take brief notes and sort evidence **SL.3.4** Report on a topic or text with facts and details
Irregular words	An Irregular Handshake, p. 159	Greeting	None
	Irregular Thinking, p. 159	Sharing	**SL.3.1** Engage in collaborative discussions **L.3.1i** Produce simple, compound, and complex sentences
	Step and Spell, p. 159	Group activity	**RF.3.3d** Read irregularly spelled words **L.3.2** Demonstrate command of standard capitalization, punctuation, and spelling
	What's the Word? p. 159	Morning message	**RF.3.3d** Read irregularly spelled words **RF.3.4b** Read prose and poetry orally
Limericks	Lively Limericks, p. 83	Group activity	**RL.3.5** Refer to parts of stories, dramas, and poems; describe how each part builds on earlier sections **RF.3.4b** Read prose and poetry orally **W.3.4** Produce well-organized, purposeful writing

Language Arts Content	Activity Title & Page	Morning Meeting Component	Common Core Standards
Listening	Inquiring Minds, p. 81	Group activity	**RI.3.1** Ask/answer questions to demonstrate understanding of a text **RI.3.7** Use information gained from illustrations/words to demonstrate understanding **RF.3.4a** Read with purpose and understanding **SL.3.1c** Ask questions to check understanding, stay on topic, and link comments
Modifiers	Show, Don't Tell, p. 163	Greeting	**SL.3.1b** Follow discussion rules
	Why, Oh Why? p. 163	Sharing	**SL.3.1** Engage in collaborative discussions
	The Laughing Tissue, p. 163	Group activity	**SL.3.1** Engage in collaborative discussions **L.3.1a** Explain the function of nouns, pronouns, verbs, adjectives, and adverbs
	Fill in the Modifier, p. 163	Morning message	**RF.3.4** Read accurately and fluently **SL.3.1** Engage in collaborative discussions **L.3.3a** Choose words and phrases for effect
Multisyllabic words	Multisyllabic Madness, p. 88	Morning message	**RF.3.3** Use phonics and word analysis skills to decode words **RF.3.3c** Decode multisyllable words
Narratives	Weekend Focus, p. 77	Sharing	**W.3.3** Write narratives using effective technique, descriptive details, and clear sequences **W.3.3c** Use temporal words and phrases to signal event order **W.3.5** Develop and strengthen writing by planning, revising, and editing **SL.3.4** Report on a topic or text with facts and details
Nonfiction	Fountain of Knowledge, p. 157	Greeting	**RI.3.1** Ask/answer questions to demonstrate understanding of a text **W.3.2** Write informative/explanatory texts **SL.3.1** Engage in collaborative discussions
	Nifty Nonfiction, p. 157	Sharing	**RI.3.1** Ask/answer questions to demonstrate understanding of a text **W.3.2** Write informative/explanatory texts **SL.3.1** Engage in collaborative discussions
	News Anchor Antics, p. 157	Group activity	**RI.3.1** Ask/answer questions to demonstrate understanding of a text **W.3.2** Write informative/explanatory texts **SL.3.1** Engage in collaborative discussions
	Writing Preview, p. 157	Morning message	**W.3.8** Recall/gather information; take brief notes and sort evidence **SL.3.1** Engage in collaborative discussions

Language Arts Content	Activity Title & Page	Morning Meeting Component	Common Core Standards
Nouns	Hi, Group! p. 161	Greeting	**SL.3.1b** Follow discussion rules **L.3.1b** Form and use regular and irregular plural nouns **L.3.5b** Connect words to real-life uses
	Gabbing About Groups, p. 161	Sharing	**SL.3.1** Engage in collaborative discussions **L.3.1b** Form and use regular and irregular plural nouns **L.3.5b** Connect words to real-life uses
	A Clutch of Clues, p. 161	Group activity	**SL.3.1b** Follow discussion rules **L.3.1b** Form and use regular and irregular plural nouns **L.3.5b** Connect words to real-life uses
	Collective Nouns, p. 161	Morning message	**RF.3.4b** Read prose and poetry orally **SL.3.1** Engage in collaborative discussions **L.3.1b** Form and use regular and irregular plural nouns **L.3.5b** Connect words to real-life uses
Opinions	State Your Opinion, p 76	Sharing/Group activity combination	**RI.3.2** Determine main idea and key details **RI.3.6** Distinguish own point of view from that of author **SL.3.1** Engage in collaborative discussions **SL.3.2** Determine main ideas and supporting details of text read aloud
Questioning	Interview and Introduce, p. 73	Greeting/ sharing combination	**SL.3.1** Engage in collaborative discussions **SL.3.3** Ask/answer questions about information from a speaker **SL.3.6** Speak in complete sentences when appropriate to task and situation
	Inquiring Minds, p. 81	Group activity	**RI.3.1** Ask/answer questions to demonstrate understanding of a text **RI.3.7** Use information gained from illustrations/words to demonstrate understanding **RF.3.4a** Read with purpose and understanding **SL.3.1c** Ask questions to check understanding, stay on topic, and link comments
Research	Five-Minute Sleuths, p. 79	Group activity	**RI.3.5** Use text features and search tools to locate information efficiently **RI.3.7** Use information gained from illustrations/words to demonstrate understanding **W.3.7** Conduct short research projects **W.3.8** Recall/gather information; take brief notes and sort evidence **SL.3.4** Report on a topic or text with facts and details
Rhyme	Lively Limericks, p. 83	Group activity	**RL.3.5** Refer to parts of stories, dramas, and poems; describe how each part builds on earlier sections **RF.3.4b** Read prose and poetry orally **W.3.4** Produce well-organized, purposeful writing

Language Arts Content	Activity Title & Page	Morning Meeting Component	Common Core Standards
Staying on topic	Special Interest Sharing, p. 75	Sharing	**W.3.2** Write informative/explanatory texts **SL.3.1** Engage effectively in collaborative discussions on grade 3 topics and texts **SL.3.1c** Ask questions to check understanding, stay on topic, and link comments **SL.3.3** Ask/answer questions about information from a speaker **SL.3.4** Report on a topic or text with facts and details
Story elements	On the Case, p. 165	Greeting	**SL.3.1b** Follow discussion rules
	Mysterious Experience, p. 165	Sharing	**SL.3.1** Engage in collaborative discussions **SL.3.4** Report on a topic or text with facts and details
	Mystery Winker, p. 165	Group activity	None
	Sneaking Suspicion, p. 165	Morning message	**SL.3.1** Engage in collaborative discussions **SL.3.4** Report on a topic or text with facts and details
Text parts	Big Ideas, Small Details, p. 86	Morning message	**RI.3.1** Ask/answer questions to demonstrate understanding of a text **RI.3.2** Determine main idea and key details **SL.3.2** Determine main ideas and supporting details of text read aloud
Word parts	The Affix Effect, p. 85	Group activity	**RF.3.3** Use phonics and word analysis skills to decode words **L.3.4** Determine or clarify meaning of unknown words **L.3.4b** Determine meaning of word plus affix

Fourth Grade

Activities Listed by Language Arts Content

Language Arts Content	Activity Title & Page	Morning Meeting Component	Common Core Standards
Alliteration	Alliterative Aloha, p. 171	Greeting	**SL.4.1a** Come to discussions prepared **L.4.5** Understand figurative language, word relationships, and nuances in meaning **L.4.6** Acquire and accurately use words
	Noticing Author's Craft, p. 171	Sharing	**RL.4.4** Determine word meanings in text **RF.4.4b** Read prose and poetry **SL.4.1** Engage in collaborative discussions **L.4.5** Understand figurative language, word relationships, and nuances in meaning
	Sound Says, p. 171	Group activity	None
	Circling Sounds, p. 171	Morning message	**SL.4.1** Engage in collaborative discussions **L.4.5** Understand figurative language, word relationships, and nuances in meaning
Character	Answering As . . . p. 95	Sharing	**RL.4.1** Refer to text details and examples when explaining/drawing inferences **RL.4.3** Describe character, setting, or event using text details **W.4.9** Draw evidence from literary/informational texts **SL.4.1b** Follow discussion rules
	Author as Character, p. 97	Sharing	**RL.4.3** Describe character, setting, or event using text details **W.4.3a** Orient readers by using story elements **W.4.3b** Use dialogue and description to develop experiences/events or show characters' responses
Commas	Comma Commotion, p. 167	Greeting	**L.4.2** Demonstrate command of standard capitalization, punctuation, and spelling
	My To-Do List, p. 167	Sharing	**SL.4.6** Understand when to use formal vs. informal English **L.4.2** Demonstrate command of standard capitalization, punctuation, and spelling
	Where's the Comma? p. 167	Group activity	**L.4.2** Demonstrate command of standard capitalization, punctuation, and spelling
	Pause Accordingly! p. 167	Morning message	**SL.4.1** Engage in collaborative discussions **L.4.2** Demonstrate command of standard capitalization, punctuation, and spelling

Language Arts Content	Activity Title & Page	Morning Meeting Component	Common Core Standards
Dramatizing	What Are You Doing? p. 93	Greeting	**RL.4.3** Describe character, setting, or event using text details **W.4.3b** Use dialogue and description to develop experiences/events or show characters' responses **SL.4.1b** Follow discussion rules
	Ten-Line Scene, p. 106	Group activity	**RL.4.5** Refer to structural elements of poems and drama when writing or speaking about a text **RL.4.7** Connect written, visual and oral presentations of text **W.4.4** Produce appropriate writing **SL.4.1** Engage in collaborative discussions
Modifiers	Show, Don't Tell, p. 163	Greeting	**SL.4.1b** Follow discussion rules
	Why, Oh Why? p. 163	Sharing	**SL.4.1** Engage in collaborative discussions
	The Laughing Tissue, p. 163	Group activity	**SL.4.1** Engage in collaborative discussions **L.4.1** Demonstrate command of standard grammar and usage
	Fill in the Modifier, p. 163	Morning message	**RF.4.4** Read with accuracy and fluency **SL.4.1** Engage in collaborative discussions **L.4.3a** Choose words to convey ideas precisely
Onomatopoeia	Chugga-Chugga, p. 169	Greeting	**SL.4.1b** Follow discussion rules
	Bing Bang Boom, p. 169	Sharing	**SL.4.1** Engage in collaborative discussions **L.4.5** Understand figurative language, word relationships, and nuances in meaning
	The Onomatopoeia Machine, p. 169	Group activity	**SL.4.1** Engage in collaborative discussions **SL.4.6** Understand when to use formal vs. informal English **L.4.5** Understand figurative language, word relationships, and nuances in meaning
	A Melody of Sounds! p. 169	Morning message	**RF.4.4b** Read prose and poetry **L.4.5** Understand figurative language, word relationships, and nuances in meaning
Opinions	Problem Solvers to the Rescue, p. 108	Morning message	**RF.4.4b** Read prose and poetry **W.4.1** Write opinion pieces **SL.4.1** Engage in collaborative discussions
Organizing information	Precious Paragraphs, p. 107	Morning message	**RI.4.5** Describe the overall structure of events, ideas, concepts, or information **W.4.3** Write narratives **W.4.5** Develop and strengthen writing by planning, revising, editing

Fourth Grade, continued

Language Arts Content	Activity Title & Page	Morning Meeting Component	Common Core Standards
Paraphrasing	Seconds to Respond, p. 99	Sharing	**W.4.4** Produce appropriate writing **SL.4.1** Engage in collaborative discussions **SL.4.2** Paraphrase text read aloud or information presented in diverse media **L.4.3a** Choose words to convey ideas precisely
Personal narratives	Of Utmost Importance, p. 98	Sharing	**W.4.3** Write narratives **W.4.8** Recall relevant information from experiences/gather relevant information **SL.4.1** Engage in collaborative discussions **SL.4.1b** Follow discussion rules
Point of view	Spoken Duet, p. 105	Group activity	**RL.4.1** Refer to text details and examples when explaining/drawing inferences **RL.4.2** Determine theme and summarize text **RF.4.4** Read with accuracy and fluency **W.4.4** Produce appropriate writing **SL.4.1** Engage in collaborative discussions
Questioning	What's Your Scoop? p. 94	Greeting/sharing combination	**W.4.4** Produce appropriate writing **W.4.7** Conduct short research projects **SL.4.1b** Follow discussion rules **SL.4.4** Report information or tell a story
Reading comprehension	Book Talk, p. 100	Group activity	**RF.4.4a** Read text with purpose and understanding **SL.4.1** Engage in collaborative discussions
Revising for clarity	Scrambled Sentence, p. 103	Group activity	**W.4.5** Develop and strengthen writing by planning, revising, editing **L.4.1** Demonstrate command of standard grammar and usage **L.4.2** Demonstrate command of standard capitalization, punctuation, and spelling
Spelling	Sparkle, p. 104	Group activity	**L.4.2** Demonstrate command of standard capitalization, punctuation, and spelling **L.4.2d** Spell correctly
Story elements	On the Case, p. 165	Greeting	**SL.4.1b** Follow discussion rules
	Mysterious Experience, p. 165	Sharing	**SL.4.1** Engage in collaborative discussions **SL.4.4** Report information or tell a story
	Mystery Winker, p. 165	Group activity	None
	Sneaking Suspicion, p. 165	Morning message	**SL.4.1** Engage in collaborative discussions **SL.4.4** Report information or tell a story

Language Arts Content	Activity Title & Page	Morning Meeting Component	Common Core Standards
Storytelling	A Time of Change, p. 96	Sharing	**W.4.3** Write narratives **SL.4.1** Engage in collaborative discussions **SL.4.4** Report information or tell a story
Usage	Too Many Twos, p. 110	Morning message	**RF.4.4c** Use context to confirm/self-correct word recognition and understanding **W.4.5** Develop and strengthen writing by planning, revising, editing **SL.4.1c** Pose/respond to questions; make comments that contribute to the discussion **L.4.1g** Correctly use frequently confused words (e.g., to, too, two; there, their)
Vocabulary	Hi-Definition, p. 91	Greeting	**RF.4.4c** Use context to confirm/self-correct word recognition and understanding **SL.4.1** Engage in collaborative discussions **L.4.4a** Use context as a clue to word meaning
	The Root of It, p. 92	Greeting	**SL.4.1** Engage in collaborative discussions **L.4.4b** Use Greek/Latin affixes and roots as clues to word meaning
	On My Back, p. 101	Group activity	**RL.4.3** Describe character, setting, or event using text details **RF.4.4c** Use context to confirm/self-correct word recognition and understanding **L.4.4a** Use context as a clue to word meaning
	Say It! p. 102	Group activity	**SL.4.1b** Follow discussion rules **L.4.5** Understand figurative language, word relationships, and nuances in meaning
	Sophisticated Synonyms, p. 109	Morning message	**RI.4.4** Determine meaning of words in text **RF.4.4** Read with accuracy and fluency **L.4.4** Determine or clarify word meanings **L.4.5** Understand figurative language, word relationships, and nuances in meaning

Fifth Grade

Activities Listed by Language Arts Content

Language Arts Content	Activity Title & Page	Morning Meeting Component	Common Core Standards
Affixes	I'm Speaking Greek and Latin! p. 114	Greeting	**RF.5.3a** Use knowledge of morphology to read multisyllabic words **SL.5.6** Adapt speech to a variety of contexts and tasks **L.5.4b** Use Greek/Latin affixes and roots as clues to word meaning
Alliteration	Alliterative Aloha, p. 171	Greeting	**SL.5.1a** Come to discussions prepared **L.5.5** Understand figurative language, word relationships, and nuances in meaning **L.5.6** Accurately use academic and domain-specific words
	Noticing Author's Craft, p. 171	Sharing	**RL.5.4** Determine word meanings in text **RF.5.4b** Read prose and poetry orally **SL.5.1** Engage in collaborative discussions **L.5.5** Understand figurative language, word relationships, and nuances in meaning
	Sound Says, p. 171	Group activity	None
	Circling Sounds, p. 171	Morning message	**SL.5.1** Engage in collaborative discussions **L.5.5** Understand figurative language, word relationships, and nuances in meaning
Character	Tell Me About It, p. 118	Sharing	**RL.5.1** Quote accurately from a text when explaining/drawing inferences **RI.5.1** Quote accurately from a text when explaining/drawing inferences **W.5.4** Produce clear and coherent writing **SL.5.1** Engage in collaborative discussions **L.5.5b** Recognize and explain common idioms
	Cascading Characteristics, p. 120	Group activity	**RL.5.3** Compare and contrast two or more characters **RI.5.3** Explain relationships or interactions between individuals **W.5.9** Draw evidence from literary/informational texts **SL.5.4** Report on a topic/text or present an opinion
	Character Traits, p. 121	Group activity	**RL.5.1** Quote accurately from a text when explaining/drawing inferences **RI.5.1** Quote accurately from a text when explaining/drawing inferences **RF.5.4** Read accurately and fluently **SL.5.4** Report information or present an opinion **L.5.4** Determine word meaning

Language Arts Content	Activity Title & Page	Morning Meeting Component	Common Core Standards
Commas	Comma Commotion, p. 167	Greeting	**L.5.2c** Use commas
	My To-Do List, p. 167	Sharing	**SL.5.6** Adapt speech to a variety of contexts and tasks **L.5.2a** Punctuate items in a series
	Where's the Comma? p. 167	Group activity	**L.5.2** Demonstrate command of standard capitalization, punctuation, and spelling
	Pause Accordingly! p. 167	Morning message	**SL.5.1** Engage in collaborative discussions **L.5.2** Demonstrate command of standard capitalization, punctuation, and spelling
Communication skills	Blink 1-2-4, p. 111	Greeting	**SL.5.1b** Follow discussion rules
Conjunctions	You Can Call Me, p. 115	Greeting	**SL.5.1b** Follow discussion rules **L.5.1e** Use correlative conjunctions
Dramatizing	Human Slide Show, p. 123	Group activity	**RL.5.2** Determine theme and summarize text **RL.5.5** Explain how a series of chapters, scenes, or stanzas fits together **RF.5.4b** Read prose and poetry orally **SL.5.5** Include multimedia/visual displays to enhance development of main ideas or themes
Figurative language	Broadcast Views, p. 112	Greeting/sharing combination	**RL.5.1** Quote accurately from a text when explaining/drawing inferences **W.5.4** Produce clear and coherent writing **SL.5.1** Engage in collaborative discussions **L.5.5b** Recognize and explain common idioms
Fluency	Read. Rinse. Repeat., p. 125	Group activity	**RF.5.4b** Read prose and poetry orally **SL.5.1** Engage in collaborative discussions **SL.5.6** Adapt speech to a variety of contexts and tasks
Interjections	Say What?! p. 116	Sharing	**RF.5.4a** Read text with purpose and understanding **W.5.5** Develop and strengthen writing by revising/editing **W.5.7** Conduct short research projects **SL.5.1c** Pose and respond to questions **L.5.1a** Explain the function of interjections

Language Arts Content	Activity Title & Page	Morning Meeting Component	Common Core Standards
Onomatopoeia	Chugga-Chugga, p. 169	Greeting	**SL.5.1b** Follow discussion rules
	Bing Bang Boom, p. 169	Sharing	**SL.5.1** Engage in collaborative discussions **L.5.5** Understand figurative language, word relationships, and nuances
	The Onomato-poeia Machine, p. 169	Group activity	**SL.5.1** Engage in collaborative discussions **SL.5.6** Adapt speech to a variety of contexts and tasks **L.5.5** Understand figurative language, word relationships, and nuances in meaning
	A Melody of Sounds! p. 169	Morning message	**RF.5.4b** Read prose and poetry orally **L.5.5** Understand figurative language, word relationships, and nuances in meaning
Opinions	Take a Stand, p. 117	Sharing	**RI.5.2** Determine main ideas of a text and explain supporting details **W.5.1** Write opinion pieces on topics/texts, supporting point of view with reasons and information **SL.5.1** Engage in collaborative discussions **SL.5.4** Report on a topic/text or present an opinion
Punctuation	You Don't Say, p. 119	Sharing	**W.5.5** Develop and strengthen writing by editing **SL.5.1** Engage in collaborative discussions **L.5.2d** Use underlining, quotation marks, or italics to indicate titles of works
	Say What You Mean to Say, p. 128	Morning message	**W.5.5** Develop and strengthen writing by editing **SL.5.1b** Follow discussion rules **L.5.2** Demonstrate command of standard capitalization, punctuation, and spelling **L.5.4** Determine word meaning
Spelling	Human Tic Tac Toe, p. 124	Group activity	**L.5.2e** Spell words correctly; consult references as needed **L.5.5** Understand figurative language, word relationships, and nuances in meaning
	Witch Won? p. 130	Morning message	**RF.5.3** Apply grade-level phonics and word analysis skills in decoding words **W.5.5** Develop and strengthen writing by editing **SL.5.1** Engage in collaborative discussions **L.5.2e** Spell words correctly; consult references as needed
	Say What You Mean to Say, p. 128	Morning message	**W.5.5** Develop and strengthen writing by editing **SL.5.1b** Follow discussion rules **L.5.2** Demonstrate command of standard capitalization, punctuation, and spelling **L.5.4** Determine word meaning

Language Arts Content	Activity Title & Page	Morning Meeting Component	Common Core Standards
Story elements	On the Case, p. 165	Greeting	**SL.5.1b** Follow discussion rules
	Mysterious Experience, p. 165	Sharing	**SL.5.1** Engage in collaborative discussions **SL.5.4** Report information or present an opinion
	Mystery Winker, p. 165	Group activity	None
	Sneaking Suspicion, p. 165	Morning message	**SL.5.1** Engage in collaborative discussions **SL.5.4** Report information or present an opinion
Summarizing	Heeeeeeere's Johnny! p. 113	Greeting	**SL.5.1** Engage in collaborative discussions **SL.5.4** Report on a topic/text or present an opinion
Verb tense	Check That Verb Past, p. 126	Morning message	**RF.5.4** Read with sufficient accuracy and fluency to support comprehension **W.5.3** Write narratives to develop real/imagined experiences or events **L.5.1c** Use verb tense to convey times, sequences, states, and conditions **L.5.1d** Recognize inappropriate shifts in verb tense
Vocabulary	Eeek, It's a . . ., p. 122	Group activity	**RF.5.3a** Use knowledge of morphology to read multisyllabic words **SL.5.1** Engage in collaborative discussions **L.5.4** Determine word meaning **L.5.4b** Use common Greek/Latin affixes and roots as clues to word meaning
	Consult as Needed, p. 127	Morning message	**RI.5.10** Read and comprehend informational texts **RF.5.4b** Read prose and poetry orally **SL.5.1c** Pose and respond to questions **L.5.4c** Consult reference materials to find pronunciation and meaning
	Where's That Thesaurus? p. 129	Morning message	**RF.5.4c** Use context to confirm/self-correct word recognition and understanding **W.5.5** Plan, revise, edit, rewrite, try new approaches **L.5.4c** Consult reference materials to find pronunciation and meaning **L.5.6** Accurately use academic and domain-specific words

Sixth Grade

Activities Listed by Language Arts Content

Language Arts Content	Activity Title & Page	Morning Meeting Component	Common Core Standards
Alliteration	Alliterative Aloha, p. 171	Greeting	**SL.6.1a** Come to discussions prepared **L.6.5** Understand figurative language, word relationships, and nuances in meaning **L.6.6** Accurately use academic and domain-specific words
	Noticing Author's Craft, p. 171	Sharing	**RL.6.4** Determine literal, figurative, and connotative word meanings **SL.6.1** Engage in collaborative discussions **L.6.5** Understand figurative language, word relationships, and nuances in meaning
	Sound Says, p. 171	Group activity	None
	Circling Sounds, p. 171	Morning message	**SL.6.1** Engage in collaborative discussions **L.6.5** Understand figurative language, word relationships, and nuances in meaning
Auditory recognition	Sound Symphony, p. 145	Group activity	**SL.6.4** Use appropriate eye contact and adequate volume **L.6.2b** Spell correctly **L.6.3** Use knowledge of language conventions **L.6.4** Determine or clarify word meanings
Character	Superhero Greeting, p. 133	Greeting	**W.6.3a** Engage and orient readers **W.6.3b** Use narrative techniques **SL.6.1b** Follow discussion rules **SL.6.4** Use appropriate eye contact and adequate volume
	Character Interrogation, p. 138	Group activity	**RI.6.1** Cite textual evidence **W.6.7** Conduct short research projects **SL.6.1a** Come to discussions prepared **SL.6.1c** Pose and respond to specific questions
	Character Timeline, p. 139	Group activity	**RL.6.3** Describe how plot unfolds and characters respond **W.6.4** Produce clear and coherent writing **W.6.7** Conduct short research projects **SL.6.1** Engage in collaborative discussions
	Mood Orchestra, p. 143	Group activity	**RL.6.3** Describe how plot unfolds and characters respond **W.6.3** Use narrative techniques **SL.6.4** Present findings; use appropriate eye contact/volume

Language Arts Content	Activity Title & Page	Morning Meeting Component	Common Core Standards
Commas	Comma Commotion, p. 167	Greeting	**L.6.2** Demonstrate command of standard capitalization, punctuation, and spelling
	My To-Do List, p. 167	Sharing	**SL.6.6** Adapt speech to a variety of contexts and tasks **L.6.2** Demonstrate command of standard capitalization, punctuation, and spelling
	Where's the Comma? p. 167	Group activity	**L.6.2** Demonstrate command of standard capitalization, punctuation, and spelling
	Pause Accordingly, p. 167	Morning message	**SL.6.1** Engage in collaborative discussions **L.6.2** Demonstrate command of standard capitalization, punctuation, and spelling
Fact vs. fiction	Fact or Fiction, p. 141	Group activity	**RI.6.1** Cite textual evidence **W.6.9** Draw evidence from literary or informational texts **SL.6.4** Present findings; use appropriate eye contact/volume **RH.6–8.8** Distinguish among fact, opinion, and reasoned judgment in a text
Figurative language	Go Figure, p. 142	Group activity	**RL.6.4** Determine meaning of words and phrases, including figurative and connotative meanings **SL.6.1** Engage in collaborative discussions **L.6.4** Determine or clarify word meanings **L.6.5** Understand figurative language, word relationships, and nuances in meaning
	Worlds Apart? p. 150	Morning message	**RI.6.1** Cite textual evidence **RI.6.4** Determine meaning of words in text **W.6.4** Produce clear and coherent writing **SL.6.1** Engage in collaborative discussions
Idioms	Idiomatic Handshakes, p. 131	Greeting	**RL.6.4** Determine meaning of words and phrases, including figurative and connotative meanings **SL.6.4** Use appropriate eye contact and adequate volume **L.6.5** Understand figurative language, word relationships, and nuances in meaning
Main idea	Headline News, p. 135	Sharing	**RI.6.2** Determine a central idea and provide a summary **W.6.4** Produce clear and coherent writing **SL.6.1** Engage in collaborative discussions
Narrative	What's Your Perspective? p. 148	Morning message	**RL.6.5** Analyze how sentence, chapter, scene, or stanza fits into the overall structure **RI.6.3** Analyze how individual, event, or idea is introduced, illustrated, and elaborated **W.6.9** Draw evidence from literary or informational texts **SL.6.1** Engage in collaborative discussions

Language Arts Content	Activity Title & Page	Morning Meeting Component	Common Core Standards
Onomatopoeia	Chugga-Chugga, p. 169	Greeting	**SL.6.1b** Follow discussion rules
	Bing Bang Boom, p. 169	Sharing	**SL.6.1** Engage in collaborative discussions **L.6.5** Understand figurative language, word relationships, and nuances in meaning
	The Onomatopoeia Machine, p. 169	Group activity	**SL.6.1** Engage in collaborative discussions **SL.6.6** Adapt speech to a variety of contexts and tasks **L.6.5** Understand figurative language, word relationships, and nuances in meaning
	A Melody of Sounds! p. 169	Morning message	**L.6.5** Understand figurative language, word relationships, and nuances in meaning
Opinions	Lend Me Your Ear, p. 136	Sharing/ group activity combination	**RI.6.8** Trace and evaluate the argument in a text **W.6.1** Write arguments to support claims with reasons and evidence **SL.6.1** Engage in collaborative discussions **SL.6.3** Delineate a speaker's argument
Persuasive writing	Creating Commercials, p. 140	Group activity	**W.6.4** Produce clear and coherent writing **SL.6.1** Engage in collaborative discussions **SL.6.5** Include multimedia components and visual displays in presentations
	Finish This, p. 146	Morning message	**RI.6.6** Determine author's point of view and explain how it is conveyed **W.6.1** Write arguments to support claims with reasons and evidence **W.6.1e** Provide a concluding statement or section **SL.6.1** Engage in collaborative discussions
Point of view	Picture This, p. 137	Sharing	**RI.6.6** Determine author's point of view and explain how it is conveyed **RI.6.7** Integrate information in different media or formats **SL.6.2** Interpret information presented in diverse media **SL.6.5** Include multimedia components and visual displays in presentations **RH.6–8.7** Integrate visual and other information in print and digital texts
Reading comprehension	In the Voice Of, p. 132	Greeting	**SL.6.4** Use appropriate eye contact and adequate volume **SL.6.6** Adapt speech to a variety of contexts and tasks

Language Arts Content	Activity Title & Page	Morning Meeting Component	Common Core Standards
Story elements	On the Case, p. 165	Greeting	**SL.6.1b** Follow discussion rules
	Mysterious Experience, p. 165	Sharing	**SL.6.1** Engage in collaborative discussions **SL.6.4** Present claims and findings orally
	Mystery Winker, p. 165	Group activity	None
	Sneaking Suspicion, p. 165	Morning message	**SL.6.1** Engage in collaborative discussions **SL.6.4** Present claims and findings orally
Themes	Thinking Themes, p. 134	Greeting/ sharing combination	**RL.6.2** Determine theme/central idea of a text **RL.6.9** Compare and contrast texts **W.6.4** Produce clear and coherent writing **SL.6.1** Engage in collaborative discussions
Topic-related ideas	List and Tell, p. 147	Morning message	**W.6.2a** Introduce a topic and use organizing strategies **W.6.7** Conduct short research projects **SL.6.1** Engage in collaborative discussions **RH.6–8.1** Cite specific textual evidence to support analysis
Visual information	What's Your Point? p. 149	Morning message	**RI.6.7** Integrate information in different media or formats **SL.6.1a** Come to discussions prepared **SL.6.5** Include multimedia components and visual displays in presentations **RH.6–8.5** Describe how a text presents information **RH.6–8.7** Integrate visual and other information in print and digital texts
Vocabulary	Quadrilateral Quandary, p. 144	Group activity	**L.6.4b** Use Greek/Latin affixes and roots as clues to word meaning **L.6.5** Understand figurative language, word relationships, and nuances in meaning **L.6.6** Accurately use academic and domain-specific words

Kindergarten

Reading: Literature

RL.K.1 With prompting and support, ask and answer questions about key details in a text.
- *Book Share (Sharing)*, p. 16

RL.K.6 With prompting and support, name the author and illustrator of a story and define the role of each in telling the story.
- *Author? Illustrator? You Decide (Sharing)*, p. 15

RL.K.10 Actively engage in group reading activities with purpose and understanding.
- *Book Share (Sharing)*, p. 16
- *Reading Rates (Group activity)*, p. 155

Reading: Informational Text

RI.K.1 With prompting and support, ask and answer questions about key details in a text
- *Fountain of Knowledge (Greeting)*, p. 157
- *News Anchor Antics (Group activity)*, p. 157
- *Nifty Nonfiction (Sharing)*, p. 157

RI.K.5 Identify the front cover, back cover, and title page of a book.
- *The Bookey Pokey (Group activity)*, p. 24

RI.K.10 Actively engage in group reading activities with purpose and understanding.
- *A Capital Idea (Morning message)*, p. 27
- *Give Me Space (Morning message*, p. 28

- *Phoneme Fun (Morning message)*, p. 29
- *Punctuation Play (Morning message)*, p. 155
- *Typewriter (Morning message)*, p. 30

Reading: Foundational Skills

RF.K.1 Demonstrate understanding of the organization and basic features of print.
- *The Bookey Pokey (Group activity)*, p. 24
- *Hey Readers (Greeting)*, p. 12
- *Reading Rates (Group activity)*, p. 155

RF.K.1a Follow words from left to right, top to bottom, and page by page.
- *A Capital Idea (Morning message)*, p. 27
- *Give Me Space (Morning message)*, p. 28
- *Hey Readers (Greeting)*, p. 12
- *Phoneme Fun (Morning message)*, p. 29
- *Typewriter (Morning message)*, p. 30

RF.K.1b Recognize that spoken words are represented in written language by specific sequences of letters.
- *Set Your Sights on a Word (Greeting)*, p. 13
- *What's That Sound? (Group activity)*, p. 26

RF.K.1c Understand that words are separated by spaces in print.
- *Give Me Space (Morning message)*, p. 28

RF.K.1d Recognize upper- and lowercase letters of the alphabet.
- *Everything's in Order (Greeting)*, p. 11
- *If Your Letter's on the Card (Group activity)*, p. 20

RF.K.2 Demonstrate understanding of spoken words, syllables, and sounds (phonemes).
- *Hey Readers (Greeting)*, p. 12
- *Phoneme Fun (Morning message)*, p. 29

RF.K.2a Recognize and produce rhyming words.
- *1, 2, 3, Rhyme With Me (Group activity)*, p. 19

RF.K.2b Count, pronounce, blend, and segment syllables in spoken words.
- *Hickety Pickety Bumble Bee (Greeting)*, p. 153
- *Syllable Count (Morning message)*, p. 153
- *Syllable Drama (Group activity)*, p. 153
- *Syllables in Names (Sharing)*, p. 153

RF.K.2d Isolate and pronounce the initial, medial vowel, and final sounds (phonemes) in three-phoneme (consonant-vowel-consonant, or CVC) words. (This does not include CVCs ending with /l/, /r/, or /x/.)
- *The Long and Short of It (Group activity)*, p. 25
- *What's That Sound? (Group activity)*, p. 26

***Note: Because this book is intended not as a curriculum, but as a supplement to whatever curriculum you're using, it does not address every Common Core standard.*

203

Language

L.K.1a Print many upper- and lower-case letters.
- *A Capital Idea (Morning message)*, p. 27
- *Everything's in Order (Greeting)*, p. 11
- *If Your Letter's on the Card (Group activity)*, p. 20

L.K.1b Use frequently occurring nouns and verbs.
- *One Is Never Enough (Group activity)*, p. 23

L.K.1c Form regular plural nouns orally by adding /s/ or /es/.
- *One Is Never Enough (Group activity)*, p. 23

L.K.1d Understand and use question words (who, what, where, when, why, how).
- *Author? Illustrator? You Decide (Sharing)*, p. 15
- *Book Share (Sharing)*, p. 16

- *Reading Inquiry (Sharing)*, p. 17
- *That's the Point! (Greeting)*, p. 14

L.K.1f Produce and expand complete sentence in shared language activities.
- *I See (Group activity)*, p. 21
- *Reading Inquiry (Sharing)*, p. 17
- *Syllables in Names (Sharing)*, p. 153

L.K.2a Capitalize the first word in a sentence and the pronoun I.
- *A Capital Idea (Morning message)*, p. 27

L.K.2b Recognize and name end punctuation.
- *A Capital Idea (Morning message)*, p. 27
- *Punctuation Play (Morning message)*, p. 155
- *That's the point! (Greeting)*, p. 14

L.K.2d Spell simple words phonetically, drawing on knowledge of sound-letter relationships.
- *Phoneme Fun (Morning message)*, p. 29

L.K.4 Determine or clarify the meaning of unknown and multiple-meaning words and phrases based on kindergarten reading and content.
- *Syllable Drama (Group activity)*, p. 153

L.K.5b Demonstrate understanding of frequently occurring verbs and adjectives by relating them to their opposites (antonyms).
- *Let's All Do the Opposite (Group activity)*, p. 22

L.K.5c Identify real-life connections between words and their use.
- *I See (Group activity)*, p. 21

L.K.6 Use words and phrases acquired through conversations, reading and being read to, and responding to texts.
- *Let's All Do the Opposite (Group activity)*, p. 22
- *Let's Get Emotional (Greeting)*, p. 155

First Grade

Reading: Literature

RL.1.3 Describe characters, settings, and major events in a story, using key details.
- *Are You Curious, George? (Greeting)*, p. 31
- *Character Comparisons (Sharing)*, p. 35

RL.1.4 Identify words and phrases in stories or poems that suggest feelings or appeal to the senses.
- *Lazy Mary (Group activity)*, p. 44

RL.1.6 Identify who is telling the story at various points in a text.
- *Lazy Mary (Group activity)*, p. 44

RL.1.7 Use illustrations and details in a story to describe its characters, setting, or events.
- *Are You Curious, George? (Greeting)*, p. 31
- *My Son John (Group activity)*, p. 45

RL.1.9 Compare and contrast the adventures and experiences of characters in stories.
- *Character Comparisons (Sharing)*, p. 35
- *Lazy Mary (Group activity)*, p. 44

RL.1.10 With prompting and support, read prose and poetry of appropriate complexity for grade 1.
- *My Son John (Group activity)*, p. 45
- *Reading Rates (Group activity)*, p. 155

Reading: Informational Text

RI.1.1 Ask and answer questions about key details in a text.
- *Fact Finding (Sharing)*, p. 36
- *Fountain of Knowledge (Greeting)*, p. 157
- *News Anchor Antics (Group activity)*, p. 157
- *Nifty Nonfiction (Sharing)*, p. 157

RI.1.2 Identify the main topic and retell key details of a text.
- *Fact Finding (Sharing)*, p. 36

RI.1.4 Ask and answer questions to help determine or clarify the meaning of words and phrases in a text.
- *What Do You Mean? (Morning message)*, p. 50

RI.1.5 Know and use various text features to locate key facts or information in a text.
- *Fact Finding (Sharing)*, p. 36
- *Greetings, Digraph Detectives (Morning message)*, p. 48

RI.1.10 With prompting and support, read informational texts appropriately complex for grade 1.
- *Punctuation Play (Morning message)*, p. 155

Reading: Foundational Skills

RF.1.1a Recognize the distinguishing features of a sentence.

- *Sentence Structure Models (Morning message)*, p. 49

RF.1.2 Demonstrate understanding of spoken words, syllables, and sounds (phonemes).

- *Final-E Decoded (Greeting)*, p. 32
- *Hickety Pickety Bumble Bee (Greeting)*, p. 153
- *Syllable Count (Morning message)*, p. 153
- *Syllable Drama (Group activity)*, p. 153
- *Syllables in Names (Sharing)*, p. 153

RF.1.2b Orally produce single-syllable words by blending sounds (phonemes), including consonant blends.

- *Greetings, Digraph Detectives (Morning message)*, p. 48

RF.1.3 Know and apply grade-level phonics and word analysis skills in decoding words.

- *Just Say the Word (Group activity)*, p. 43

RF.1.3a Know spelling-sound correspondences for common consonant digraphs.

- *Greetings, Digraph Detectives (Morning message)*, p. 48

RF.1.3b Decode regularly spelled one-syllable words.

- *Final-E Decoded (Greeting)*, p. 32

RF.1.3c Know final -e and common vowel team conventions for representing long vowel sounds.

- *Final-E Decoded (Greeting)*, p. 32

RF.1.3d Use knowledge that every syllable must have a vowel sound to determine the number of syllables in a printed word.

- *Syllable Count (Morning message)*, p. 153
- *Syllable Drama (Group activity)*, p. 153

RF.1.3g Recognize and read grade-appropriate irregularly spelled words.

- *Just say the Word (Group activity)*, p. 43
- *Step and Spell (Group activity)*, p. 159
- *What's the Word? (Morning message)*, p. 159

RF.1.4 Read with sufficient accuracy and fluency to support comprehension.

- *Lazy Mary (Group activity)*, p. 44
- *Syllable Count (Morning message)*, p. 153

RF.1.4a Read grade-level text with purpose and understanding.

- *Have I Got a Preposition for You! (Group activity)*, p. 40

RF.1.4b Read grade-level text orally with accuracy, appropriate rate, and expression on successive readings.

- *Reading Rates (Group activity)*, p. 155
- *Punctuation Play (Morning message)*, p. 155
- *What's the Word? (Morning message)*, p. 159

RF.1.4c Use context to confirm or self-correct word recognition and understanding, rereading as necessary.

- *Shades of Meaning (Group activity)*, p. 46

Writing

W.1.1 Write opinion pieces in which they introduce the topic or name the book they are writing about, state an opinion, supply a reason for the opinion, and provide some sense of closure.

- *Are You Curious, George? (Greeting)*, p. 31
- *Character Comparisons (Sharing)*, p. 35
- *Proud Publishers (Sharing)*, p. 37

W.1.2 Write informative/explanatory texts in which they name a topic,

supply some facts about the topic, and provide some sense of closure.

- *Fountain of Knowledge (Greeting)*, p. 157
- *News Anchor Antics (Group activity)*, p. 157
- *Nifty Nonfiction (Sharing)*, p. 157

W.1.3 Write narratives in which they recount two or more appropriately sequenced events, include some details regarding what happened, use temporal words to signal event order, and provide some sense of closure.

- *First, Next, Last (Group activity)*, p. 39
- *If You're Jovial and You Know It (Group activity)*, p. 41
- *That's Not Nellie's (Greeting)*, p. 34

W.1.6 With guidance and support from adults, use a variety of digital tools to produce and publish writing, including in collaboration with peers.

- *Have I Got a Preposition for You! (Group activity)*, p. 40

W.1.7 Participate in shared research and writing projects.

- *Fact Finding (Sharing)*, p. 36
- *First, Next, Last (Group activity)*, p. 39
- *Me, Myself, and I (Greeting)*, p. 33

W.1.8 With guidance and support from adults, recall information from experiences or gather information from provided sources to answer a question.

- *Lazy Mary (Group activity)*, p. 44
- *My Son John (Group activity)*, p. 45
- *Writing Preview (Morning message)*, p. 157

Speaking and Listening

SL.1.1 Participate in collaborative conversations with diverse partners about grade 1 topics and texts with peers and adults in small and larger groups.

- *Fact Finding (Sharing)*, p. 36
- *Fluency Matters (Sharing)*, p. 155
- *Fountain of Knowledge (Greeting)*, p. 157

L.1.5d Distinguish shades of meaning among verbs differing in manner and adjectives differing in intensity by defining or choosing them or by acting out the meanings.

- *If You're Jovial and You Know It (Group activity)*, p. 41
- *Shades of Meaning (Group activity)*, p. 46

L.1.6 Use words and phrases acquired through conversations, reading and being read to, and responding to texts, including using frequently occurring conjunctions to signal simple relationships.

- *Have I Got a Preposition for You! (Group activity)*, p. 40
- *I'm Thinking Of (Group activity)*, p. 42

- *Let's Get Emotional (Greeting)*, p. 155
- *Me, Myself, and I (Greeting)*, p. 33
- *Proud Publishers (Sharing)*, p. 37
- *Shades of Meaning (Group activity)*, p. 46

Second Grade

Reading: Literature

RL.2.1 Ask and answer such questions as who, what, where, when, why, and how to demonstrate understanding of key details in a text.

- *Question Quest (Morning meeting)*, p. 68
- *ReACT! (Group activity)*, p. 63
- *Readers Recommend (Sharing)*, p. 57

RL.2.2 Recount stories, including fables and folktales from diverse cultures, and determine their central message, lesson, or moral.

- *Just Say Venn! (Morning message)*, p. 66

RL.2.3 Describe how characters in a story respond to major events and challenges.

- *Commonalities (Group activity)*, p. 60
- *ReACT! (Group activity)*, p. 63
- *What a Character! (Group activity)*, p. 64

RL.2.6 Acknowledge differences in the points of view of characters, including by speaking in a different voice for each character when reading dialogue aloud.

- *Commonalities (Group activity)*, p. 60
- *What a Character! (Group activity)*, p. 64

RL.2.7 Use information gained from the illustrations and words in a print or digital text to demonstrate under-

standing of its characters, setting, or plot.

- *Commonalities (Group activity)*, p. 60
- *Question Quest (Morning message)*, p. 68
- *ReACT! (Group activity)*, p. 63
- *Worth a Thousand Words (Morning message)*, p. 70

RL.2.9 Compare and contrast two or more versions of the same story by different authors or from different cultures.

- *Just Say Venn! (Morning message)*, p. 66

RL.2.10 By the end of the year, read and comprehend literature, including stories and poetry, in the grades 2–3 text complexity band proficiently, with scaffolding as needed at the high end of the range.

- *Reading Rates (Group activity)*, p. 155

Reading: Informational Text

RI.2.1 Ask and answer such questions as who, what, where, when, why, and how to demonstrate understanding of key details in a text.

- *Fountain of Knowledge (Greeting)*, p. 157
- *News Anchor Antics (Group activity)*, p. 157
- *Nifty Nonfiction (Sharing)*, p. 157

RI.2.2 Identify the main topic of a multiparagraph text as well as the

focus of specific paragraphs within the text.

- *What's It All About? (Morning message)*, p. 69

RI.2.5 Know and use various text features to locate key facts or information in a text efficiently.

- *Heading Hello (Greeting)*, p. 52

RI.2.7 Explain how specific images contribute to and clarify a text.

- *Worth a Thousand Words (Morning message)*, p. 70

RI.2.8 Describe how reasons support specific points the author makes in a text.

- *What's It All About? (Morning message)*, p. 69

RI.2.10 By the end of year, read and comprehend informational texts, including history/social studies, science, and technical texts, in the grades 2–3 text complexity band proficiently, with scaffolding as needed at the high end of the range.

- *Punctuation Play (Morning message)*, p. 155

Reading: Foundational Skills

RF.2.3 Know and apply grade-level phonics and word analysis skills in decoding words.

- *Compound Charades (Group activity)*, p. 61
- *Irregular Plural Hello (Greeting)*, p. 54

- *Syllable Hunt (Morning message)*, p. 67
- *Syllable Sharing (Sharing)*, p. 58

RF.2.3a Distinguish long and short vowels when reading regularly spelled one-syllable words.
- *What's in a Name? (Greeting)*, p. 55

RF.2.3b Know spelling-sound correspondences for additional common vowel teams.
- *What's in a Name? (Greeting)*, p. 55

RF.2.3c Decode regularly spelled two-syllable words with long vowels.
- *Syllable Hunt (Morning message)*, p. 67

RF.2.3f Recognize and read grade-appropriate irregularly spelled words.
- *Step and Spell (Group activity)*, p. 159
- *What's the Word? (Morning message)*, p. 159

RF.2.4 Read with sufficient accuracy and fluency to support comprehension.
- *In the Manner of the Adverb (Greeting)*, p. 53
- *Just Say Venn! (Morning message)*, p. 66

RF.2.4b Read grade-level text orally with accuracy, appropriate rate, and expression on successive readings.
- *Collective Nouns (Morning message)*, p. 161
- *Emphatic Exclamations (Greeting)*, p. 51
- *Punctuation Play (Morning message)*, p. 155
- *Reading Rates (Group activity)*, p. 155
- *What's the Word? (Morning message)*, p. 159

RF.2.4c Use context to confirm or self-correct word recognition and understanding, rereading as necessary.
- *Question Quest (Morning message)*, p. 68

Writing

W.2.1 Write opinion pieces in which they introduce the topic or book they are writing about, state an opinion, supply reasons that support the opinion, use linking words to connect opinion and reasons, and provide a concluding statement or section.
- *Readers Recommend (Sharing)*, p. 57
- *Would You Rather? (Group activity)*, p. 65

W.2.2 Write informative/explanatory texts in which they introduce a topic, use facts and definitions to develop points, and provide a concluding statement or section.
- *Fountain of Knowledge (Greeting)*, p. 157
- *News Anchor Antics (Group activity)*, p. 157
- *Nifty Nonfiction (Sharing)*, p. 157

W.2.3 Write narratives in which they recount a well-elaborated event or short sequence of events, include details to describe actions, thoughts, and feelings, use temporal words to signal event order, and provide a sense of closure.
- *It's All in the Details (Sharing)*, p. 56

W.2.5 With guidance and support from adults and peers, focus on a topic and strengthen writing as needed by revising and editing.
- *Readers Recommend (Sharing)*, p. 57

W.2.8 Recall information from experiences or gather information from provided sources to answer a question.
- *Describe It! (Group activity)*, p. 62
- *It's All in the Details (Sharing)*, p. 56
- *ReACT! (Group activity)*, p. 63
- *What a Character! (Group activity)*, p. 64
- *What's It All About? (Morning message)*, p. 69
- *Writing Preview (Morning message)*, p. 157

Speaking and Listening

SL.2.1 Participate in collaborative conversations with diverse partners about grade 2 topics and texts with peers and adults in small and larger groups.
- *Collective Nouns (Morning message)*, p. 161
- *Commonalities (Group activity)*, p. 60
- *Fluency Matters (Sharing)*, p. 155
- *Fountain of Knowledge (Greeting)*, p. 157
- *Gabbing About Groups (Sharing)*, p. 161
- *Irregular Thinking (Sharing)*, p. 159
- *News Anchor Antics (Group activity)*, p. 157
- *Nifty Nonfiction (Sharing)*, p. 157
- *Readers Recommend (Sharing)*, p. 57
- *Worth a Thousand Words (Morning message)*, p. 70
- *Writing Preview (Morning message)*, p. 157

SL.2.1a Follow agreed-upon rules for discussions.
- *A Clutch of Clues (Group activity)*, p. 161
- *Describe It! (Group activity)*, p. 62
- *Hi, Group! (Greeting)*, p. 161
- *Syllable Sharing (Sharing)*, p. 58

SL.2.1b Build on others' talk in conversations by linking comments to the remarks of others.
- *Describe It! (Group activity)*, p. 62

SL.2.1c Ask for clarification and further explanation as needed about the topic and texts under discussion..
- *Would You Rather? (Group activity)*, p. 65

SL.2.2 Recount or describe key ideas or details from a text read aloud or information presented orally or through other media.
- *Just Say Venn! (Morning message)*, p. 66
- *Question Quest (Morning message)*, p. 68
- *What's It All About? (Morning message)*, p. 69

SL.2.3 Ask and answer questions about what a speaker says in order to clarify comprehension, gather additional information, or deepen understanding of a topic or issue.
- *It's All in the Details (Sharing)*, p. 56
- *Readers Recommend (Sharing)*, p. 57
- *Worth a Thousand Words (Morning message)*, p. 70
- *Would You Rather? (Group activity)*, p. 65

SL.2.4 Tell a story or recount an experience with appropriate facts and relevant, descriptive details, speaking audibly in coherent sentences.
- *It's All in the Details (Sharing)*, p. 56

SL.2.6 Produce complete sentences when appropriate to task and situation in order to provide requested detail or clarification.
- *Commonalities (Group activity)*, p. 60
- *Describe It! (Group activity)*, p. 62
- *Fluency Matters (Sharing)*, p. 155
- *It's All in the Details (Sharing)*, p. 56
- *Let's Get Emotional (Greeting)*, p. 155

Language

L.2.1 Demonstrate command of the conventions of standard English grammar and usage when writing or speaking.
- *Alphabet Aerobics (Group activity)*, p. 59
- *Irregular Plural Hello (Greeting)*, p. 54

L.2.1a Use collective nouns.
- *A Clutch of Clues (Group activity)*, p. 161
- *Collective Nouns (Morning message)*, p. 161
- *Gabbing About Groups (Sharing)*, p. 161
- *Hi, Group! (Greeting)*, p. 161

L.2.1b Form and use frequently occurring irregular plural nouns.
- *Irregular Plural Hello (Greeting)*, p. 54

L.2.1e Use adjectives and adverbs, and choose between them depending on what is to be modified.
- *In the Manner of the Adverb (Greeting)*, p. 53

L.2.1f Produce, expand, and rearrange complete simple and compound sentences.
- *Irregular Thinking (Sharing)*, p. 159

L.2.2 Demonstrate command of the conventions of standard English capitalization, punctuation, and spelling when writing.
- *Alphabet Aerobics (Group activity)*, p. 59
- *Emphatic Exclamations (Greeting)*, p. 51

L.2.2d Generalize learned spelling patterns when writing words.
- *Irregular Plural Hello (Greeting)*, p. 54
- *Step and Spell (Group activity)*, p. 159
- *Syllable Hunt (Morning message)*, p. 67

L.2.2e Consult reference materials, including beginning dictionaries, as needed to check and correct spellings.
- *Heading Hello (Greeting)*, p. 52

L.2.3 Use knowledge of language and its conventions when writing, speaking, reading, or listening.
- *Emphatic Exclamations (Greeting)*, p. 51
- *Punctuation Play (Morning message)*, p. 155

L.2.4d Use knowledge of the meaning of individual words to predict the meaning of compound words.
- *Compound Charades (Group activity)*, p. 61

L.2.5 Demonstrate understanding of word relationships and nuances in word meanings.
- *In the Manner of the Adverb (Greeting)*, p. 53

L.2.5a Identify real-life connections between words and their use.
- *A Clutch of Clues (Group activity)*, p. 161
- *Collective Nouns (Morning message)*, p. 161
- *Gabbing About Groups (Sharing)*, p. 161
- *Hi, Group! (Greeting)*, p. 161
- *Let's Get Emotional (Greeting)*, p. 155

L.2.6 Use words and phrases acquired through conversations, reading and being read to, and responding to texts, including using adjectives and adverbs to describe.
- *Compound Charades (Group activity)*, p. 61

Third Grade

Reading: Literature

RL.3.1 Ask and answer questions to demonstrate understanding of a text, referring explicitly to the text as the basis for the answers.

- *Character Corners (Group activity)*, p. 78
- *Fountain of Knowledge (Greeting)*, p. 157
- *Radio Hour (Group activity)*, p. 84
- *What's the Motive? (Morning message)*, p. 89

RL.3.3 Describe characters in a story (e.g., their traits, motivations, or feelings) and explain how their actions contribute to the sequence of events.

- *Character Corners (Group activity)*, p. 78
- *How Are You Feeling Today? (Greeting)*, p. 72
- *It's How You Do It (Group activity)*, p. 82
- *What's the Motive? (Morning message)*, p. 89

RL.3.4 Determine the meaning of words and phrases as they are used in a text, distinguishing literal from nonliteral language.

- *Idiom-ania (Group activity)*, p. 80

RL.3.5 Refer to parts of stories, dramas, and poems when writing or speaking about a text, using terms such as chapter, scene, and stanza; describe how each successive part builds on earlier sections.

- *Lively Limericks (Group activity)*, p. 83

Reading: Informational Text

RI.3.1 Ask and answer questions to demonstrate understanding of a text, referring explicitly to the text as the basis for the answers.

- *Big Ideas, Small Details (Morning message)*, p. 86
- *Inquiring Minds (Group activity)*, p. 81

- *News Anchor Antics (Group activity)*, p. 157
- *Nifty Nonfiction (Sharing)*, p. 157

RI.3.2 Determine the main idea of a text; recount the key details and explain how they support the main idea.

- *Big Ideas, Small Details (Morning message)*, p. 86
- *State Your Opinion (Sharing and group activity)*, p. 76

RI.3.4 Determine the meaning of general academic and domain-specific words and phrases in a text relevant to a grade 3 topic or subject area.

- *Wonderful Words (Morning message)*, p. 90

RI.3.5 Use text features and search tools to locate information relevant to a given topic efficiently.

- *Five-Minute Sleuths (Group activity)*, p. 84

RI.3.6 Distinguish their own point of view from that of the author of a text.

- *State Your Opinion (Sharing and group activity)*, p. 76

RI.3.7 Use information gained from illustrations and the words in a text to demonstrate understanding of the text.

- *Five-Minute Sleuths (Group activity)*, p. 84
- *Inquiring Minds (Group activity)*, p. 81

Reading: Foundational Skills

RF.3.3 Know and apply grade-level phonics and word analysis skills in decoding words.

- *Comparatively Speaking (Group activity)*, p. 71
- *Multisyllabic Madness (Morning message)*, p. 88
- *The Affix Effect (Group activity)*, p. 85

RF.3.3c Decode multisyllable words.

- *Multisyllabic Madness (Morning message)*, p. 88

RF.3.3d Read grade-appropriate irregularly spelled words.

- *Step and Spell (Group activity)*, p. 159
- *What's the Word? (Morning message)*, p. 159

RF.3.4 Read with sufficient accuracy and fluency to support comprehension.

- *Fill In the Modifier (Morning message)*, p. 163

RF.3.4a Read grade-level text with purpose and understanding.

- *Inquiring Minds (Group activity)*, p. 81

RF.3.4b Read grade-level prose and poetry orally with accuracy, appropriate rate, and expression on successive readings.

- *Collective Nouns (Morning message)*, p. 161
- *Comma Hunt (Morning message)*, p. 87
- *Lively Limericks (Group activity)*, p. 83
- *Radio Hour (Group activity)*, p. 84
- *What's the Word? (Morning message)*, p. 159

RF.3.4c Use context to confirm or self-correct word recognition and understanding, rereading as necessary.

- *Wonderful Words (Morning message)*, p. 90
- *Idiom-ania (Group activity)*, p. 80

Writing

W.3.1 Write opinion pieces on topics or texts, supporting a point of view with reasons.

- *If I Were (Sharing)*, p. 74

W.3.1a Introduce the topic or text they are writing about, state an opinion, and create an organizational structure that lists reasons.
- *If I Were (Sharing)*, p. 74

W.3.1b Provide reasons that support the opinion.
- *If I Were (Sharing)*, p. 74

W.3.1c Use linking words and phrases to connect opinion and reasons.
- *If I Were (Sharing)*, p. 74

W.3.2 Write informative/explanatory texts to examine a topic and convey ideas and information clearly.
- *Fountain of Knowledge (Greeting)*, p. 157
- *News Anchor Antics (Group activity)*, p. 157
- *Nifty Nonfiction (Sharing)*, p. 157
- *Special Interest Sharing (Sharing)*, p. 75

W.3.3 Write narratives to develop real or imagined experiences or events using effective technique, descriptive details, and clear event sequences.
- *Weekend Focus (Sharing)*, p. 77

W.3.3c Use temporal words and phrases to signal event order.
- *Weekend Focus (Sharing)*, p. 77

W.3.4 With guidance and support from adults, produce writing in which development and organization are appropriate to task and purpose.
- *Lively Limericks (Group activity)*, p. 83

W.3.5 With guidance and support from peers and adults, develop and strengthen writing as needed by planning, revising, and editing.
- *Weekend Focus (Sharing)*, p. 77

W.3.7 Conduct short research projects that build knowledge about a topic.

- *Five-Minute Sleuths (Group activity)*, p. 84
- *Writing Preview (Morning message)*, p. 157

W.3.8 Recall information from experiences or gather information from print and digital sources; take brief notes on sources and sort evidence into provided categories.
- *Five-Minute Sleuths (Group activity)*, p. 84

Speaking and Listening

SL.3.1 Engage effectively in a range of collaborative discussions (one-on-one, in groups, and teacher-led) with diverse partners on grade 3 topics and texts, building on others' ideas and expressing their own clearly.
- *Collective Nouns (Morning message)*, p. 161
- *Fill In the Modifier (Morning message)*, p. 163
- *Fountain of Knowledge (Greeting)*, p. 157
- *Gabbing About Groups (Sharing)*, p. 161
- *Interview and Introduce (Greeting and sharing)*, p. 73
- *Irregular Thinking (Sharing)*, p. 159
- *It's How You Do It (Group activity)*, p. 82
- *Mysterious Experience (Sharing)*, p. 165
- *News Anchor Antics (Group activity)*, p. 157
- *Nifty Nonfiction (Sharing)*, p. 157
- *Radio Hour (Group activity)*, p. 84
- *Sneaking Suspicion (Morning message)*, p. 165
- *Special Interest Sharing (Sharing)*, p. 75
- *State Your Opinion (Sharing and group activity)*, p. 76
- *The Laughing Tissue (Group activity)*, p. 163
- *Why, Oh Why? (Sharing)*, p. 163

- *Writing Preview (Morning message)*, p. 157

SL.3.1a Come to discussions prepared, having read or studied required material; explicitly draw on that preparation and other information known about the topic to explore ideas under discussion.
- *Character Corners (Group activity)*, p. 78
- *Comma Hunt (Morning message)*, p. 87
- *What's the Motive? (Morning message)*, p. 89

SL.3.1b Follow agreed-upon rules for discussions.
- *A Clutch of Clues (Group activity)*, p. 161
- *Hi, Group! (Greeting)*, p. 161
- *On the Case (Greeting)*, p. 165
- *Show, Don't Tell (Greeting)*, p. 163

SL.3.1c Ask questions to check understanding of information presented, stay on topic, and link their comments to the remarks of others.
- *How Are You Feeling Today? (Greeting)*, p. 72
- *Inquiring Minds (Group activity)*, p. 81
- *Special Interest Sharing (Sharing)*, p. 75

SL.3.1d Explain their own ideas and understanding in light of the discussion.
- *If I Were (Sharing)*, p. 74
- *What's the Motive? (Morning message)*, p. 89

SL.3.2 Determine the main ideas and supporting details of a text read aloud or information presented in diverse media and formats, including visually, quantitatively, and orally.
- *Big Ideas, Small Details (Morning message)*, p. 86
- *State Your Opinion (Sharing and group activity)*, p. 76

SL.3.3 Ask and answer questions about information from a speaker, offering appropriate elaboration and detail.

- *How Are You Feeling Today? (Greeting)*, p. 72
- *Interview and Introduce (Greeting and sharing)*, p. 73
- *Special Interest Sharing (Sharing)*, p. 75

SL.3.4 Report on a topic or text, tell a story, or recount an experience with appropriate facts and relevant, descriptive details, speaking clearly at an understandable pace.

- *Five-Minute Sleuths (Group activity)*, p. 84
- *Mysterious Experience (Sharing)*, p. 165
- *Sneaking Suspicion (Morning message)*, p. 165
- *Special Interest Sharing (Sharing)*, p. 75
- *Weekend Focus (Sharing)*, p. 77

SL.3.5 Create engaging audio recordings of stories or poems that demonstrate fluid reading at an understandable pace; add visual displays when appropriate to emphasize or enhance certain facts or details.

- *Radio Hour (Group activity)*, p. 84

SL.3.6 Speak in complete sentences when appropriate to task and situation in order to provide requested detail or clarification.

- *Interview and Introduce (Greeting and sharing)*, p. 73

Language

L.3.1a Explain the function of nouns, pronouns, verbs, adjectives, and adverbs in general and their functions in particular sentences.

- *How Are You Feeling Today? (Greeting)*, p. 72
- *It's How You Do It (Group activity)*, p. 82
- *The Laughing Tissue (Group activity)*, p. 163

L.3.1b Form and use regular and irregular plural nouns.

- *A Clutch of Clues (Group activity)*, p. 161
- *Collective Nouns (Morning message)*, p. 161
- *Gabbing About Groups (Sharing)*, p. 161
- *Hi, Group! (Greeting)*, p. 161

L.3.1g Form and use comparative and superlative adjectives and adverbs, and choose between them depending on what is to be modified.

- *Comparatively Speaking (Greeting)*, p. 71

L.3.1i Produce simple, compound, and complex sentences.

- *Irregular Thinking (Sharing)*, p. 159

L.3.2 Demonstrate command of the conventions of standard English capitalization, punctuation, and spelling when writing.

- *Comma Hunt (Morning message)*, p. 87
- *Step and Spell (Group activity)*, p. 159

L.3.2c Use commas and quotation marks in dialogue.

- *Comma Hunt (Morning message)*, p. 87

L.3.3a Choose words and phrases for effect.

- *Fill In the Modifier (Morning message)*, p. 163

L.3.4 Determine or clarify the meaning of unknown and multiple-meaning words and phrases based on grade 3 reading and content, choosing flexibly from a range of strategies.

- *The Affix Effect (Group activity)*, p. 85

L.3.4a Use sentence-level context as a clue to the meaning of a word or phrase.

- *Wonderful Words (Morning message)*, p. 90

L.3.4b Determine the meaning of the new word formed when a known affix is added to a known word.

- *The Affix Effect (Group activity)*, p. 85

L.3.5a Distinguish the literal and nonliteral meanings of words and phrases in context.

- *Idiom-ania (Group activity)*, p. 80

L.3.5b Identify real-life connections between words and their use.

- *A Clutch of Clues (Group activity)*, p. 161
- *Collective Nouns (Morning message)*, p. 161
- *Gabbing About Groups (Sharing)*, p. 161
- *Hi, Group! (Greeting)*, p. 161

Fourth Grade

Reading: Literature

RL.4.1 Refer to details and examples in a text when explaining what the text says explicitly and when drawing inferences from the text.
- *Answering As … (Sharing)*, p. 95
- *Spoken Duet (Group activity)*, p. 105

RL.4.2 Determine a theme of a story, drama, or poem from details in the text; summarize the text.
- *Spoken Duet (Group activity)*, p. 105

RL.4.3 Describe in depth a character, setting, or event in a story or drama, drawing on specific details in the text.
- *Answering As … (Sharing)*, p. 95
- *Author as Character (Sharing)*, p. 97
- *On My Back (Group activity)*, p. 101
- *What Are You Doing? (Greeting)*, p. 93

RL.4.4 Determine the meaning of words and phrases as they are used in a text, including those that allude to significant characters found in mythology.
- *Noticing Author's Craft (Sharing)*, p. 171

RL.4.5 Explain major differences between poems, drama, and prose, and refer to the structural elements of poems and drama when writing or speaking about a text.
- *Ten-Line Scene (Group activity)*, p. 106

RL.4.7 Make connections between the text of a story or drama and a visual or oral presentation of the text, identifying where each version reflects specific descriptions and directions in the text.
- *Ten-Line Scene (Group activity)*, p. 106

Reading: Informational Text

RI.4.4 Determine the meaning of general academic and domain-specific words or phrases in a text relevant to a grade 4 topic or subject area.

- *Sophisticated Synonyms (Morning message)*, p. 109

RI.4.5 Describe the overall structure of events, ideas, concepts, or information in a text or part of a text.
- *Precious Paragraphs (Morning message)*, p. 107

Reading: Foundational Skills

RF.4.4 Read with sufficient accuracy and fluency to support comprehension.
- *Fill In the Modifier (Morning message)*, p. 163
- *Sophisticated Synonyms (Morning message)*, p. 109
- *Spoken Duet (Group activity)*, p. 105

RF.4.4a Read grade-level text with purpose and understanding.
- *Book Talk (Group activity)*, p. 100

RF.4.4b Read grade-level prose and poetry orally with accuracy, appropriate rate, and expression on successive readings.
- *A Melody of Sounds! (Morning message)*, p. 169
- *Noticing Author's Craft (Sharing)*, p. 171
- *Problem Solvers to the Rescue (Morning message)*, p. 108

RF.4.4c Use context to confirm or self-correct word recognition and understanding, rereading as necessary.
- *Hi-Definition (Greeting)*, p. 91
- *Too Many Twos (Morning message)*, p. 110
- *On My Back (Group activity)*, p. 101

Writing

W.4.1 Write opinion pieces on topics or texts, supporting a point of view with reasons and information.
- *Problem Solvers to the Rescue (Morning message)*, p. 108

W.4.3 Write narratives to develop real or imagined experiences or events using effective technique, descriptive details, and clear event sequences.
- *A Time of Change (Sharing)*, p. 96
- *Of Utmost Importance (Sharing)*, p. 98
- *Precious Paragraphs (Morning message)*, p. 107

W.4.3a Orient the reader by establishing a situation and introducing a narrator and/or characters; organize an event sequence that unfolds naturally.
- *Author as Character (Sharing)*, p. 97

W.4.3b Use dialogue and description to develop experiences and events or show the responses of characters to situations.
- *Author as Character (Sharing)*, p. 97
- *What Are You Doing? (Greeting)*, p. 93

W.4.4 Produce clear and coherent writing in which the development and organization are appropriate to task, purpose, and audience.
- *Seconds to Respond (Sharing)*, p. 99
- *Spoken Duet (Group activity)*, p. 105
- *Ten-Line Scene (Group activity)*, p. 106
- *What's Your Scoop? (Greeting and sharing)*, p. 94

W.4.5 With guidance and support from peers and adults, develop and strengthen writing as needed by planning, revising, and editing.
- *Precious Paragraphs (Morning message)*, p. 107
- *Scrambled Sentence (Group activity)*, p. 103
- *Too Many Twos (Morning message)*, p. 110

W.4.7 Conduct short research projects that build knowledge through investigation of different aspects of a topic.
- *What's Your Scoop? (Greeting and sharing)*, p. 94

L.4.4a Use context as a clue to the meaning of a word or phrase.
- *Hi-Definition (Greeting)*, p. 91
- *On My Back (Group activity)*, p. 101

L.4.4b Use common, grade-appropriate Greek and Latin affixes and roots as clues to the meaning of a word.
- *The Root of It (Greeting)*, p. 92

L.4.5 Demonstrate understanding of figurative language, word relationships, and nuances in word meanings.
- *Alliterative Aloha (Greeting)*, p. 171
- *A Melody of Sounds! (Morning message)*, p. 169
- *Bing Bang Boom (Sharing)*, p. 169
- *Circling Sounds (Morning message)*, p. 171
- *Noticing Author's Craft (Sharing)*, p. 171
- *Say It! (Group activity)*, p. 102

- *Sophisticated Synonyms (Morning message)*, p. 109
- *The Onomatopoeia Machine (Group activity)*, p. 169

L.4.6 Acquire and use accurately grade-appropriate general academic and domain-specific words and phrases, including those that signal precise actions, emotions, or states of being and that are basic to a particular topic.
- *Alliterative Aloha (Greeting)*, p. 171

Fifth Grade

Reading: Literature

RL.5.1 Quote accurately from a text when explaining what the text says explicitly and when drawing inferences from the text.
- *Broadcast Views (Greeting and sharing)*, p. 112
- *Character Traits (Group activity)*, p. 121
- *Tell Me About It (Sharing)*, p. 118

RL.5.2 Determine a theme of a story, drama, or poem from details in the text, including how characters in a story or drama respond to challenges or how the speaker in a poem reflects upon a topic; summarize the text.
- *Human Slide Show (Group activity)*, p. 123

RL.5.3 Compare and contrast two or more characters, settings, or events in a story or drama, drawing on specific details in the text.
- *Cascading Characteristics (Group activity)*, p. 120

RL.5.4 Determine the meaning of words and phrases as they are used in a text, including figurative language such as metaphors and similes.
- *Noticing Author's Craft (Sharing)*, p. 171

RL.5.5 Explain how a series of chapters, scenes, or stanzas fits together to provide the overall structure of a particular story, drama, or poem.
- *Human Slide Show (Group activity)*, p. 123

Reading: Informational Text

RI.5.1 Quote accurately from a text when explaining what the text says explicitly and when drawing inferences from the text.
- *Character Traits (Group activity)*, p. 121
- *Tell Me About It (Sharing)*, p. 118

RI.5.2 Determine two or more main ideas of a text and explain how they are supported by key details; summarize the text.
- *Take a Stand (Sharing)*, p. 117

RI.5.3 Explain the relationships or interactions between two or more individuals, events, ideas, or concepts in a historical, scientific, or technical text based on specific information in the text.
- *Cascading Characteristics (Group activity)*, p. 120

RI.5.10 By the end of the year, read and comprehend informational texts, including history/social studies, science, and technical texts, at

the high end of the grades 4–5 text complexity band independently and proficiently.
- *Consult as Needed (Morning message)*, p. 127

Reading: Foundational Skills

RF.5.3 Know and apply grade-level phonics and word analysis skills in decoding words.
- *Witch Won? (Morning message)*, p. 130

RF.5.3a Use combined knowledge of all letter-sound correspondences, syllabication patterns, and morphology (e.g., roots and affixes) to read accurately unfamiliar multisyllabic words in context and out of context.
- *Eeek, It's a … (Group activity)*, p. 122
- *I'm Speaking Greek and Latin! (Greeting)*, p. 114

RF.5.4 Read with sufficient accuracy and fluency to support comprehension.
- *Character Traits (Group activity)*, p. 121
- *Check That Verb Past (Morning message)*, p. 126

RF.5.4a Read grade-level text with purpose and understanding.
- *Say What?! (Sharing)*, p. 116

RF.5.4b Read grade-level prose and poetry orally with accuracy, appropriate rate, and expression on successive readings.

- *A Melody of Sounds! (Morning message)*, p. 169
- *Consult as Needed (Morning message)*, p. 127
- *Human Slide Show (Group activity)*, p. 123
- *Noticing Author's Craft (Sharing)*, p. 171
- *Read. Rinse. Repeat. (Group activity)*, p. 125

RF.5.4c Use context to confirm or self-correct word recognition and understanding, rereading as necessary.

- *Where's That Thesaurus? (Morning message)*, p. 129

Writing

W.5.1 Write opinion pieces on topics or texts, supporting a point of view with reasons and information.

- *Take a Stand (Sharing)*, p. 117

W.5.3 Write narratives to develop real or imagined experiences or events using effective technique, descriptive details, and clear event sequences.

- *Check That Verb Past (Morning message)*, p. 126

W.5.4 Produce clear and coherent writing in which the development and organization are appropriate to task, purpose, and audience.

- *Broadcast Views (Greeting and sharing)*, p. 112
- *Tell Me About It (Sharing)*, p. 118

W.5.5 With guidance and support from peers and adults, develop and strengthen writing as needed by planning, revising, editing, rewriting, or trying a new approach.

- *Say What?! (Sharing)*, p. 116
- *Say What You Mean to Say (Morning message)*, p. 128

- *Where's That Thesaurus? (Morning message)*, p. 129
- *Witch Won? (Morning message)*, p. 130
- *You Don't Say (Sharing)*, p. 119

W.5.7 Conduct short research projects that use several sources to build knowledge through investigation of different aspects of a topic.

- *Say What?! (Sharing)*, p. 116

W.5.9 Draw evidence from literary or informational texts to support analysis, reflection, and research.

- *Cascading Characteristics (Group activity)*, p. 120

Speaking and Listening

SL.5.1 Engage effectively in a range of collaborative discussions (one-on-one, in groups, and teacher-led) with diverse partners on grade 5 topics and texts, building on others' ideas and expressing their own clearly.

- *Bing Bang Boom (Sharing)*, p. 169
- *Broadcast Views (Greeting and sharing)*, p. 112
- *Circling Sounds (Morning message)*, p. 171
- *Eeek, It's a … (Group activity)*, p. 122
- *Heeeeeeere's Johnny! (Greeting and sharing)*, p. 113
- *Mysterious Experience (Sharing)*, p. 165
- *Noticing Author's Craft (Sharing)*, p. 171
- *Pause Accordingly! (Morning message)*, p. 167
- *Read. Rinse. Repeat. (Group activity)*, p. 125
- *Sneaking Suspicion (Morning message)*, p. 165
- *Take a Stand (Sharing)*, p. 117
- *Tell Me About It (Sharing)*, p. 118
- *The Onomatopoeia Machine (Group activity)*, p. 169
- *Witch Won? (Morning message)*, p. 130
- *You Don't Say (Sharing)*, p. 119

SL.5.1a Come to discussions prepared, having read or studied required material; explicitly draw on that preparation and other information known about the topic to explore ideas under discussion.

- *Alliterative Aloha (Greeting)*, p. 171

SL.5.1b Follow agreed-upon rules for discussion and carry out assigned roles.

- *Blink 1-2-4 (Greeting)*, p. 111
- *Chugga-Chugga (Greeting)*, p. 169
- *On the Case (Greeting)*, p. 165
- *Say What You Mean to Say (Morning message)*, p. 128
- *You Can Call Me (Greeting)*, p. 115

SL.5.1c Pose and respond to questions by making comments that contribute to the discussion and elaborate on the remarks of others.

- *Consult as Needed (Morning message)*, p. 127
- *Say What?! (Sharing)*, p. 116

SL.5.4 Report on a topic or text or present an opinion, sequencing ideas logically and using appropriate facts and relevant, descriptive details to support main ideas or themes; speak clearly at an understandable pace.

- *Character Traits (Group activity)*, p. 121
- *Heeeeeeere's Johnny! (Greeting and sharing)*, p. 113
- *Mysterious Experience (Sharing)*, p. 165
- *Sneaking Suspicion (Morning message)*, p. 165
- *Take a Stand (Sharing)*, p. 117

SL.5.5 Include multimedia components (e.g., graphics, sound) and visual displays in presentations when appropriate to enhance the development of main ideas or themes.

- *Human Slide Show (Group activity)*, p. 123

Sixth Grade

Reading: Literature

RL.6.2 Determine a theme or central idea of a text and how it is conveyed through particular details; provide a summary of the text distinct from personal opinions or judgments.
- *Thinking Themes (Greeting and sharing)*, p. 134

RL.6.3 Describe how a particular story's or drama's plot unfolds in a series of episodes as well as how the characters respond or change as the plot moves toward a resolution.
- *Character Timeline (Group activity)*, p. 139
- *Mood Orchestra (Group activity)*, p. 143

RL.6.4 Determine the meaning of words and phrases as they are used in a text, including figurative and connotative meanings; analyze the impact of a specific word choice on meaning and tone.
- *Go Figure (Group Activity)*, p. 142
- *Idiomatic Handshakes (Greeting)*, p. 131
- *Noticing Author's Craft (Sharing)*, p. 171

RL.6.5 Analyze how a particular sentence, chapter, scene, or stanza fits into the overall structure of a text and contributes to the development of the theme, setting, or plot.
- *What's Your Perspective? (Morning message)*, p. 148

RL.6.9 Compare and contrast texts in different forms or genres (e.g., stories and poems; historical novels and fantasy stories) in terms of their approaches to similar themes and topics.
- *Thinking Themes (Greeting and sharing)*, p. 134

Reading: Informational Text

RI.6.1 Cite textual evidence to support analysis of what the text says explicitly as well as inferences drawn from the text.
- *Character Interrogation (Group activity)*, p. 138
- *Fact or Fiction (Group activity)*, p. 141
- *Worlds Apart? (Morning message)*, p. 150

RI.6.2 Determine a central idea of a text and how it is conveyed through particular details; provide a summary of the text distinct from personal opinions or judgments.
- *Headline News (Sharing)*, p. 135

RI.6.3 Analyze in detail how a key individual, event, or idea is introduced, illustrated, and elaborated in a text.
- *What's Your Perspective? (Morning message)*, p. 148

RI.6.4 Determine the meaning of words and phrases as they are used in a text, including figurative, connotative, and technical meanings.
- *Go Figure (Group activity)*, p. 142
- *Worlds Apart? (Morning message)*, p. 150

RI.6.6 Determine an author's point of view or purpose in a text and explain how it is conveyed in the text.
- *Finish This (Morning message)*, p. 146
- *Picture This (Sharing)*, p. 137

RI.6.7 Integrate information presented in different media or formats well as in words to develop a coherent understanding of a topic or issue.
- *Picture This (Sharing)*, p. 137
- *What's Your Point (Morning message)*, p. 149

RI.6.8 Trace and evaluate the argument and specific claims in a text, distinguishing claims that are supported by reasons and evidence from claims that are not.
- *Lend Me Your Ear (Sharing and group activity)*, p. 136

Writing

W.6.1 Write arguments to support claims with clear reasons and relevant evidence.
- *Finish This (Morning message)*, p. 146
- *Lend Me Your Ear (Sharing and group activity)*, p. 136

W.6.1e Provide a concluding statement or section that follows from the argument presented.
- *Finish This (Morning message)*, p. 146

W.6.2a Introduce a topic; organize ideas, concepts, and information, using strategies such as definition, classification, comparison/contrast, and cause/effect; include formatting, graphics, and multimedia when useful to aiding comprehension.
- *List and Tell (Morning message)*, p. 147

W.6.3 Write narratives to develop real or imagined experiences or events using effective technique, relevant descriptive details, and well-structured event sequences.
- *Mood Orchestra (Group activity)*, p. 143

W.6.3a Engage and orient the reader by establishing a context and introducing a narrator and/or characters; organize an event sequence that unfolds naturally and logically.
- *Superhero Greeting (Greeting)*, p. 133

W.6.3b Use narrative techniques, such as dialogue, pacing, and description, to develop experiences, events, and/or characters.
- *Superhero Greeting (Greeting)*, p. 133

Language

L.6.2 Demonstrate command of the conventions of standard English capitalization, punctuation, and spelling when writing.

- *Comma Commotion (Greeting)*, p. 167
- *My To-Do List (Sharing)*, p. 167
- *Pause Accordingly! (Morning message)*, p. 167
- *Where's the Comma? (Group activity)*, p. 167

L.6.2b Spell correctly.

- *Sound Symphony (Group activity)*, p. 145

L.6.3 Use knowledge of language and its conventions when writing, speaking, reading, or listening.

- *Sound Symphony (Group activity)*, p. 145

L.6.4 Determine or clarify the meaning of unknown and multiple-meaning words and phrases based on grade 6 reading and content, choosing flexibly from a range of strategies.

- *Go Figure (Group activity)*, p. 142
- *Sound Symphony (Group activity)*, p. 145

L.6.4b Use common, grade-appropriate Greek or Latin affixes and roots as clues to the meaning of a word.

- *Quadrilateral Quandary (Group activity)*, p. 144

L.6.5 Demonstrate understanding of figurative language, word relationships, and nuances in word meanings.

- *Alliterative Aloha (Greeting)*, p. 171
- *A Melody of Sounds! (Morning message)*, p. 169
- *Bing Bang Boom (Sharing)*, p. 169
- *Circling Sounds (Morning message)*, p. 171
- *Go Figure (Group activity)*, p. 142
- *Idiomatic Handshakes (Greeting)*, p. 131
- *Noticing Author's Craft (Sharing)*, p. 171
- *Quadrilateral Quandary (Group activity)*, p. 144
- *The Onomatopoeia Machine (Group activity)*, p. 169

L.6.6 Acquire and use accurately grade-appropriate general academic and domain-specific words and phrases; gather vocabulary knowledge when considering a word or phrase important to comprehension or expression.

- *Alliterative Aloha (Greeting)*, p. 171
- *Quadrilateral Quandary (Group activity)*, p. 144

Reading: History/Social Studies

RH.6–8.1 Cite specific textual evidence to support analysis of primary and secondary sources.

- *List and Tell (Morning message)*, p. 147

RH.6–8.5 Describe how a text presents information.

- *What's Your Point? (Morning message)*, p. 149

RH.6–8.7 Integrate visual information with other information in print and digital texts.

- *Picture This (Sharing)*, p. 137
- *What's Your Point? (Morning message)*, p. 149

RH.6–8.8 Distinguish among fact, opinion, and reasoned judgment in a text.

- *Fact or Fiction (Group activity)*, p. 141

Index of Activities

Additional Resources

All the activities in this book are consistent with the *Responsive Classroom* approach to education, in which Morning Meeting is a key practice. *Responsive Classroom* is an evidence-based approach associated with greater teacher effectiveness, higher student achievement, and improved school climate. *Responsive Classroom* practices help educators build competencies in four interrelated domains: engaging academics, positive community, effective management, and developmentally appropriate teaching.

To learn more about Morning Meeting and other key *Responsive Classroom* practices, see the following selected resources published by Center for Responsive Schools and available from **www.responsiveclassroom.org** ▪ 800-360-6332.

The Morning Meeting Book, 3rd ed., by Roxann Kriete and Carol Davis. 2014.

Doing Math in Morning Meeting: 150 Quick Activities That Connect to Your Curriculum by Andy Dousis and Margaret Berry Wilson. 2010.

Doing Science in Morning Meeting: 150 Quick Activities That Connect to Your Curriculum by Lara Webb and Margaret Berry Wilson. 2013.

80 Morning Meeting Ideas for Grades K–2 by Susan Lattanzi Roser. 2012.

80 Morning Meeting Ideas for Grades 3–6 by Carol Davis. 2012.

Morning Meeting Messages K–6: 180 Sample Charts from Three Classrooms by Rosalea S. Fisher, Eric Henry, and Deborah Porter. 2006.

99 Activities and Greetings: Great for Morning Meeting . . . and other meetings, too! by Melissa Correa-Connolly. 2004.

Morning Meeting Professional Development Kit. 2008.

Energizers! 88 Quick Movement Activities That Refresh and Refocus, K–6, by Susan Lattanzi Roser. 2009.

The Power of Our Words: Teacher Language That Helps Children Learn, 2nd ed., by Paula Denton, EdD. 2014.

The Language of Learning: Teaching Students Core Thinking, Listening, and Speaking Skills by Margaret Berry Wilson. 2014.

Interactive Modeling: A Powerful Technique for Teaching Children by Margaret Berry Wilson. 2012.

Closing Circles: 50 Activities for Ending the Day in a Positive Way by Dana Januszka and Kristen Vincent. 2012.

Acknowledgments

Thank you to the people who influence my thinking about teaching and learning: My students, workshop participants, colleagues, and co-authors Joan and Kate. I am grateful to Tim Keefe and Joan Riordan who guided my creative progress for this book. Thanks to Lisa Cody, who first mentored me in the *Responsive Classroom* approach. To my husband, Matthew, thank you for being my biggest fan!

—*Jodie Luongo*

Thanks to Ruth Charney, Chip Wood, Marlynn Clayton, and Linda Crawford for being my teachers, mentors, and inspiration. Thanks also to the colleagues and administrators in Stamford, Connecticut, who have supported me and the use of the *Responsive Classroom* approach for so many years. Finally, thank you to Kate, dedicated co-author, and to Jodie, collaborator, cheerleader, and friend.

—*Joan Riordan*

I am grateful to my students, past and present, for making Morning Meeting one of my favorite parts of the school day. You have helped me see just how enriching and engaging a meeting can be. A big thank-you to my co-authors, Joan and Jodie, for their enthusiasm and creativity, and to my family, Christine, Jack, Maureen, and Rob, for their support and curiosity. To my husband, Kendall: I could not have completed this project without your encouragement and love.

—*Kate Umstatter*

The authors would also like to thank manuscript readers Patricia Pendleton and Earl Hunter II for their time and valuable suggestions for improving the book. The authors are also grateful for the skill and artistry of the members of the Center for Responsive Schools publications team who worked on this book—Mary Beth Forton, Alice Yang, Elizabeth Nash, Jim Brissette, Cathy Hess, and Helen Merena—and the many *Responsive Classroom* program developers and consultants who helped shape Morning Meeting into the powerful teaching practice that it is today.

 **JODIE LUONGO** began her journey as an educator in the Stamford, Connecticut, Public Schools sixteen years ago. She now teaches at Cider Mill School in Wilton, Connecticut. She lives in Connecticut with her husband, Matthew. Together they run a yoga studio and dog-sit incredible furry friends.

 **JOAN RIORDAN** began her career as an educator in 1990 after a brief time in the financial world. She has been teaching kindergarten ever since. Joan is a team leader, cooperating teacher, and mentor for new teachers at Newfield Elementary School in Stamford, Connecticut. When Joan is not teaching, you might find her reading, baking, or writing for children.

 **KATE UMSTATTER** has taught students ages three through ten throughout her career. She has worked in both independent and public schools in New York City and is currently a third grade teacher at PS 503 in Sunset Park, Brooklyn. She lives with her husband, Kendall, in Brooklyn, New York.

About the Publisher

Center for Responsive Schools, Inc., a not-for-profit educational organization, is the developer of *Responsive Classroom®*, an evidence-based education approach associated with greater teacher effectiveness, higher student achievement, and improved school climate. *Responsive Classroom* practices help educators build competencies in four interrelated domains: engaging academics, positive community, effective management, and developmentally appropriate teaching. We offer the following resources for educators:

PROFESSIONAL DEVELOPMENT SERVICES

- Workshops for teachers and administrators (locations around the country and on-site)

- On-site consulting services to support implementation

- Resources for site-based study

- National conference for school and district leaders

PUBLICATIONS AND RESOURCES

- Books and videos for teachers and school leaders

- Professional development kits for school-based study

- Website with extensive library of free articles: www.responsiveclassroom.org

- Free newsletter for educators

- The *Responsive®* blog, with news, ideas, and advice from and for educators

FOR DETAILS, CONTACT:

Responsive Classroom

Center for Responsive Schools, Inc.
85 Avenue A, P.O. Box 718
Turners Falls, Massachusetts 01376-0718

800-360-6332 ■ www.responsiveclassroom.org
info@responsiveclassroom.org

More Books in the Series

Doing Math in Morning Meeting: 150 Quick Activities That Connect to Your Curriculum

- 264 pp., Item 130
  5–49 copies $21.25 ea; 50+ $20 ea.

25 activities for each grade (K–5). Correlates activities with Common Core State Standards.

Doing Science in Morning Meeting: 150 Quick Activities That Connect to Your Curriculum

- 222 pp., Item 149
  5–49 copies $21.25 ea; 50+ $20 ea.

20 activities for each grade (K–6) plus 10 themed meetings. Correlates activities with Next Generation Science Standards and *A Framework for K–12 Science Education*.